GREGG SHORTHAND

Functional Method

Diamond Jubilee Series

GREGG
SHORTHAND

Functional Method

Louis A. Leslie
Charles E. Zoubek
Shorthand written by Charles Rader

Diamond Jubilee Series

GREGG DIVISION

McGRAW-HILL BOOK COMPANY

New York   St. Louis   Dallas   San Francisco

Toronto   London   Sydney

GREGG SHORTHAND, FUNCTIONAL METHOD
DIAMOND JUBILEE SERIES

Copyright © 1963, 1955, by McGraw-Hill, Inc. All Rights Reserved.
Copyright 1949 by McGraw-Hill, Inc. All Rights Reserved.
Printed in the United States of America. This book, or parts thereof, may not be
reproduced in any form without permission of the publishers.

4 5 6 7 8 9 0 RRD-63 9 8 7 6 5

37310

Library of Congress Catalog Card No. 62-15522

PREFACE

Gregg Shorthand, the Universal System

To most people, the terms "shorthand" and "Gregg" are synonymous. Since its publication in 1888, Gregg Shorthand has been learned and used by millions of people not only in the English language but in many foreign languages as well. Today Gregg Shorthand is truly the universal system of shorthand.

The success of any shorthand system rests on the merits of its alphabet; the Gregg alphabet is the most efficient shorthand alphabet devised in more than two thousand years of shorthand history. The fact that this alphabet, virtually without change, has been the basis of Gregg Shorthand for three-quarters of a century is indeed a tribute to the genius of its inventor, John Robert Gregg.

Functional Method

The Functional Method of teaching Gregg Shorthand has for many years been used with great success by thousands of teachers of the system. The Functional Method type of presentation, fundamentally a language-art type of teaching, allows much scope for the ingenuity of the individual teacher within the framework of language-art teaching. It is distinguished, in general, by the use of a reading approach of approximately 20 class periods, by the provision of a printed key to the shorthand plates, and by the absence of verbalizations of rules or principles.

Gregg Shorthand, Diamond Jubilee Series

This edition of Gregg Shorthand, issued during the Diamond Jubilee year of the publication of the system, has two primary objectives:

1. To enable the student to learn Gregg Shorthand more quickly and easily. This ease of learning is accomplished through the revision of the shorthand system, which reduces the "learning load."

2. To provide for transcription readiness by increased emphasis on vocabulary development, spelling, punctuation, and application of correct principles of grammar — all concurrently with the teaching of shorthand.

Revision of the System

Gregg Shorthand, Diamond Jubilee Series, represents the first revision of the Gregg Shorthand system since 1949. The changes in the system are based on research by the authors, on suggestions of experi-

5

enced teachers, and on a study of the application of the principles by the stenographer in the office.

The major changes in the system concern:

Brief Forms. Those brief forms with a low frequency of business use have been eliminated; the words they represented are now written in full. The outlines for some brief forms have been modified for easier joining and greater legibility. A few new brief forms have been added.

In all, there are now 129 brief forms representing 148 meanings.

Phrases. An analysis of the notes of hundreds of students and stenographers revealed that many phrasing principles that had been taught were very seldom applied. These have been eliminated.

Word Beginnings and Endings. The word beginnings and endings that are infrequently used or that apply only to a limited number of words have been omitted.

Principles. Those word-building principles that had presented both teaching and learning problems have been eliminated or modified.

Building Transcription Skills

Spelling and Punctuation. A very popular and helpful innovation in an elementary shorthand manual was introduced in 1949 in the form of "marginal reminders," which taught the student spelling and punctuation concurrently with shorthand. This new edition retains this helpful learning device with three slight, but useful, modifications:

1. The punctuation marks are encircled in color in the shorthand plates of the Reading and Writing Practice; in addition, the reason for their use is given above the circle. Thus, the student is saved the many eye movements that were previously necessary when the reason was given in the left margin of the page.

2. The words singled out from the Reading and Writing Practice for spelling attention are now syllabicated. Thus, the student is better able to learn correct word division as well as correct spelling.

3. Only one principle of punctuation is presented at a time in each assignment rather than several, as in the previous edition.

Business Vocabulary Builder. Beginning with Chapter 2, each assignment contains a Business Vocabulary Builder consisting of several business words or expressions for which meanings are provided. The expressions are selected from the Reading and Writing Practice.

Similar-Words Drill. These drills teach the student the difference in meaning between similar words that stenographers often confuse: for example, *it's, its; their, there; accept, except.*

Spelling Families. An effective device for improving spelling is to study words in related groups, or spelling families. In *Gregg Shorthand, Functional Method, Diamond Jubilee Series,* the student studies six of these families.

Common Word Roots. A mastery of some of the more common Latin and Greek word roots is an effective device for the student wishing to increase his command of words. In this volume the student studies five of these common word roots.

Grammar Checkup. In a number of assignments, drills are provided on rules of grammar that stenographers often apply incorrectly. Examples illustrating the correct applications of these rules are given in the Reading and Writing Practice.

Transcription Quiz. Beginning with Assignment 57, each assignment contains a Transcription Quiz consisting of a letter in which the student has to supply the internal punctuation. This provides him with a daily test of how well he has mastered the punctuation rules presented in earlier assignments.

Organization of Textbook

Gregg Shorthand, Functional Method, Diamond Jubilee Series, is organized into 3 parts, 10 chapters, and 70 assignments. These 70 assignments provide ample material for a typical semester.

PART 1: *Principles* — Chapters 1 — 8. Each chapter contains six assignments — the first five assignments are devoted to the presentation of principles, and the sixth assignment is a recall. The last of the new principles is presented in Assignment 47.

PART 2: *Reinforcement* — Chapter 9. Chapter 9 contains eight assignments, each of which reviews intensively the principles in one of the chapters in Part 1.

PART 3: *Shorthand and Transcription Skill Building* — Chapter 10. This chapter consists of 14 assignments, each of which is designed to strengthen the student's grasp of a major principle of Gregg Shorthand. In addition, each assignment continues to develop the student's vocabulary and to improve his ability to spell, to punctuate, and to apply rules of grammar correctly.

Organization of Lessons

In *Gregg Shorthand, Functional Method, Diamond Jubilee Series,* the order of presentation of principles has been reorganized to introduce as early as possible the most frequently used alphabetic characters, brief forms, and word-building principles. Because of this reorganization, smooth, natural connected shorthand practice material is available in the very early assignments. In addition, the principles have been distributed more equally among the assignments, so that the student is not confronted wih a lengthy assignment one day and a very short one the next.

Brief forms are presented in groups of nine and never in two consecutive assignments.

Reading and Writing Practice

All the shorthand practice material in the Reading and Writing Practice is completely new, fresh, and up to date. A careful balance of business letters and interesting, informative articles has been maintained. Two new features have been introduced into the Reading and Writing Practice:

1. A brief-form letter at the beginning of each assignment in which a group of brief forms has been introduced. This letter contains one or more uses of all the brief forms, or their derivatives, of the assignment.

2. An occasional "Chuckle" that both teacher and students will enjoy as a relief from business material.

Other Features

Chapter Openings. Each chapter is introduced by a beautifully illustrated spread that not only paints for the student a vivid picture of the life and duties of a secretary but also inspires and encourages him in his efforts to acquire the necessary skills.

Student Helps. To be sure that the student gets the greatest benefit from each phase of his shorthand study, he is given step-by-step suggestions on how to handle it when it is first introduced.

Reading Scoreboards. At various points in the text, the student is given an opportunity to determine his reading speed by means of a scoreboard. The scoreboard enables him to calculate the number of words a minute he is reading.

Recall Charts. In the last assignment of each chapter in Part 1, a unique recall chart is provided. This chart contains illustrations of all the theory taught in the chapter. It also contains illustrations of all the theory the student has studied up to that assignment.

Check Lists. To keep the student constantly reminded of the importance of good practice procedures, an occasional check list is provided. These check lists deal with writing shorthand, reading shorthand, homework, proportion, etc.

Recall Drills. On pages 426-433 is a series of Recall Drills that review the word beginnings, word endings, and phrasing principles of Gregg Shorthand.

The authors and publishers wish to express their gratitude for the suggestions and advice they have received from so many teachers "on the firing line." They are confident that because of this help all teachers will derive even greater satisfaction from their teaching and will obtain better results than they have ever obtained before.

The Publishers

CONTENTS

YOUR PRACTICE PROGRAM

To make the most rapid progress in your study of shorthand, you must practice efficiently. By practicing efficiently, you will achieve two important results: First, you will get the greatest benefit from the material on which you practice; second, and no doubt very important to you, you will be able to complete each assignment in the shortest possible time.

To begin with, choose a quiet place in which to practice — and resist that temptation to turn on the radio or the television set! Then follow these easy steps:

Reading Word Lists

1. With the type key exposed, pronounce and spell aloud — if possible — each word and shorthand outline in the list, thus: *see, s-e; fee, f-e*. By reading aloud, you will be sure that you are concentrating on each word as you study. Repeat this procedure with all the words in the list until you feel you can read the shorthand outlines without referring to the type key.

The student studies the word lists by placing a card or slip of paper over the key and reading the shorthand words aloud.

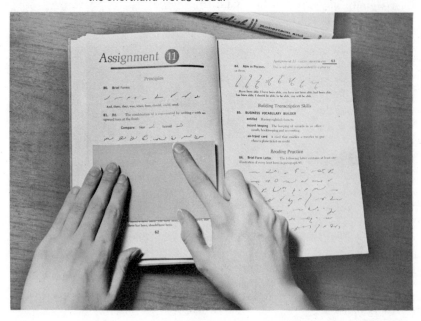

2. Cover the type key with a card or slip of paper. Then spell and pronounce aloud, thus: *s-e, see; f-e, fee.*

3. If the spelling of a shorthand outline does not immediately give you the meaning, refer to the type key. Do not spend more than a few seconds trying to decipher an outline.

4. After you have read all the words in the paragraph, reread them in the same way. This reading should be easier and you should not have to refer to the key so often.

5. In reading brief forms and phrases, it is not necessary to spell.

Reading Letters and Articles

1. Place your left index finger under the shorthand outline you are about to read.

2. Place your right index finger on the type key to that shorthand outline. The key begins on page 434.

3. Read the shorthand, aloud if possible, until you come to a shorthand outline that you cannot read. Spell the outline. If the spelling does not *immediately* give you the meaning, anchor your finger on the outline and turn to the key in the back, where your right index finger is resting near the point at which you are reading.

4. Determine the meaning of the outline that you cannot read, and then place your right index finger on it.

5. Turn back to the shorthand from which you are reading, where your left index finger has kept your place for you.

This procedure is vitally important, as it will enable you to save countless hours that you might otherwise waste finding your place in the shorthand and in the key.

6. If time permits, read the Reading Practice a second time.

Remember, during the early stages your shorthand reading may not be very rapid. That is only natural, as you are, in a sense, learning a new language. If you do every day's assignment faithfully, however, you will find your reading rate increasing almost from day to day.

Writing Shorthand

Before you do any writing of shorthand, you should give careful consideration to the tools of your trade — your notebook and your pen.

Your Notebook. The best notebook for shorthand writing is one that measures 6 by 9 inches and has a vertical rule down the middle of each sheet. If the notebook has a Spiral binding, so much the better, as the Spiral binding enables you to keep the pages flat at all times. The paper, of course, should take ink well.

Your Pen. If it is at all possible, use a fountain pen or a good ball-point pen for your shorthand writing. Why a pen for shorthand writing?

It requires less effort to write with a pen; consequently, you can write for long periods of time without fatigue. On the other hand, the point of a pencil soon becomes blunt; and the blunter it gets, the more effort you have to expend as you write with it. Pen-written notes remain readable almost indefinitely; pencil notes soon become blurred and hard to read. Pen-written notes are easier to read under artificial light.

Having selected your writing tools, you should follow these steps in working with each Reading and Writing Practice:

1. Read the material you are going to write. Follow the suggestions given on page 11. Always read everything before you copy it, referring to the key whenever you cannot read an outline after you have spelled it.

2. Place a card in the proper place in the key so that if you must refer to the key for an outline you cannot read you will be able to do so with the minimum loss of time.

3. Read a convenient group of words from the printed shorthand; then write the group, reading aloud as you write.

In the early stages your writing may not be very rapid, nor will your notes be so pretty as those in the book. With regular practice, however, you will soon become so proud of your shorthand notes that you won't want to write any more longhand!

The student reads the Reading Practice, referring to the key whenever he cannot read an outline. Notice how the left index finger is anchored on the place in the shorthand; the right index finger, on the place in the key.

When copying, the student reads a convenient group of words aloud and then writes that group in his notebook. Notice how he keeps his place in the shorthand with his left index finger.

PRINCIPLES

PART

1

Shorthand—Door Opener to Careers

You have your own reasons for learning shorthand. Everyone does. Maybe the title of <u>secretary</u> appeals to you, and you know that shorthand is an absolute "must" if you are to earn that title. Maybe you have your heart set on becoming a shorthand reporter. Or maybe you have some personal reason for wanting to acquire shorthand skill.

One very big reason why many people study shorthand is that shorthand opens doors that might otherwise remain closed to them. How can shorthand open doors? Let's cite an example. Janet Greene has considerable talent in art and is very anxious to get into advertising, where she can put her talent and training to use. But Janet found out quickly that competition is keen in this field, and jobs for beginners are not easy to get. After pounding the pavement and being given the "No Help Wanted" treatment time after time, she asked a personnel counselor, "How do I go about getting into advertising?" The answer was direct: "Study shorthand and develop a good stenographic skill. You can always get a job as a stenographer—a good-paying job, too. Get your foot in the door of an advertising agency by working there as a stenographer. Then, when you have made a niche for yourself, let it be known that you have artistic talents and ambitions. Chances are that the opportunity to employ those talents will be given to you."

Good advice!

Every year countless young women—and men—use their shorthand skill to open doors to varied and interesting careers. They may be careers in art, in television, in medicine, in publishing, or in management. Competition is very keen in these fields, but many people find shorthand the magic key that opens the door wide.

Even the young lady who isn't really interested in a career—only in the title of "Mrs."—finds shorthand and secretarial training valuable. Thousands of young women continue to work even after they are married—to help earn money for a new home, to save for vacation travel, or to help meet unexpected expenses.

Chapter

1

Assignment ①

GREGG SHORTHAND IS EASY TO LEARN

If you can write longhand, you can write Gregg Shorthand — it's as simple as that!

The strokes you will use in writing Gregg Shorthand are the same as those that you have been accustomed to writing in longhand. Actually, in some ways Gregg Shorthand is easier to learn than longhand. Skeptical? Well, just this one illustration should convince you. In longhand there are many different ways to express the letter *f*, all of which you had to learn. Here are six of them:

$$F \; f \; f \; \mathcal{F} \; \mathcal{F} \; \mathcal{F}$$

In Gregg Shorthand there is only one way to write *f*, as you will discover in this lesson.

Practice regularly and your shorthand skill will develop rapidly!

Principles

GROUP A

1. S-Z. The first stroke you will learn is the shorthand *s*, which is one of the most frequently used letters in the English language. The shorthand *s* is a tiny downward curve that resembles the longhand comma in shape.

Because in English *s* often has the sound of *z*, as in *saves*, the same downward curve is used to express *z*.

S-Z

2. A.   The next stroke you will learn is the shorthand *a*, which is simply the longhand *a* with the final connecting stroke omitted.

A   *a* ₊ *o*

3. Silent Letters Omitted.   In the English language, many words contain letters that are not pronounced. In shorthand, these silent letters are omitted; and we write only the sounds that are actually pronounced in a word. For example, in the word *say*, the *y* would not be written because it is not pronounced. For the word *face*, we would write *f-a-s*; the *e* would be omitted because it is not pronounced, and the *c* would be represented by the shorthand *s* because it has the sound of *s*.

What letters in the following words would not be written in shorthand because they are not pronounced?

day	**eat**	**main**
mean	**save**	**steam**

4. S-A Words.   With the strokes for *a* and *s*, you can now form two words.

say, *s-a*   ⟋   **ace,** *a-s*   ⟋

Notice that the *c* in *ace* is represented by the shorthand *s* because it has the *s* sound.

5. F, V.   The shorthand stroke for *f* is the same shape as the stroke for *s* except that it is larger — about half the height of the space between the lines in your shorthand notebook.

The shorthand stroke for *v* is the same shape as *f* except that it is much larger — almost the full height of the space between the lines of your shorthand notebook. Note the difference in the sizes of *s, f, v*.

Face, safe, safes, vase, save, saves.

6.   E.   The shorthand stroke for *e* is a tiny circle. It is simply the longhand *e* with the two connecting strokes omitted.

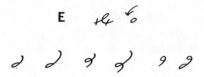

E

See, fee, sees, fees, ease, easy.

Notice in pronouncing the word *easy* that the *y* sounds like *e;* therefore, in shorthand it is represented by the *e* circle.

Suggestion: At this point, take a few moments to read the procedures outlined for practicing word lists on page 10. By following those procedures, you will derive the greatest benefit from your practice.

GROUP B

7.   N, M.   The shorthand stroke for *n* is a very short forward straight line.

The shorthand stroke for *m* is a longer forward straight line.

N $\xrightarrow{\;\;}$ M $\xrightarrow{\;\;\;\;}$

N

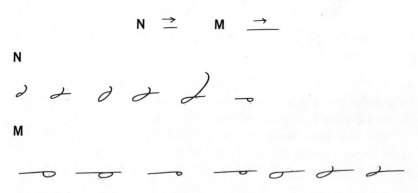

M

See, seen, say, sane, vain, knee.
May, main, me, mean, aim, same, seem.

Notice that the *k* in *knee* is not written; it is not written because it is not pronounced.

8. T, D.   The shorthand stroke for *t* is a short upward straight line.

The shorthand stroke for *d* is a longer upward straight line.

T ⟋⟍   **D** ⟋⟍

T

Eat, tea, team, neat, seat, stay, steam, meet.
Day, date, aid, made, need, seed, feed, saved, deed.

9. Punctuation and Capitalization

| period | ⟍ | paragraph | > | parentheses | ⟨ ⟩ |
| question mark | × | dash | ═ | hyphen | ⁼ |

For all other punctuation marks, the regular longhand forms are used.

Capitalization is indicated by two upward dashes underneath the word to be capitalized.

Dave   **Fay**   **May**

Reading Practice

Do you realize that, with the strokes you have learned and with the help of an occasional longhand word, you can already read complete sentences?

In the following sentences, spell each shorthand word aloud as you read it, thus: *D-a-v, Dave; s-t-a-d, stayed.* If you cannot read a word after you have spelled it, refer to the key.

1. [shorthand] all [shorthand] , 2. [shorthand]
[shorthand] for [shorthand] , 3. [shorthand] [shorthand] the
[shorthand] , 4. The [shorthand] is [shorthand] 12 ,
5. [shorthand] the [shorthand] ,
6. [shorthand] the [shorthand] on
the [shorthand] , 7. [shorthand] on
[shorthand] , 8. [shorthand]
on [shorthand] 10 , 9. [shorthand] gave [shorthand]
a [shorthand] , 10. [shorthand] with [shorthand] ,
11. [shorthand] for [shorthand] ,
12. [shorthand] all [shorthand]

---

1. Dave stayed all day.
2. Fay made tea for me.
3. Amy saved the fee.
4. The date is May 12.
5. Dave made the Navy team.
6. Dean made the Navy team on the same day.
7. Meet me on East Main.
8. Dave may see me on May 10.
9. Fay gave me a vase.
10. Amy stayed with me.
11. Fay made me stay for tea.
12. Dean may stay all day.

Assignment ②

Principles

10. Alphabet Review.　In Assignment 1 you studied the following nine shorthand strokes. How quickly can you read them?

11. O, R, L.　The shorthand stroke for *o* is a small deep hook.

The shorthand stroke for *r* is a short forward curve.

The shorthand stroke for *l* is a longer forward curve about three times as long as the stroke for *r*.

Note how these shorthand strokes are derived from their longhand forms.

O

R

L

No, snow, toe, so, phone, note, own, stone, tone, dome.
Ray, rate, ear, near, dear, free, fair, store, more.
Lay, late, laid, ail, nail, mail.
Deal, feel, fail, low, roll, stole.

21

Notice that in the last four *o* words on the first line the *o* is placed on its side when it comes before *n, m*. By placing it on its side when it precedes *n, m*, we can make a much easier, faster joining.

12. H, -ing. The letter *h* is simply a dot placed above the vowel. With few exceptions, *h* occurs at the beginning of a word.

Ing, which almost always occurs at the end of a word, is also expressed by a dot.

He, hair, hail, hear, hole, heating, heeding, hearing.

13. Long Ī. The shorthand stroke for the long sound of *ī*, as in *my*, is a large broken circle.

My, might, fine, line, right-write, light, side, tire.

14. Omission of Minor Vowels. Sometimes a vowel in a word is slightly sounded or slurred. Such a vowel may be omitted if it does not contribute to speed or legibility.

Reader, leader, meter, total, heater, later, even.

Reading Practice

With the aid of a few words in longhand, you can now read the following sentences. Remember to spell each shorthand word aloud as you read it and to refer to the key when you cannot read a word.

1.

2. ⟋⟍ ⟋ ⟋ ⟋ at ⟋ ＞

3. ⟋ ⟍ ⟍ has a ⟋ ⟋.
⟋ ＞ 4. ⟋⟍ ⟋ is ⟋ ＞

5. ⟋ ⟍ ⟋ ⟍ for ⟍ ＞

6. ⟋ ⟍ ⟋ buy ⟋⟍ ⟋
⟋ ＞ 7. ⟋ ⟋⟍ ⟋ ⟋⟍ ⟍ ＞

8. ⟋⟍ ⟋ ⟋ is icy ＞ 9. ⟋
⟋ a ⟍ score ＞ 10. ⟋ ⟋⟍
⟋ ⟍ ＞ 11. ⟋ ⟋ ⟋⟍ ⟍
⟋ at ⟋ ＞ 12. ⟋ ⟍ a ⟋
⟍ ⟋ ⟋ ⟍

---

1. He may drive me home later.
2. My train leaves late at night.
3. Ray Taylor has a fine writing style.
4. My mail is late.
5. Ray might fly home for Easter.
6. Lee Stone may buy my steel safe.
7. I may dye my hair.
8. My side road is icy.
9. Ray made a high score.
10. Lee may stay home.
11. Ray drove me home late at night.
12. I own a fine home near Erie.

Assignment ③

Principles

15. Alphabet Review.   How rapidly can you read the following shorthand strokes that you studied in Assignments 1 and 2?

16. Brief Forms.   The English language contains many words that are used again and again in all the writing and speaking that we do.

As an aid to rapid shorthand writing, special abbreviations, called "brief forms," are provided for many of these common words. For example, we write *m* for *am, v* for *have.*

You are already familiar with the process of abbreviation in longhand — *Mr.* for *Mister, memo* for *memorandum, Ave.* for *Avenue.*

Because these brief forms occur so frequently, you will be wise to learn them well!

I, Mr., have, are-our-hour, will-well, a-an, am, it-at, in-not.

Notice that some of the strokes represent more than one word. You will have no difficulty selecting the correct word in a sentence; the sense of the sentence will give you the answer.

17. Phrases.   By using brief forms for common words, we are able to save writing time. Another device that helps save writing time is called "phrasing," or the writing of two or more shorthand outlines together. Here are a number of useful phrases built with the brief forms you have just studied.

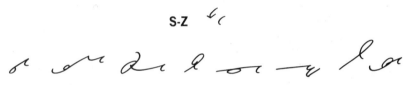

I have, I have not, I will, he will, he will not, in our, I am, in it.

18. Left S-Z. In Assignment 1 you learned one stroke for *s* and *z*. Another stroke for *s* and *z* is also used in order to provide an easy joining in any combination of strokes — a backward comma, which is also written downward. For convenience it is called the "left *s*."

At this point you need not try to decide which *s* stroke to use in any given word; this will become clear to you as your study of shorthand progresses.

S-Z

Eats, readers, files, ties, names, most, days, writes.

19. P, B. The shorthand stroke for *p* is the same shape as the stroke for *s* given in paragraph 18, except that it is larger — approximately half the height of the space between the lines in your shorthand notebook.

The shorthand stroke for *b* is also the same shape, except that it is much larger — almost the full height of the space between the lines in your shorthand notebook. Both *p* and *b* are written downward.

Notice the difference in the sizes of *s*, *p*, and *b*.

S **P** **B**

P

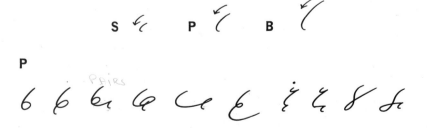

B

6 6 6 6 6 6 6 6 6 6

Pay, pays, pairs, price, please, people, hopes, opens, paid, pains.
Bay, base, boats, brains, blames, blows, able, neighbors, beat.

Notice that *pr, pl, br, bl* are written with one sweep of the pen without a pause between the *p* or *b* and the *r* or *l*.

Reading Practice

You have already reached the point where you can read sentences written entirely in shorthand.

Suggestion: Before you start your work on the Reading Practice, read the practice procedures for reading shorthand on page 11. By following the procedures given there for using the Key to Shorthand, you will get the most benefit out of the Reading Practice.

GROUP A

1.

2.

3.

4.

5.

6.

7. (52)

GROUP B

8. [shorthand outlines]

9. [shorthand outlines]

10. [shorthand outlines]

11. [shorthand outlines]

12. [shorthand outlines]

13. [shorthand outlines]

14. [shorthand outlines] 60

[shorthand outlines] (61)

GROUP C

15. [shorthand outlines]

16. [shorthand outlines]

17. [shorthand outlines]

18. [shorthand outlines]

19. [shorthand outlines] (38)

Assignment 4

Principles

20. Alphabet Review.   In Assignments 1 through 3, you studied 17 shorthand strokes. How rapidly can you read these strokes?

21. Sh, Ch, J.   The shorthand stroke for *sh* (called "ish") is a very short downward straight stroke.

The shorthand stroke for *ch* (called "chay") is a longer downward straight stroke approximately half the height of the space between the lines in your shorthand notebook.

The shorthand stroke for the sound of *j*, as in *James* and *age*, is a long downward straight stroke almost the full height of the space between the lines in your shorthand notebook.

Sh　/ᶜ　　Ch　/ᶜ　　J　/ᶜ

Sh

Ch

J

She, show, shown, shows, showed, shade, shape, sheep, shine, shore.
Each, teach, reached, cheese, chain, chair, chairs, cheap, cheaper, speech.
Age, page, stage, change, changed, range, strange, jail.

22.   OO, K, G.   The shorthand stroke for the sound of *oo*, as in *to*, is a tiny upward hook.

The shorthand stroke for *k* is a short forward curve.

The shorthand stroke for the hard sound of *g*, as in *gain*, is a much longer forward curve. It is called "gay."

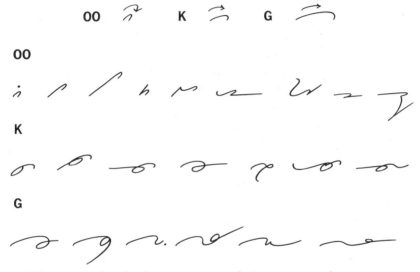

Who, to-too-two, do, shoe, true, room, fruit, noon, moved.
Ache, take, make, came, keep, like, maker.
Gain, gave, going, grade, goal, gleam.

Notice:

a. The *oo* hook is placed on its side when it follows *n* or *m*, as in *noon, moved.* By placing it on its side when it follows these letters, we can make a smoother joining.

b. Kr and gl are written with one smooth, wavelike motion.

c. Kl and gr are written with a hump between the *k* and the *l* and the *g* and the *r.*

Reading Practice

The following sentences contain many illustrations of the new shorthand strokes you studied in Assignment 4. They also review all the strokes and brief forms you studied in Assignments 1 through 3.

Remember, you will get the most benefit from this Reading Practice and complete it in the shortest possible time if you follow the suggestions on page 11 for using the Key to Shorthand. Take a few moments now to reread those suggestions.

GROUP A

(50)

GROUP B

8. [shorthand outlines] (47)

GROUP C

11. [shorthand outlines]

12. [shorthand outlines]

13. [shorthand outlines]

14. [shorthand outlines]

15. [shorthand outlines] (38)

GROUP D

16. [shorthand outlines]

17. [shorthand outlines]

18. [shorthand outlines]

19. [shorthand outlines] (28)

Assignment 5

Principles

23. Alphabet Review. Here are all the shorthand strokes you have studied in Assignments 1 through 4. See how rapidly you can read them.

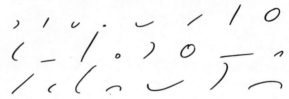

24. Ă, Ä. The large *a* circle also represents the sounds of *ă*, as in *has*, and *ä*, as in *mark*.

Ă

Ä

Has, had, man, acting, facts, matters, passed-past, last.
Mark, parked, large, far, cars, harm, starting.

25. Ĕ, Ĭ, Obscure Vowel. The tiny *e* circle also represents the sound of *ĕ*, as in *let*, the sound of *ĭ*, as in *trim*, and the obscure vowel heard in *her, church*.

Ĕ

32

Reading Practice

Your progress has been so rapid that you can already read business letters written entirely in shorthand.

28. Brief-Form Letter. This letter contains one or more illustrations of all the brief forms you studied in this assignment.

[shorthand outlines] (58)

....

29. *[shorthand outlines]*

ĭ

Obscure Vowel

Let, letter, test, best, rest, checked, selling, any.
Trim, him, did, gives, bills, remits, shipped.
Her, hurry, urge, earns, hurt, learn, search, served, church.

26.   Th.   Two tiny curves, written upward, are provided for the
sounds of *th*. These curves are called "ith."

At this time you need not try to decide which *th* stroke to use in
any given word; this will become clear to you as your study of shorthand progresses.

         Over Th   **Under Th**

Over Th

Under Th

These, thick, thicker, then, thinner, theme, bath, teeth.
Though, throw, three, both, health, earth, cloth, thorough.

27.   Brief Forms.   Here is another group of brief forms for very
frequently used business words. Learn them well.

Is-his, the, that, can, you-your, Mrs., of, with, but.

ah (64)

30.

65

31,

ch (57)

31.

(40)

Assignment 6 RECALL

Assignment 6 contains no new strokes for you to learn. In this assignment you will find a helpful Recall Chart and a Reading Practice based on the shorthand devices of Assignments 1 through 5.

32. Recall Chart. The following chart, which reviews all the shorthand devices you studied in Assignments 1 through 5, is divided into three parts: (1) words that illustrate the principles, (2) brief forms, (3) phrases.

Spell out each word aloud, thus: *a-k-t, act.* You need not spell the brief forms and phrases.

The chart contains 84 words and phrases. Can you read the entire chart in 9 minutes or less? If you can, you are making good progress.

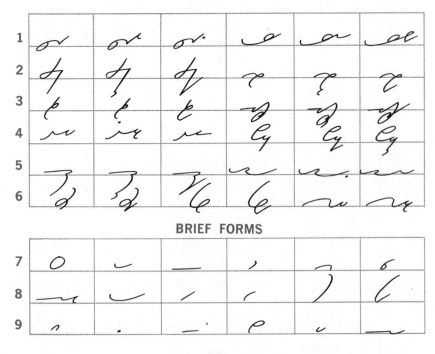

WORDS

BRIEF FORMS

PHRASES

10					
11					
12					
13					
14					

Reading Practice

33. *[shorthand outlines]* (51)

....

34. *[shorthand outlines]*

[Gregg shorthand outlines] 4–1212 *[shorthand outlines]* (64)

....

35. *[Gregg shorthand outlines]* (65)

....

36. *[Gregg shorthand outlines]*

[Gregg shorthand outlines] (73)

....

37. *[Gregg shorthand outlines]* (61)

Shorthand in the Business Office

"Miss Phillips, please bring in your notebook. I want to dictate some letters . . ."

". . . and, John, be sure to send a copy of that report to Mr. Castle in Denver, and two copies to Ed Smith in Toledo—no, better send him three. By the way, when you send Smith's copies, include a list of our recent price changes. A copy of the report should go to Alison, too; I think he is in Miami this week. Be sure that everything goes airmail special. . . ."

"When Mrs. Cochran calls, tell her our group will meet her at the National Airport, South Terminal, at 3:30. Ask her to bring along the photographs and news releases on the Wilson project. Tell her she should plan to stay over in Wichita an extra day or two—Fred Toffi wants her to see the public relations people at Boeing. . . ."

Many times during the day secretaries and other office employees are given instructions or dictation by their bosses or supervisors, such as in the three examples cited above. Only if these employees can write shorthand rapidly can they be sure of getting the facts—all of them—down on paper. Studies show that almost half of our communicating time in the office is spent in listening to others, and much of what the business employee hears must be recorded word for word. Nearly all business employees have occasional need for a fast writing ability. For the stenographer or secretary, however, such a skill is a constant need. Shorthand is as important to her (or him) as the ability to type. Taking things down in shorthand is so much a part of her daily routine that when she is summoned by her boss—either directly, or by buzzer or telephone—she automatically picks up her notebook and pen.

Every year hundreds of thousands of people in all parts of the country learn shorthand. Most of them study shorthand because they want to become secretaries. Secretarial work is perhaps the most popular—and frequently the most important—career in the world for young women.

Chapter

2

More and more young men are learning shorthand, too. Some executives in such fields as transportation, engineering, and manufacturing hire men exclusively as secretaries or shorthand reporters. Frequently men who do not intend to become secretaries or reporters learn shorthand and find it a valuable skill in helping them to advance more rapidly in their chosen field. Thousands have found shorthand the open-sesame to administrative positions.

And speaking of business offices, the United States Government runs perhaps the largest "business office" in the world. The armed services alone need thousands of stenographers to record the many details of military activities. Many of these stenographers are civilians employed in the different branches of the armed forces. Other Government installations, in Washington and throughout the free world, employ hundreds of thousands of civilian office personnel and offer an almost unlimited choice of fields of work for the skilled shorthand writer.

Assignment 7

Principles

38. Ŏ, Aw.   The small hook that represents *o*, as in *row*, also represents the sounds heard in *hot* and *drawing*.

Ŏ

Aw

Hot, top, drop, job, copy, doctor, sorry, stock, body.
Drawing, law, cause, taught, brought, all, call, small.

39. Common Business-Letter Salutations and Closings

Dear Sir, Dear Madam, Yours truly, Sincerely yours, Yours very truly, Very truly yours.

Building Transcription Skills

40. BUSINESS VOCABULARY BUILDER

Words are the stenographer's tools of her trade. The more words she knows and understands, the easier her task of taking dictation and transcribing will be.

To help you increase your knowledge and understanding of words, each assignment hereafter will contain a Business Vocabulary Builder consisting of words or expressions, selected from the Reading Practice,

43

that should be part of your everyday vocabulary. A brief definition, as it applies in the sentence in which it occurs, will be given for each such word or expression.

Before you begin your work on the Reading Practice, be sure you understand the meaning of the words and expressions in the Business Vocabulary Builder.

bursar   A treasurer of a school, such as a college.

semester   A school term consisting, usually, of eighteen weeks.

draft   A tentative first copy, or outline, usually intended to be revised.

Reading Practice

41.

(71)

42.

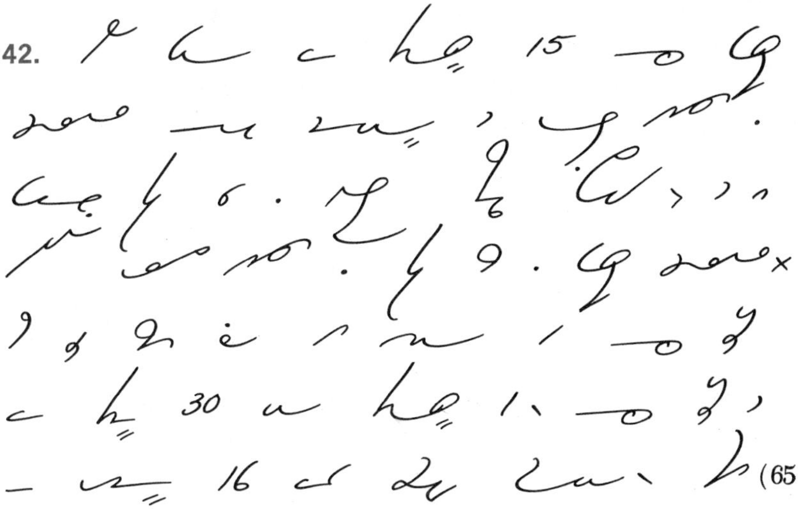

(65)

43.

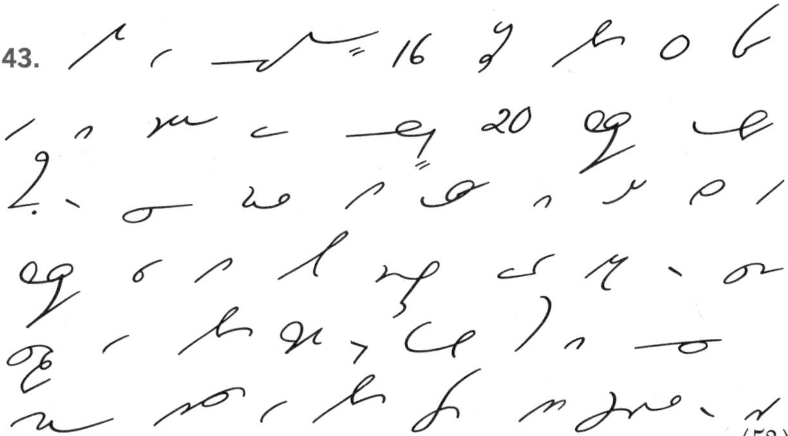

(53)

44.

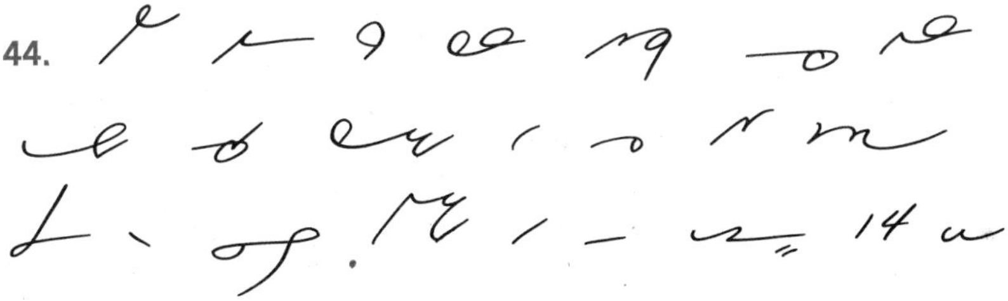

[Gregg shorthand outlines] 15 [outlines] (44)

·····························

45. [Gregg shorthand outlines] (73)

·····························

46. [Gregg shorthand outlines] 30 [outlines] 15 [outlines] (24)

Assignment 8

Principles

47. Brief Forms. Here is the third group of brief forms for frequently used words.

For, shall, which, be-by, put, would, there-their, this, good.

48. Word Ending -ly. The very common word ending -*ly* is expressed by the *e* circle.

Briefly, only, mostly, nearly, merely, totally, highly, daily.

Notice how the circle for *ly* in *daily* is added to the other side of the *d* after the *a* has been written.

49. Amounts and Quantities. In business you will frequently have to take dictation in which amounts and quantities are used. Here is a quick way to express them.

400; 4,000; 400,000; $4; $4,000; $400,000; four o'clock; $4.50; 4 per cent.

Notice that the *n* for *hundred* and the *th* for *thousand* are placed underneath the figure.

Building Transcription Skills

50. BUSINESS VOCABULARY BUILDER

earnestly Sincerely.

billing machines Machines used in the preparation of bills or invoices.

gross Twelve dozen (144).

minor (*adjective*) Of less importance. (Do not confuse with *miner*, which means "one who works in a mine.")

Reading Practice

51. Brief-Form Letter. This letter contains one or more illustrations of the brief forms in this assignment.

52. [Gregg shorthand outlines]

15,

5,

(109)

....

53. [Gregg shorthand outlines]

30.

10.

(shorthand outlines) (61)

·····························

54. *(shorthand outlines)*

(shorthand outlines) (60)

·····························

55. *(shorthand outlines)*

[Gregg shorthand outlines]

15. *[shorthand outlines]* (70)

....

56. *[shorthand outlines]*

[shorthand outlines]

5 *[shorthand outlines]* 5

[shorthand outlines]

[shorthand outlines] 2^{50} .

[shorthand outlines]

[shorthand outlines]

[shorthand outlines] (65)

....

57. *[shorthand outlines]*

[shorthand outlines]

[shorthand outlines]

[shorthand outlines]

[shorthand outlines]

[shorthand outlines] (47)

Assignment 9

Principles

58. Word Ending -tion. The word ending *-tion* (sometimes spelled *-sion, -cian,* or *-shion*) is represented by *sh.*

(shorthand outlines)

Action, portions, occasion, physician, fashions, nation, national, cautioned.

59. Word Endings -cient, -ciency. The word ending *-cient* (or *-tient*) is represented by *sh-t; -ciency,* by *sh-s-e.*

(shorthand outlines)

Patient, efficient, proficient, efficiency, proficiency.

60. Word Ending -tial. The word ending *-tial* (or *-cial*) is represented by *sh.*

(shorthand outlines)

Official, essential, social, financial, initial, special, initialed, specially, especially.

61. T for to in Phrases. In phrases, *to* is represented by *t* when it is followed by a downstroke.

(shorthand outlines)

To be, to have, to see, to plan, to pay, to show, to change, to buy, to feel.

Building Transcription Skills

62. **BUSINESS VOCABULARY BUILDER**

ranch-type home   A dwelling in which all the rooms are on one floor.

corporation   A type of business organization that is owned by stockholders.

data   Information; facts. (*Note:* The word *data* is the plural form of the word *datum.*)

financial position   The worth of a company at a given time.

essential   Necessary.

Reading Practice

63.

(82)

64. [Gregg shorthand outlines] (68)

....

65. [Gregg shorthand outlines] (103)

66. [Gregg shorthand outlines]

1960

15 16 × 9 0

1959

(94)

....

67. [Gregg shorthand outlines]

4

950/

(shorthand outlines) (79)

....

68. *(shorthand outlines)* (98)

Assignment 10

Principles

69. Nd. The shorthand strokes for *n-d* are joined without an angle to form the *nd* blend, as in *lined*.

Nd

Compare: line   lined

Trained, planned, signed, find, friendly, kind, mind, spend.

70. Nt. The stroke for *nd* also represents *nt,* as in *sent.*

Sent, events, prevent, renting, painted, parent, agent, into, entirely.

71. Ses. The sound of *ses,* as in *senses,* is represented by joining the two forms of *s.* The similar sounds of *sis,* as in *sister,* and *sus,* as in *versus,* are represented in the same way.

Compare: sense   senses

face   faces

Addresses, promises, passes, losses, causes, places, offices, leases.
Cases, guesses, basis, assist, sister, versus, census.

Building Transcription Skills

72. **BUSINESS VOCABULARY BUILDER**

> **initial** First.
>
> **premises** A piece of land or real estate.
>
> **current** Belonging to the present time.

Reading Practice

73. *[shorthand outlines]* (82)

....

74. *[shorthand outlines]*

[Gregg shorthand outlines]

(84)

....

75. [Gregg shorthand outlines]

25

4-5112

(65)

....

76. [Gregg shorthand outlines]

[Shorthand outlines] ①

[Shorthand outlines]

[Shorthand outlines] ② 120/ ③

[Shorthand outlines] 28

[Shorthand outlines]

[Shorthand outlines] 10

12 × [outline] (67)

·····························

77. [Shorthand outlines]

[Shorthand outlines]

[Shorthand outlines]

[Shorthand outlines]

[Shorthand outlines]

[Shorthand outlines]

[Shorthand outlines] 15

16 [Shorthand outlines] (67)

·····························

78. [Shorthand outlines]

[Gregg shorthand outlines]

(54)

·····························

79. [Gregg shorthand outlines]

10, ; —

= 12, >

ah (77)

Assignment 11

Principles

80.   Brief Forms

And, them, they, was, when, from, should, could, send.

81.   Rd.   The combination *rd* is represented by writing *r* with an upward turn at the finish.

Compare: fear *↗*   **feared** *↗*

Stored, tired, hired, appeared, record, heard, toward, harder.

82.   Ld.   The combination *ld* is represented by writing the *l* with an upward turn at the finish.

Compare: nail *↗*   **nailed** *↗*

Failed, old, settled, mailed, child, build, told.

83.   Been in Phrases.   The word *been* is represented by *b* after *have, has, had.*

Had been, have been, I have been, you have been, I have not been, has been, it has been, there has been, should have been.

84. Able in Phrases. The word *able* is represented by *a* after *be* or *been.*

Have been able, I have been able, you have not been able, had been able, has been able, I should be able, to be able, you will be able.

Building Transcription Skills

85. BUSINESS VOCABULARY BUILDER

entitled Having rightful claim to.

record keeping The keeping of records in an office — usually bookkeeping and accounting.

air-travel card A card that enables a traveler to purchase a plane ticket on credit.

Reading Practice

86. Brief-Form Letter. The following letter contains at least one illustration of every brief form in paragraph 80.

(shorthand outlines) (104)

87. *(shorthand outlines)* (78)

88. *(shorthand outlines)*

[Gregg shorthand outlines]

(81)

- -

89. *[Gregg shorthand outlines]* 12

(61)

- -

90. *[Gregg shorthand outlines]* 30

(93)

91. (64)

Assignment ⑫

Assignment 12 is a "breather" for you; it presents no new shorthand devices for you to learn. It contains a helpful Recall Chart and several short letters in shorthand that you should have no difficulty reading.

92. Recall Chart. The following chart contains all the brief forms in Chapter 2 and one or more illustrations of all the shorthand devices you have studied in Chapters 1 and 2.

Can you read the entire chart in 9 minutes or less?

BRIEF FORMS

1					
2					
3					

WORDS

4					
5					
6					
7					
8					
9					
10					
11					

PHRASES AND AMOUNTS

12					
13					
14					
15	4/	4	4	4/	5,	6

Building Transcription Skills

93. BUSINESS VOCABULARY BUILDER

parcel post   A department of the post office that collects and delivers packages; a method of shipping merchandise.

pamphlet   A small book, usually with a paper cover.

foreign operations   A company's customers and branch office overseas.

Reading Practice

94.

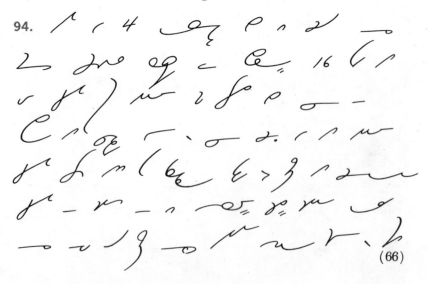

(66)

95. [Gregg shorthand outlines] **15.**

[Gregg shorthand outlines] **16.**

[Gregg shorthand outlines]

[Gregg shorthand outlines]

[Gregg shorthand outlines]

[Gregg shorthand outlines] 10 × (59)

....

96. [Gregg shorthand outlines]

[Gregg shorthand outlines]

[Gregg shorthand outlines]

[Gregg shorthand outlines]

[Gregg shorthand outlines]

10 [Gregg shorthand outlines]

[Gregg shorthand outlines]

[Gregg shorthand outlines]

[Gregg shorthand outlines] × (83)

97.

(94)

·····················

98.

[Gregg shorthand outlines] ... 14 ...

... 16 ... (78)

....

99. *[Gregg shorthand outlines]* ... 30/

... 15 ... ... 15; ...

... (59)

....

100. *[Gregg shorthand outlines]* ...

... ...) 15/ ... 26 ...

... ... 5 ... ...

...) 15/ ... (64)

Why Be a Secretary?

Why do young people choose secretarial work as a career? If you were to ask ten different secretaries, you would be likely to get ten different answers! Their answers, though, could be "capsuled" into five primary reasons why secretaries like their jobs:

1. "The work is interesting." The secretary in a travel-agency office gave this reason. Would you find it exciting to work in an organization that makes and sells phonograph records? broadcasts radio and television programs? produces advertisements for radio, TV, magazines, and newspapers? operates an airline? These are only a few of the types of firms that need secretaries.

2. "A secretary often has dealings with important people." This was the reason given by a secretary to a lawyer. Secretaries do work for and with important people. These important people, and those with whom they come in contact, make the decisions that turn the wheels of industry, of business, of the professions, and of the arts. The secretary is brought into the "inner circle" of management where she can observe big things happening.

3. "An office is a pleasant place in which to work." Does this sound like a strange reason for choosing secretarial work? Not if you consider the fact that more of a secretary's waking hours are spent in the office than at home. The important people in an office rate the best accommodations. If the executive for whom the secretary works has a choice location, she is likely to have one, too.

4. "The salary is good." The secretary who gave this reason works in an engineering firm that manufactures electronic devices for rockets. In comparison with general office employees, the secretary receives excellent pay; often, the magic word "shorthand" makes the difference between a medium-paying job and a well-paying one!

5. "The work has variety." Most secretaries won't argue with the one who gave that reason. The secretary has dozens of opportunities for variety every day. The alert secretary will find all the variety she can possibly want—one day is never like another!

Chapter

3

Assignment 13

Principles

101. Brief Forms

Glad, work, yesterday, very, thank, order, soon, enclose, were-year.

*In phrases, the dot is omitted from *thank*. *Thanks* is written with a disjoined left *s* in the dot position.

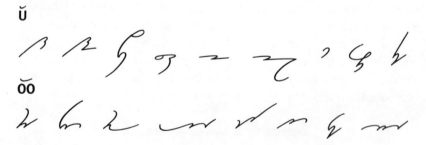

Thank you, thank you for, thank you for the, I thank you, I thank you for the, thanks.

102. Ŭ, O͞O.
The hook that expresses the sound of *oo*, as in *to*, also represents the sound of *ŭ*, as in *does*, and the sound of *oͦo*, as in *foot*.

Ŭ

OͦO

Does, dozen, above, enough, none, number, us, precious, just.
Foot, book, full, looked, stood, took, pushed, cooked.

Notice that the *oo* in *enough, none, number* is turned on its side; that *oo* and *s* join without an angle in *us, precious, just*.

103. W, Sw.
At the beginning of words, *w* is represented by the *oo* hook; *sw*, by *s-oo*.

74

We, way, wait, week-weak, wash, want, wood, sweet, swim, swear.

Building Transcription Skills

104. BUSINESS VOCABULARY BUILDER

> **apparel**   Clothing; garments.
>
> **cruise**   A pleasure trip by boat.
>
> **booklet**   A little book, usually bound in paper covers.

Reading Practice

105. Brief-Form Letter.   In the following letter, all the brief forms presented in this assignment are used at least once.

(shorthand outlines) (88)

....

106. *(shorthand outlines)* (85)

....

107. *(shorthand outlines)*

[Gregg shorthand outlines]

(94)

....

108. *[Gregg shorthand outlines]*

(70)

....

109. *[Gregg shorthand outlines]*

[Shorthand outlines] ah (76)

....

110. *[Shorthand outlines]* (64)

Assignment 14

Principles

111. Wh. *Wh*, as in *while*, is pronounced *hw* — the *h* is pronounced first. Therefore, in shorthand, we write the *h* first.

While, white, wheel, whale, whip, wheat.

112. W in the Body of a Word. When the sound of *w* occurs in the body of a word, as in *quick*, it is represented by a short dash underneath the vowel following the *w* sound. The dash is inserted after the rest of the outline has been written.

Quick, quit, quite, twice, equipped, always, roadway, Broadway.

113. Ted. The combination *ted* is represented by joining *t* and *d* into one long upward stroke.

Ted

Compare: heat   heed   heated

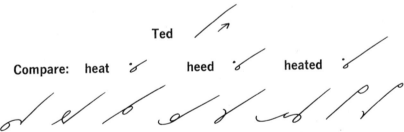

Acted, tested, dated, rated, seated, located, today, steady.

114. Ded, Det, Dit. The long upward stroke that represents *ted* also represents *ded, det, dit*.

Traded, needed, added, guided, detail, credit, edit, deduct.

79

Building Transcription Skills

115. BUSINESS VOCABULARY BUILDER

auditor   A person who checks the accuracy of accounting and financial records.

queries   Questions.

portion   A part of a whole.

in vain   Without any result; to no purpose.

Reading Practice

116.

[Gregg shorthand outlines] (93)

....

117. *[Gregg shorthand outlines]* (87)

....

118. *[Gregg shorthand outlines]* 250/ *[Gregg shorthand outlines]*

[Gregg shorthand outlines] (67)

························

119. *[Gregg shorthand outlines]* (87)

························

120. *[Gregg shorthand outlines]*

[Gregg shorthand outlines] (73)

---

121. *[Gregg shorthand outlines]* (63)

---

122. *[Gregg shorthand outlines]* (45)

Assignment 15

Principles

123. Brief Forms

Value, than, one-won, what, about, great, think-thing, why, business.

124. Brief-Form Derivatives and Phrases

Once, greater, greatest, thinking, things, businessman, businesses.
About the, about that, about them, about these, I think, if you think, what is, what are, what will.

Notice that a disjoined left *s* is used to express *things, thinks;* that the plural of *business* is formed by adding another left *s*.

125. Word Ending -ble.   The word ending *-ble* is represented by *b*.

Payable, available, reliable, sensible, terrible, possible, troubled, cabled.

126. Word Beginning Re-.   The word beginning *re-* is represented by *r*.

Received, revise, repaired, receipted, resisted, research, reappear, reopen.

84

Building Transcription Skills

127. BUSINESS VOCABULARY BUILDER

> **asset** Anything of value owned by a company, e.g., cash, equipment, furniture, etc.

> **receipt** A written acknowledgment of the taking or receiving of goods or money.

> **severely** Harshly, gravely.

Reading Practice

128. Brief-Form Letter. All the brief forms in this assignment are used at least once in this letter.

(shorthand outlines) (127)

························

129. *(shorthand outlines)*

① *(shorthand outlines)*

② *(shorthand outlines)*

③ *(shorthand outlines)*

(shorthand outlines) 20 *(shorthand outlines)*

(shorthand outlines) × ah *(shorthand outlines)* (93)

························

130. *(shorthand outlines)* 15 *(shorthand outlines)*

(Gregg shorthand outlines)

(76)

· ·

131. (Gregg shorthand outlines)

(102)

132.

(shorthand outlines) 15x

(shorthand outlines)

(shorthand outlines) 15

(shorthand outlines)

(shorthand outlines) (76)

133.   Chuckle

(shorthand outlines) (44)

Assignment 16

Principles

134. Oi. The sound of *oi*, as in *toy*, is represented by ⟋ .

Toy, oil, joy, join, noise, appoint, annoy, voice, choice.

135. Men, Mem. The combinations *men, mem* are represented by joining *m* and *n* into one long forward stroke.

Men, Mem

Compare: knee _____   me _____   many _____

Men

Men, mentioned, meant, mentally, mended.
Mends, amended, menace, women.
Member, remember, memory, memorize.

136. Min, Mon, Mun, etc. The long forward stroke used for *men, mem* also represents *min, mon, mun,* etc.

Minute, month, money, managed, manner.

137. **Word Beginning Be-.** The word beginning *be-* is represented by *b*.

Became, begin, belief, believed, because, below, beneath.

Building Transcription Skills

138. **BUSINESS VOCABULARY BUILDER**

    credit manager   A person who is in charge of a credit department in a company or store.

    treasurer   An official in charge of the funds of a company or organization.

    succeeding   Filling a vacancy left by someone.

Reading Practice

139.

(88)

----

140. (84)

141.

[Gregg shorthand outlines]

(112)

....

142. *[Gregg shorthand outlines]*

(84)

143. *[shorthand outlines]* (70)

SHORTHAND READING CHECK LIST

When you read shorthand, do you

1. Read aloud so that you know you are concentrating on each outline that you read?

2. Spell each outline that you cannot immediately read?

3. Refer to the key in the back of the book when the spelling does not give you the meaning?

4. Keep your left index finger on your place in the shorthand and your right index finger on the proper spot in the key so that you can look up the meaning of an outline quickly and without losing your place in the shorthand?

Assignment 17

Principles

144. Brief Forms

Gentlemen, morning, important-importance, those, where, manufacture.

145. Word Beginnings Per-, Pur-.

The word beginnings *per-*, *pur-* are represented by *pr*.

Person, permit, perhaps, perfect, persist, purchase, purchaser, purple.

146. Word Beginnings De-, Dĭ-.

The word beginnings *de-*, *dĭ-* are represented by *d*.

Decide, delay, deposit, desired, deserves, derive, direct, diploma.

147. Past Tense.

As you have perhaps already noticed from your study of Assignments 1 through 16, the past tense of a verb is formed by adding the stroke for the sound that is heard in the past tense. In some words, the past tense will have the sound of *t*, as in *baked;* in others, it will have the sound of *d*, as in *saved*.

Saved, changed, showed, flowed, missed, faced, traced, baked.

Building Transcription Skills

148. BUSINESS VOCABULARY BUILDER

personnel records Information concerning the people who work for a company.

proceed To go ahead; to advance (do not confuse with *precede*, which means "to come before").

deprived Denied; kept from.

collection agency A firm that specializes in collecting accounts for a company such as a department store.

149. SIMILAR-WORDS DRILL

In the English language there are many groups of words that sound or look alike, but each member of the group is spelled differently and each has its own meaning.

Example: **cite** (to quote), **sight** (the ability to see), **site** (place).

There are many other groups of words that sound or look *almost* alike.

Example: **defer** (to put off), **differ** (to disagree).

The unwary or careless stenographer will sometimes select the wrong member of the group when transcribing, with the result that her transcript does not make sense.

From time to time in the assignments ahead, you will be given a similar-words exercise designed to help you select the correct word, so that when you become a stenographer you will not suffer the embarrassment of having your letters returned for correction.

Read carefully the definitions and the illustrative sentences in each similar-words exercise.

It's, its

it's The contraction of *it is.*

It's a fine day.

its (*no apostrophe*)   Possessive form meaning *belonging to it.*

Its operating efficiency has been proven.

Reading Practice

150.   Brief-Form Letter.   This letter contains one or more examples of all the brief forms in this assignment.

(119)

151. *[shorthand outlines]* (62)

....

152. *[shorthand outlines]* (104)

153. *[shorthand outlines]* (110)

....

154. *[shorthand outlines]*

(shorthand outlines) (107)

155. Chuckle

(shorthand outlines) (64)

Assignment 18 RECALL

Assignment 18 is another "breather" for you; it contains no new shorthand devices for you to learn. In this assignment you will find a Recall Chart and a Reading Practice that you will find not only interesting but informative as well.

156. Recall Chart. This chart reviews all the brief forms in Chapter 3 as well as the shorthand devices you studied in Chapters 1, 2, and 3.

The chart contains 90 words and phrases. Can you read the entire chart in 8 minutes or less?

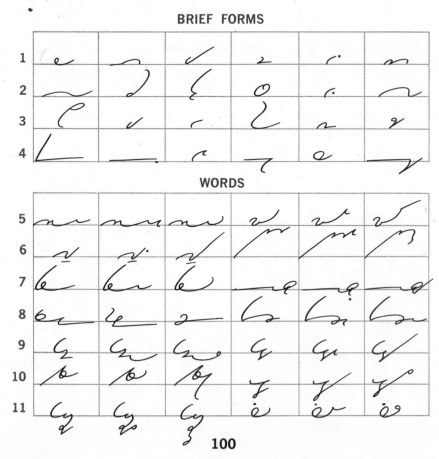

BRIEF FORMS

WORDS

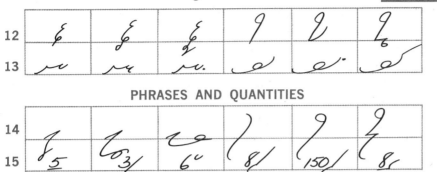

PHRASES AND QUANTITIES

Building Transcription Skills

157. BUSINESS VOCABULARY BUILDER

traits   Qualities of mind and character.

poised (*adjective*)   Able to meet embarrassing situations calmly.

teamwork   Co-operation among members of a working group.

Reading Practice

Reading Scoreboard.   One of the factors in measuring your progress in shorthand is the rate at which you read shorthand. Wouldn't you like to determine your reading rate on the *first reading* of the articles in Assignment 18? The following table will help you.

Assignment 18 contains 469 words.

If you read Assignment 18 in	your reading rate is
19 MINUTES	25 WORDS A MINUTE
21 MINUTES	22 WORDS A MINUTE
23 MINUTES	20 WORDS A MINUTE
26 MINUTES	17 WORDS A MINUTE
28 MINUTES	16 WORDS A MINUTE
31 MINUTES	15 WORDS A MINUTE

If you can read Assignment 18 through the first time in less than 19 minutes, you are doing well indeed. If you take considerably longer than 31 minutes, here are some questions you should ask yourself:

1. Am I spelling each outline I cannot read immediately?

2. Am I referring to the key when the spelling does not give me the meaning?

3. Should I perhaps reread the directions for reading shorthand on page 11?

After you have determined your reading rate, make a record of it in some convenient place. You can then watch your reading rate grow as you time yourself on the Reading Scoreboards in later assignments.

158.   Desirable Traits

[Gregg shorthand outlines] (161)

159. Good Health

[Gregg shorthand outlines]

(shorthand outlines) ④

(shorthand outlines)

(shorthand outlines)

(shorthand outlines)

(shorthand outlines) ①

(shorthand outlines)

(shorthand outlines) ②

(shorthand outlines)

(shorthand outlines) ③

(shorthand outlines)

(shorthand outlines)

(shorthand outlines) (192)

160. The Power of a Smile

(shorthand outlines)

(shorthand outlines)

(shorthand outlines)

(shorthand outlines)

(shorthand outlines)

[Shorthand outlines] (116)

BRIEF-FORM CHECK LIST

Are you making good use of the brief-form chart that appears on the inside back cover of your textbook? Remember, the brief forms represent many of the commonest words in the language; and the better you know them, the more rapid progress you will make in developing your shorthand speed. Are you—

1. Spending a few minutes reading from the charts each day.

2. Timing yourself and trying to cut a few seconds off your reading time with each reading?

3. Reading the brief forms in a different order each time—from left to right, from right to left, from top to bottom, or from bottom to top?

The Secretary's Day

What is a typical day like in the life of a secretary? Let's suppose you are secretary to Mr. G. O. Marsden, Sales Manager. Here is what your day might be like.

8:45	Arrive at the office. Straighten and dust Mr. Marsden's desk and other furniture. Fill water decanter. Water the plants. Check appointment calendar to be sure that his agrees with yours. You notice that he has made a 9:15 appointment with Mrs. Fuller. Get necessary papers you think he might need in talking with her.
8:55	Mr. Marsden arrives. Remind him of his 9:15 appointment and a luncheon date at 12:30 with Mr. Symond at the Belle Meade Restaurant. Ask him about arrangements for a 2:30 meeting of the Advertising Committee.
9:05	The mail arrives. Open all mail (except letters marked "Personal"); read it and place it on Mr. Marsden's desk, along with any background correspondence he may need.
9:15	The receptionist calls you to say that Mrs. Fuller has arrived. You inform Mr. Marsden and then go out to the reception office to escort Mrs. Fuller in to see Mr. Marsden.
9:35	Mr. Marsden "buzzes" you on the intercom and tells you that Mrs. Fuller is leaving and asks you to get some papers that she is to take with her. You do so, bidding Mrs. Fuller good-bye at the elevator.
9:40-10:15	1. The telephone rings several times—company executives and outsiders asking for appointments and information. 2. A messenger brings you a package of books C. O. D., and you take the money from petty cash to pay him. 3. Other executives call in person to speak to Mr. Marsden.
10:15	Mr. Marsden calls you for dictation.
11:00	You return to your desk and begin transcribing.
11:15	Mr. Marsden asks for several papers that must be obtained from the files.
11:30	You call the receptionist on the third floor to be sure that the conference room has been reserved for Mr. Marsden's 2:30 meeting.

Chapter

4

12:00   You get ready to go to lunch with another secretary who works a few blocks away. Before leaving, you again remind Mr. Marsden about his luncheon date. You tell the relief receptionist that you are leaving for lunch.

12:55   Back from lunch, you return to your transcribing.

1:15-   1. You answer eight telephone calls.
1:40   2. You greet two callers who have come to see Mr. Marsden (neither has an appointment), and you persuade them to make an appointment for later in the week.
3. You duplicate the agenda for the advertising meeting and make photocopies of an advertising brochure to be discussed there.
4. You visit the conference room to see that there are enough chairs and that the room is in order; you distribute the materials for the meeting.

2:00   Mr. Marsden calls you in to dictate a short memo. He asks you to arrange to have a film and an operator in the conference room at three o'clock. You call the library for the film and Office Services to arrange for an operator.

2:25   You make sure that Mr. Marsden has all the necessary materials for the 2:30 meeting, then you return to your transcribing.

2:30-   You get out two telegrams and finish transcribing Mr. Marsden's
4:00   dictation. You telephone various people for information he needs for a report he is writing.

4:30   You prepare for Mr. Marsden's signature the letters that you have just typed and take them to him. After he has signed them, you get them ready for mailing.

4:45   You receive a call from a friend about going bowling this evening. You hurriedly agree, saying you'll be ready by 6:15.

5:00   You clear your desk, tell Mr. Marsden you are leaving (he is working late tonight), and then catch the first bus home.

As you think about the day's work, you are certain of only two things: (1) you did a good day's work, and (2) tomorrow will be entirely different!

Assignment 19

Principles

161. **Brief Forms**

Present, part, after, advertise, company, wish, immediate, must, opportunity.

162. **Ū.** The sound of $\bar{u}$, as in *view*, is represented by.

Few, refuse, reviewed, unit, united, unique, acute, usual.

163. **Word Ending -ment.** The word ending *-ment* is represented by *m*.

Arrangements, settlement, payment, assignment, shipments, elementary.

Notice that in *assignment* the *m* for *-ment* is joined to the *n* with a jog.

Building Transcription Skills

164. **BUSINESS VOCABULARY BUILDER**

partial Pertaining to a part only; not all.

tracer A follow-up investigation to locate a missing shipment of merchandise.

elements Conditions of weather, such as rain, snow, and lightning.

Reading Practice

165. **Brief-Form Letter.** This letter contains all the brief forms you studied in this assignment.

[Gregg shorthand outlines] (117)

....

166. *[Gregg shorthand outlines]*

[Gregg shorthand outlines]

(139)

....

167. *[Gregg shorthand outlines]*

(91)

168. [Gregg shorthand outlines] (84)

....

169. [Gregg shorthand outlines] (87)

170. *[shorthand outlines]* (82)

171. Chuckle

[shorthand outlines] (74)

Assignment ⓴

Principles

172. Ow.   The sound of *ow*, as in *now*, is written ⟋ .

Now, doubt, proud, found, account, ounce, house, amount.

173. Word Ending -ther.   The word ending *-ther* is represented by *th*.

Other, whether, neither, together, mother, either, rather, bother, bothered.

174. Word Beginnings Con-, Com-.   The word beginnings *con-*, *com-* are represented by *k*.

Con-

Com-

Concern, confused, consist, controlled, considerable, construct, connect.
Compose, compare, completely, complain, complaint, combine, comply.
Commerce, commit, committee, commercial, commercials, commercially.

Building Transcription Skills

175. BUSINESS VOCABULARY BUILDER

accommodate   To provide with sleeping quarters; to oblige.

confirm   To verify.

decade   Ten years.

competitor   A company that sells goods or services similar to those of another company.

Reading Practice

176.

[shorthand outlines]

(112)

177. [shorthand outlines]

(118)

....

178. [shorthand outlines]

(shorthand outlines)

(95)

179. *(shorthand outlines)*

(69)

180. *(shorthand outlines)*

(shorthand outline) (67)

181. Chuckle

(shorthand outlines) (101)

Assignment ⑳

Principles

182. Brief Forms

(shorthand outlines)

Advantage, use, big, suggest, such, several, **correspond-correspondence,** how-out, ever-every.

183. Den.   By rounding off the angle between *d-n*, we obtain the fluent *den* blend.

Den   *(shorthand outline)*

(shorthand outlines)

Sudden, wooden, deny, confident, president, dentist, danger, dinner.

184. Ten.   The stroke that represents *den* also represents *t-n.*

(shorthand outlines)

Attend, attention, written, sentences, gotten, competent, bulletins. Cotton, tonight, stands, remittances, assistance, tent, tense.

185. Tain.   The stroke that represents *d-n, t-n* also represents *tain.*

(shorthand outlines)

Obtain, certain, contain, maintain, attain, detain, container, certainly.

Building Transcription Skills

186.   BUSINESS VOCABULARY BUILDER

unique   Being the only one of its kind. (It is, therefore, incorrect to say "more unique" or "most unique.")

complimentary   Presented free.

evidently   Apparently.

council   A governing body.

Reading and Writing Practice

Suggestion: Before you start your work on this Reading and Writing Practice, read the practice procedures for writing shorthand on page 12. By following these writing procedures, you will derive the most benefit from your practice and also complete your assignment in the shortest possible time.

187.   Brief-Form Letter.   The following letter contains one or more illustrations of all the brief forms in this assignment.

[Shorthand outlines]

(138)

188. *[Shorthand outlines]*

15.

(69)

189. *[Shorthand outlines]*

4=6

[shorthand outlines] (83)

....

190. *[shorthand outlines]* (50)

....

191. *[shorthand outlines]* (53)

192. *[shorthand outlines]* 18

[shorthand outlines]

[shorthand outlines]

[shorthand outlines]

[shorthand outlines] 10

[shorthand outlines]

[shorthand outlines]

22 *[shorthand outlines]*

(94)

....

193. *[shorthand outlines]*

[shorthand outlines]

[shorthand outlines]

[shorthand outlines] 25 *[shorthand outlines]*

[shorthand outlines]

[shorthand outlines]

[shorthand outlines]

[shorthand outlines] (73)

Assignment 22

Principles

194. **Dem.**   By rounding off the angle between *d-m,* we obtain the fluent *dem* blend.

Dem

Compare: **den**   **dem**

Demonstrate, demand, condemn, seldom, domestic, damage, medium.

195. **Tem.**   The stroke that represents *dem* also represents *t-m.*

Temporary, attempt, item, system, tomorrow, automobile, customer.

196. **Business Abbreviations.**   Here are additional salutations and closings frequently used in business.

Dear Mr., Dear Mrs., Dear Miss, Yours sincerely, Cordially yours, Very cordially yours.

197. **Useful Phrases.**   With the blends just presented, we form these useful phrases.

To me, to know, to make.

198.　Days of the Week

[shorthand outlines]

Sunday, Monday, Tuesday, Wednesday, Thursday, Friday, Saturday.

199.　Months of the Year.　　You are already familiar with the outlines for several of the months, as they are written in full.

[shorthand outlines]

January, February, March, April, May, June, July, August, September, October, November, December.

Building Transcription Skills

200.　BUSINESS VOCABULARY BUILDER

justified　Proved to be wise, good.

domestic market　Customers in the United States.

estimates　Makes an approximate calculation.

Reading and Writing Practice

201.　*[shorthand outlines]*

[Shorthand outlines] (78)

....

202. [Shorthand outlines]

15

40

10 (130)

....

203. [Shorthand outlines]

[Gregg shorthand outlines]

(112)

· ·

204. [Gregg shorthand outlines]

(shorthand outlines) (130)

....

205. *(shorthand outlines)*

(shorthand outlines) (113)

Assignment 23

Principles

206. Brief Forms.   After this group, you have only five more to learn!

Time, acknowledge, general, gone, during, over, question, yet, worth.

*The outline for *over* is written above the following character. It is also used as a prefix form, as in:

Overdo, overcame, overdraw, oversee, overcoat, overtime, overtake.

207. Def, Dif.   By rounding off the angle between *d-f*, we obtain the fluent *def, dif* blend.

Def, Dif

Definite, defied, defeat, defend, different, differently, differences.

208. Div, Dev.   The stroke that represents *def, dif* also represents *div* and *dev*.

Divide, division, dividend, devoted, devised, developed, devout.

209. Ū represented by OO.   The *oo* hook is often used to represent the sound of *ū*.

New, renew, issue, avenue, suit, continued, induce, inducement.

Building Transcription Skills

210. BUSINESS VOCABULARY BUILDER

sales volume The amount of sales made to customers.

renewal An extension of a subscription.

vividly Clearly; sharply.

211. SIMILAR-WORDS DRILL

To, too, two

to (*preposition*) In the direction of. (*To* is also used as the sign of the infinitive.)

I should like to talk to you about this matter.

too Also; more than enough.

I, too, was in the Navy.

She receives too many personal telephone calls in the office.

two One plus one.

He spent two years in France.

The word in this group on which stenographers often stumble is *too*—they carelessly transcribe *to*. Don't *you* make that mistake.

Reading and Writing Practice

212. Brief-Form Letter. The following letter contains one or more illustrations of all the brief forms you studied in this assignment.

(126)

....

213.

[Gregg shorthand outlines]

ca (111)

··································

214. *[Gregg shorthand outlines]*

(84)

215.

(Gregg shorthand outlines) (150) (143)

216.

(Gregg shorthand outlines)

(shorthand outlines) (124)

217. Chuckle

(shorthand outlines) (77)

Assignment ㉔ RECALL

In Assignment 24 you will have no new shorthand devices to learn; you will have a little time to "digest" the devices that you have studied in previous assignments.

218. Recall Chart. This chart contains all the brief forms in Chapter 4 and one or more illustrations of all the shorthand devices you have studied in Chapters 1 through 4.

The chart contains 84 words. Can you read the entire chart in 7 minutes or less?

WORDS

BRIEF FORMS AND PHRASES

10						
11						
12						
13						
14						

Building Transcription Skills

219.   BUSINESS VOCABULARY BUILDER

participation   Act of taking active part in anything.

comprehend   To understand.

skim   To read quickly without concern for details.

legible   Can be read easily.

Reading and Writing Practice

220.   Check Your Study Habits

(shorthand outlines) (274)

221.   A Race with the Clock

(shorthand outlines)

[Gregg shorthand outlines] (153)

222. Chuckle

[Gregg shorthand outlines] (78)

The Secretary Takes Dictation

The number one requirement of a secretary is the ability to take dictation at a rate that enables her to keep up with the dictator <u>comfortably</u> and to transcribe it quickly and correctly. The major part of almost every executive's job is communications. Each day he must write many letters, memoranda, and reports. This is where the secretary really earns the right to her title. An efficient secretary saves her boss's time; she supplies the "hand" while he supplies the ideas —an effective combination! She quickly learns his dictating habits so that they work together as a team.

Some dictators think fast and know exactly what they want to say, and their secretaries must constantly use every ounce of skill to keep pace with them. Others think in spurts; that is, there will often be long pauses between thoughts. Then, when an idea has been framed in their minds, they are off at a fast clip for several minutes. Then, for a moment or so — nothing. Still other dictators are more deliberate. They think slowly, especially on difficult letters, and may change their minds many times during the dictation of a letter. Even so, their secretaries must be prepared for sudden bursts of speed when their ideas jell and they know what they want to say. No two executives dictate alike, and the secretary must be prepared for all types.

The good secretary has a reserve speed for any emergency. Even though a dictator's rate may be fairly low on the average, that "average" can be disastrous. Did you ever hear about the man who almost drowned in a river that averaged only six inches deep? Well, most of the river bed consisted only of sand; but there were several holes that were twelve feet deep, and it was in one of these that he almost met his sad fate!

Therefore, beware of averages. Build your skill so that you don't "drown in a cloudburst of dictation." It's good insurance to have more speed than the dictator's average.

Chapter

5

Assignment 25

Principles

223. Brief Forms

Difficult, envelope, progress, satisfy-satisfactory, success, next, state, under, request.

*The outline for *under* is written above the following character. It is also used as a prefix form, as in:

Underneath, undergo, understudy, underpay, undertake, underground, underpaid.

224. Cities and States. In your work as a stenographer and secretary, you will frequently have occasion to write geographical expressions. Here are a few important cities and states.

Cities

States

New York, Chicago, Boston, Philadelphia, Los Angeles, St. Louis, Detroit. Michigan Illinois, Massachusetts, Pennsylvania, Missouri, California.

225. Useful Business Phrases. The following phrases are used so frequently in business that special forms have been provided for them. Study these phrases as you would study brief forms.

[shorthand outlines]

Of course, as soon as, as soon as possible, to do, I hope, we hope, let us, to us, your order.

Building Transcription Skills

226.　BUSINESS VOCABULARY BUILDER

> **Manila envelope**　An envelope made of a strong brown paper.
>
> **traveler**　A salesman, representative.
>
> **progress**　Advancement to an objective.

Reading and Writing Practice

227.　Brief-Form Letter.　The following letter contains one or more illustrations of all the brief forms you studied in this assignment.

[shorthand outlines]

(shorthand outlines) (137)

....

228. *(shorthand outlines)* (91)

....

229. *(shorthand outlines)*

[shorthand outline] (122)

••••••••••••••••••••••••••••••

230. [shorthand outlines] 16^30 [shorthand outlines]

[shorthand outlines] 415 [shorthand outlines]

[shorthand outlines] 16 [shorthand outlines]

[Gregg shorthand outlines] (151)

·······························

231. *[Gregg shorthand outlines]* (101)

·······························

232. *[Gregg shorthand outlines]*

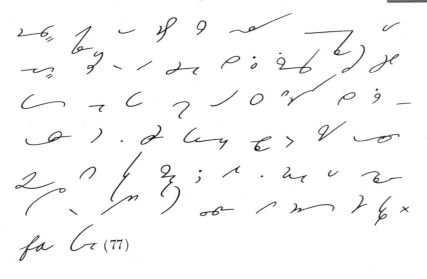

UP AND DOWN CHECK LIST

Do you always write the following strokes *upward?*

1. And   their-there

2. It-at   would

Do you always write the following strokes *down-ward?*

1. Is-his   for   have

2. Shall   which

Assignment 26

Principles

233. Long Ī and a Following Vowel. Any vowel following long *ī* is represented by a small circle within the large circle.

Compare: line ⟋ **lion** ⟋

Trial, science, prior, quietly, appliances, reliant, diet.

234. Ĭa, Ēa. The sounds of *ĭa*, as in *piano*, and *ēa*, as in *create*, are represented by a large circle with a dot placed within it.

Area, create, appreciated, piano, initiate, brilliantly, variation.

235. Word Beginnings In-, Un-, En-. The word beginnings *in-*, *un-*, *en-* are represented by *n* before a consonant.

In-

Un-

En-

Insist, increased, investment, instant, indeed, injured, intend.
Unfair, unpaid, uncertain, unfilled, until, unless, undo.
Enjoyed, engaged, endeavor, encouragement, enrolled, enlarge.

Building Transcription Skills

236.　BUSINESS VOCABULARY BUILDER

endeavor　To try.

associates (*noun*)　Fellow workers.

home appliances　Items for the home, such as refriger-
ators, stoves, washing machines, and dryers.

Reading and Writing Practice

237.

(124)

238. *[Gregg shorthand outlines]* 198

[Gregg shorthand outlines] 166/

(137)

....

239. *[Gregg shorthand outlines]*

[Gregg shorthand outlines]

(132)

....

240.

[Gregg shorthand outlines]

(shorthand outlines) (127)

....

241. *(shorthand outlines)* (79)

242. Chuckle

(shorthand outlines) (27)

Assignment 27

Principles

243. Brief Forms

[shorthand outlines]

Particular, probable, regular, speak, idea, subject, upon, street, newspaper.

244. Ng. The sound of *ng* is written ⌣ .

Compare: seen *[outline]* **sing** *[outline]*

[shorthand outlines]

Sing, sang, song, wrong, long, bring, strength, single.

245. Ngk. The sound of *ngk* (spelled *nk*) is written ⌢ .

Compare: seem *[outline]* **sink** *[outline]*

[shorthand outlines]

Rank, frankly, ink, blank, anxious, banquet, drink.

246. Omission of Vowel Preceding -tion. When *t, d, n,* or *m* is followed by *-ition, -ation,* the circle is omitted.

[shorthand outlines]

Admission, conditions, reputation, commissions, donation, addition, permission, stationed.

Building Transcription Skills

247.   BUSINESS VOCABULARY BUILDER

render   To give.

in the vicinity   Near.

beyond reproach   Cannot be criticized.

Reading and Writing Practice

248.   Brief-Form Letter.   This letter contains one or more illustrations of all the brief forms you studied in this assignment.

(129)

249. *[shorthand outlines]*

(111)

....

250. *[shorthand outlines]*

[Shorthand outlines] (116)

· ·

251. *[Shorthand outlines]* (115)

252.   Chuckle

[Shorthand outlines]

[shorthand outlines] (87)

WRITING TOOL CHECK LIST

When you write shorthand, do you —

1. Use a fountain pen, preferably one with a stiff point?

2. Leave the cap off the pen when you are copying or taking dictation?

3. Place the cap back on the pen firmly when you are not actually writing so that the ink will not clot on the point?

4. Fill your pen before you come to class each day so that you will not run out of ink in the middle of a dictation?

5. Carry a pencil "just in case"?

6. Date each day's dictation at the bottom of your notebook page, just as the stenographer does in the office?

Assignment 28

Principles

253. Ah, Aw. A dot is used for *a* in words that begin with *ah* and *aw*.

Ahead, away, await, awaited, awake, awaken, awoke, aware.

254. Y. Before *o* and *oo*, *y* is expressed by the small circle, as *y* is pronounced *e*. *Ye* is expressed by a small loop; *ya*, by a large loop.

Yawn, yacht, youth, yell, yellow, yielded, yard, yarn.

255. X. The letter *x* is usually represented by an *s* written with a slight backward slant.

Compare: miss _____ mix _____

fees _____ fix _____

Box, boxes, relax, relaxes, tax, taxes, mix, mixes.

256. Omission of Short Ŭ. In the body of a word, the sound of short *ŭ* is omitted before *n*, *m*, or a straight downstroke.

Before N

Before M

[shorthand outlines]

Before a Straight Downstroke

[shorthand outlines]

Sun, fun, ton, done, gun, begun, run, runner.
Some, summer, come, become, lumber, column.
Rush, brush, clutch, touch, much, flush, budget, judge, judged.

Building Transcription Skills

257. BUSINESS VOCABULARY BUILDER

bachelor's degree The first, or lowest, academic degree offered by a college or university.

flexible Not firm; capable of being bent.

proprietor An owner.

Reading and Writing Practice

258. *[shorthand outlines]*

[shorthand outlines] (118)

....

259. *[shorthand outlines]*

1955 *[shorthand outlines]*

[shorthand outlines] 1958

[Gregg shorthand outlines] (117)

································

260. [Gregg shorthand outlines] (125)

261.

(117)

....

262.

[Gregg shorthand outlines]

15²⁰

10/

(114)

263.   Chuckle

[Gregg shorthand outlines]

"50=50"

(84)

Assignment 29

Principles

264. Brief Forms

Purpose, regard, opinion, circular, responsible, organize, public, publish-publication, ordinary.

265. Word Beginning Ex-.   The word beginning *ex-* is represented by *e-s*.

Expense, expect, expire, expert, extend, example, extra, excuse.

266. Md, Mt.   By rounding off the angle between *m-d*, we obtain the fluent *md* blend. The same stroke also represents *mt*.

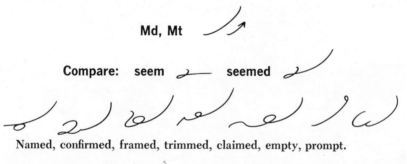

Md, Mt

Compare: seem   seemed

Named, confirmed, framed, trimmed, claimed, empty, prompt.

267. Word Ending -ful.   The word ending *-ful* is represented by *f*.

Careful, thoughtful, beautiful, useful, helpful, helpfully, helpfulness.

Building Transcription Skills

268. BUSINESS VOCABULARY BUILDER

editing   Preparing for publication.

overwhelmed   Overpowered; crushed.

major   Main; chief.

269. SIMILAR-WORDS DRILL

Addition, edition

addition   Anything added.

(shorthand outline)

This is a fine addition to my record library.

edition   All the copies of a book printed at one time.

(shorthand outline)

We have sold about 1,000 copies of the first edition of the book.

Reading and Writing Practice

270.   Brief-Form Letter.   This letter contains one or more illustrations of all the brief forms presented in this assignment.

(shorthand outline)

(124)

· ·

271.

[Gregg shorthand outlines]

(144)

·····························

272. [Gregg shorthand outlines]

(154)

273.

(shorthand outlines)

(131)

274.

(shorthand outlines)

[Gregg shorthand characters]

(170)

DID YOU KNOW THAT —

President Woodrow Wilson was an expert shorthand writer and that he drafted all his state papers in shorthand?

Samuel Pepys wrote his famous diary in shorthand? He wrote so legibly that students of literature had no difficulty making an accurate transcript of his notes.

Assignment ● 30 RECALL

After studying the new shorthand devices in Assignments 25 through 29, you have earned another breathing spell! Therefore, you will find no new shorthand strokes or principles in Assignment 30.

In this assignment you will find a Recall Chart and a Reading and Writing Practice that offers you some interesting suggestions on how to be a good conversationalist.

275. Recall Chart. This chart contains all the brief forms in Chapter 5 and one or more illustrations of the word-building principles you studied in Chapters 1 through 5.

As you read through the words in this chart, be sure to spell each word that you cannot read immediately.

Can you read the 84 words in the chart in 6 minutes or less?

BRIEF FORMS

WORDS

170

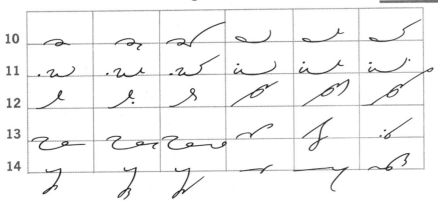

Building Transcription Skills

276.   BUSINESS VOCABULARY BUILDER

digresses   Gets off the main subject.

minute (pronounced *mĭ·nūt′*)   Very small; of little importance.

trite   Worn out; old.

Reading and Writing Practice

Reading Scoreboard.   The previous Reading Scoreboard appeared in Assignment 18. If you have been studying each Reading and Writing Practice faithfully, no doubt there has been an increase in your reading speed. Let us measure that increase on the *first reading* of the material in Assignment 30. The following table will help you:

Assignment 30 contains 514 words.

If you read Assignment 30 in	your reading rate is
18 MINUTES	29 WORDS A MINUTE
20 MINUTES	26 WORDS A MINUTE
22 MINUTES	23 WORDS A MINUTE
24 MINUTES	21 WORDS A MINUTE
26 MINUTES	20 WORDS A MINUTE
28 MINUTES	18 WORDS A MINUTE
30 MINUTES	17 WORDS A MINUTE

If you can read Assignment 30 in 18 minutes or less, you are doing well. If you take considerably longer than 30 minutes, perhaps you should review your homework procedures. For example, are you:

1. Practicing in a quiet place at home?
2. Practicing without the radio or television set on?
3. Spelling aloud any words that you cannot read immediately?

277.   Conversation Check List

[Shorthand outlines] (378)

278.   Nine Lessons in Living

[Shorthand outlines]

[shorthand outlines] (136)

SHORTHAND NOTEBOOK CHECK LIST

So that you can use your notebook efficiently, do you —

1. Write your name on the cover of your notebook?

2. Indicate on the cover the first and last days on which you used the notebook?

3. Place the date *at the bottom* of the first page of each day's dictation?

4. Place a rubber band around the completed pages of your notebook so that you lose no time finding the first blank page on which to start the day's dictation?

5. Draw a line through the shorthand notes that you have transcribed or read back so that you will know you are through with them?

English—The Secretary's "Secret Weapon"

If you are one of those who think that "English is a bore — who needs it?" then think again. The truth is that every secretary needs a solid footing in English grammar. The executive for whom you will work will doubtless know <u>what</u> he wants to say; but he may not know the correct spelling, punctuation, and grammatical construction — that is, <u>how</u> to say it. He may have a college degree in engineering, accounting, history, or chemistry; but somewhere along the line he missed the opportunity to learn the finer points of grammar. This is where you come in. The executive's request of the secretary, "Fix the letter so that it 'reads' right," is not rare. And he really means it.

Many employers are highly expert in the English language. They may dictate every punctuation mark and spell every unusual word. If you get one of these for a boss, your job of transcribing will be greatly simplified.

Then there is the dictator who <u>thinks</u> he knows grammar, but doesn't, and will expect you to transcribe everything just as it was dictated whether it is really right or not. Of course, in this case there is nothing for you to do but to follow his wishes — <u>he</u> takes the responsibility.

But if your boss says, "You know English and I don't, so you fix this letter," then you must <u>know</u>. It is <u>your</u> responsibility. Badly constructed letters can cost your company a sale or can result in the loss of good will.

No matter how rapidly you can type or can write shorthand, these skills are greatly weakened if you cannot produce a finished transcript that is grammatically perfect. The top-notch secretary must be a real expert in business English. The surer she is of the accepted rules of English, the more secure her job and the better her chances for advancement.

Don't let anyone mislead you about the importance of grammar. It's the secretary's "secret weapon."

Chapter

6

Assignment 31

Principles

279. Brief Forms

Merchant, merchandise, recognize, never, experience, between, short, quantity, situation.

280. Word Ending -ure.   The word ending *-ure* is represented by *r*.

Failure, figure, secured, pictures, nature, naturally.

281. Word Ending -ual.   The word ending *-ual* is represented by *l*.

Gradual, actual, annual, eventually, equally, annually.

Building Transcription Skills

282. PUNCTUATION PRACTICE

The first impression you get of the letter on page 179 is a good one. The letter is positioned properly; the margins are even; the date, inside address, closing, etc., are all in their proper places. If you read the letter casually, you find it makes good sense and apparently represents what the dictator said.

But if you read it carefully, you will quickly realize that the letter

The **NELSON HARDWARE** Company

 TOWER PARKWAY / NEW HAVEN 4, CONNECTICUT

March 12, 196-

Mr. Frank S. Brown
Taylor Lamp Corporation
449 Terrace Avenue
St. Louis 8, Missouri

Dear Mr. Brown,

May we ask a favor of you? The regular credit agencys
do not have your financial statement, and we assume
that is a matter of policy on your part. In view of
the friendly relationship between your fine firm and
our's however would you please co-operate with us?
One of our regular forms is enclosed for complesion
on your part.

We fully realize that submiting a finantial statement
is one of personal privilege, although we are glad
to say that most customers co-operate with us.

As you already know we want to work with you on the
best basis suited to your needs: and, of course, you
will find us helpful and genuinely interested in
serving you promply and efficiently.

Your co-operation by promptly returning the completed
form will be very much apreciated.

                    Cordially your.

                    John R. Smith
                    Credit Manager

JRS:BA
Enc.

Can you find all the errors in this letter?

will never be signed; in fact, the dictator will no doubt have something to say to the stenographer who transcribed the letter. Why? It contains several misspelled words, as well as a number of errors in punctuation.

If you are to succeed as a stenographer or secretary, your letters must not only be an accurate transcript of what the dictator said, but they must also be correctly punctuated and free of spelling errors. A stenographer or secretary who consistently turns in transcripts with errors in spelling and punctuation will not be welcome long in a business office!

To make sure that you will be able to spell and punctuate accurately when you have completed your shorthand course, you will, from this point on, give special attention to these factors in each Reading and Writing Practice.

In the assignments ahead you will review nine of the most common uses of the comma. Each time one of these uses occurs in the Reading and Writing Practice, the comma will be encircled in the shorthand, thus calling it forcefully to your attention.

On the left side of the shorthand pages, you will find a number of words selected from the Reading and Writing Practice for special spelling study; they are words that stenographers and secretaries often misspell. Each word is correctly syllabicated.

Practice Suggestions

If you follow these simple suggestions in your homework practice hereafter, your ability to spell and to punctuate should improve noticeably.

1. Read carefully the explanation of each comma usage (for example, the explanation of the parenthetical comma on page 181) to be sure that you understand it. You will encounter many illustrations of each comma usage in the Reading and Writing Practice exercises, so that eventually you will acquire the knack of applying it correctly.

2. Continue to read and copy each Reading and Writing Practice as you have always done. However, add these three important steps:

    a. Each time you see an encircled comma, note the reason for its use, which is indicated directly above the encircled comma.

    b. As you copy the Reading and Writing Practice, insert the commas in your shorthand notes, encircling them as in the textbook.

c. When spelling words appear at the left of the shorthand pages in the textbook, spell them, aloud if possible, pausing slightly after each syllable. Spelling aloud helps to impress the correct spelling more firmly on your mind.

, parenthetical

In order to make his meaning clearer, a writer sometimes inserts a comment or an explanation that could be omitted without changing the meaning of the sentence. These added comments and explanations are called *parenthetical* and are separated from the rest of the sentence by commas.

If the parenthetical word or expression occurs at the beginning or end of a sentence, only one comma is needed.

> I feel, therefore, that we should change our plans.
> Don't you think, Mr. Smith, that the price is too high?
> We shall send you a copy, of course.

Each time a parenthetical expression occurs in the Reading and Writing Practice, it will be indicated thus in the shorthand:

par

283. BUSINESS VOCABULARY BUILDER

revealing   Bringing to light something that was not evident before.

merchandising   Building sales by presenting goods to the public attractively.

accounting system   The procedures and forms used for financial record keeping.

manual   A handbook.

Reading and Writing Practice

284.   Brief-Form Letter.   All the brief forms presented in Assignment 31 are used at least once in this letter.

rec'og·nize
pleas'ant
ex·pe'ri·ence

un·hap'py
write
o'ver·due

mer'chan·dise
pur'chased

(131)

••••••••••••••••••••••••••••••

285.

nine'ty
sit'u·a'tion

[shorthand outlines]

its
of'ten

[shorthand outlines]

tact
han'dling

[shorthand outlines] (118)

························

286. [shorthand outlines]

sales
en·gaged'

[shorthand outlines]

(shorthand outlines) (95)

························

287. *(shorthand outlines)*

an·nounc'es
lec'tures

(shorthand outlines)

① *(shorthand outlines)* ②

sys'tem
man'u·al

(shorthand outlines) ③

yours
com'pli·ments
re·ceive'

(shorthand outlines) par ⊙

(120)

Assignment ③②

Principles

288. Word Ending -ily.   The word ending *-ily* is expressed by a narrow loop.

Compare: steady   *(shorthand outline)*   **steadily**   *(shorthand outline)*

(shorthand outlines)

Easily, readily, heartily, temporarily, family, busily, hastily, speedily.

289. Word Beginning Al-.   The word beginning *al-* is expressed by *o*.

(shorthand outlines)

Also, almost, altogether, already, although, alter, alteration, altered.

290. Word Beginning Mis-.   The word beginning *mis-* is represented by *m-s.*

(shorthand outlines)

Mistake, mistaken, misprint, mislead, misery.

291. Word Beginnings Dis-, Des-.   The word beginnings *dis-*, *des-* are expressed by *d-s.*

Dis-

(shorthand outlines)

Des-

(shorthand outlines)

Discuss, discussion, dispose, discouragement, discount, distances, discover.
Describe, described, description, descriptions, descriptive, despite.

Building Transcription Skills

292. BUSINESS VOCABULARY BUILDER

disturbing Troubling.

in the red Showing a net loss; losing money.

misconception An incorrect idea.

293. PUNCTUATION PRACTICE

, apposition

Sometimes a writer mentions a person or thing and then, in order
to make his meaning perfectly clear to the reader, says the same thing
again in different words.

My neighbor, Mr. Harry Green, owns a sailboat.
The meeting will be held on Friday, April 16, at the
Hotel Brown.

In many cases these constructions in apposition resemble the constructions in which the commas are used to set off parenthetical expressions. It is really immaterial whether the transcriber thinks he is using
the commas to set off an appositive or to set off a parenthetical expression, for the results are identical.

An expression in apposition is set off by two commas, except at the
end of a sentence, when only one comma is necessary.

Meet my neighbor, Harry Green.

Each time an expression in apposition occurs in the Reading and
Writing Practice, it will be indicated thus in the shorthand:

ap

⊙

Reading and Writing Practice

294.

[shorthand outlines]

in·stall'
de·scribed'
Gra'cious

[shorthand outlines]

a're·a
dis·cuss'

[shorthand outlines]

(137)

....

295.

[shorthand outlines]

dis·turb'ing
dis'con·tin'ue

[shorthand outlines]

stead'i·ly
heav'i·ly
debt

[shorthand outlines]

pub'li·ca'tion
mis'con·cep'tion

[shorthand outlines]

(159)

························

296. *[shorthand outlines]*

re·ceive'
dis·cour'ag·ing

dis'con·tin'u·ance

[Gregg shorthand outlines]

ap

tem'po·rar'i·ly
pay'roll'

(106)

∙∙∙∙∙∙∙∙∙∙∙∙∙∙∙∙∙∙∙∙∙∙∙∙∙∙∙∙

297.

par

young
mys'ter·y

(77)

298. Chuckle

(83)

PROPORTION CHECK LIST

As a result of the shorthand writing that you have already done, no doubt you have come to realize how important it is to —

1. Make the *a* circles huge; the *e* circles tiny.

2. Make the short strokes like *n* and *t* very short; the long strokes like *men* and *ted* very long.

3. Keep the straight lines straight; the curves deep.

4. Keep the *o* and *oo* hooks deep and narrow.

Assignment 33

Principles

299. Brief Forms. This is the last set of brief forms you will have to learn.

Railroad, world, throughout, object, character, govern.

300. Word Beginnings For-, Fore-. The word beginnings *for-*, *fore-* are represented by *f*.

Forgive, forget, form, informed, foreclose, force, effort, forever.

301. Word Beginning Fur-. The word beginning *fur-* is also represented by *f*.

Furnace, furnaces, further, furthermore, furnish, furnishes, furnished, furniture.

302. Ago in Phrases. In expressions of time, *ago* is represented by *g*.

Days ago, years ago, hours ago, weeks ago, months ago.

Building Transcription Skills

303. BUSINESS VOCABULARY BUILDER

character reference   One who vouches for the qualities, habits, and behavior of another.

foreman   The man in charge of a gang or crew of workers.

succeeded   Followed; took the place of.

304. PUNCTUATION PRACTICE

, series

When the last member of a series of three or more items is preceded by *and, or,* or *nor,* place a comma before the conjunction as well as between the other items.

> I bought a tie, a coat, and a pair of shoes.
> I talked to him on July 1, on July 3, and on July 18.
> Her duties consisted of receiving callers, answering the telephone, and opening the mail.

Each time a series occurs in the Reading and Writing Practice, it will be indicated thus in the shorthand:

ser

⊙

Reading and Writing Practice

305. Brief-Form Letter.   The following letter contains all the brief forms presented in Assignment 33.

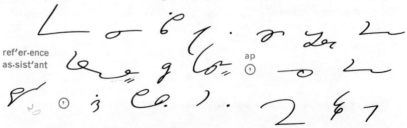

ref′er·ence
as·sist′ant

[Gregg shorthand outlines]

dis'trict
fore'man

suc·ceed'ed
fur'nish

(131)

. . . .

306.

its
o'ver·pay'ment

for'mal·ly
ac·cept'ed
as·sign'ment

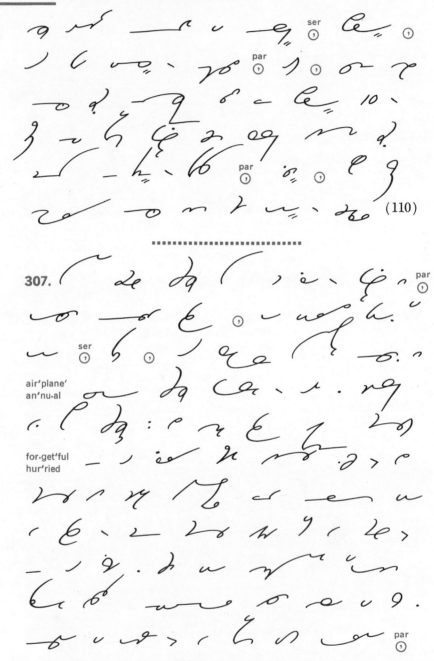

(110)

307.

air'plane'
an'nu·al

for·get'ful
hur'ried

[Gregg shorthand outlines]

bal'ance
due

(144)

....

308.

ap

ap

15

par

fur'ther
au'thor·i·za'tion

OK

par

(shorthand outlines) (134)

....

309. *(shorthand outlines)* 15

ex·hib′it
Fourth

(shorthand outlines) 50

(shorthand outlines)

(shorthand outlines)

(shorthand outlines)

ser

(shorthand outlines)

(shorthand outlines)

(shorthand outlines)

(shorthand outlines) 15 (121)

Assignment 34

Principles

310. Want in Phrases. In phrases, *want* is represented by *nt*.

I want, I wanted, you want, he wants, he wanted, who wants, if you want, do you want.

311. Ort. The *r* is omitted in the combination *ort*.

Report, export, exported, quart, quarterly, sort, mortally.

312. R Omitted in -ern, -erm. The *r* is omitted in the combinations *tern, term, thern, therm, dern, derm*.

Turn, turned, return, returned, eastern, determine, determination. Term, termed, southern, northern, thermometer, modern.

313. Word Endings -cal, -cle. The word endings *-cal, -cle* are represented by a disjoined *k*.

Chemical, practical, critical, politically, articles, physically.

197

Building Transcription Skills

314. BUSINESS VOCABULARY BUILDER

assortment   A group arranged in classes.

liberal   Generous.

practical   Useful.

distinguished   Noteworthy; famous.

Reading and Writing Practice

315.   Phrase Letter.   This letter contains many illustrations of the word *want* in phrases, as well as a review of many other phrases that you have studied.

choose
clothes
prac'ti·cal

(shorthand outlines)

lib′er·al *(shorthand outlines)* (110)

••••••••••••••••••••••••••••••

316. *(shorthand outlines)*

sight
plane
com′pa·ny's *(shorthand outlines)*

rou·tine′
tech′ni·cal
com′pa·nies *(shorthand outlines)*

(shorthand outlines) (123)

317.

[shorthand outlines]

per'son·al·ly
Chem'i·cal

[shorthand outlines]

lan'guag·es
North'ern

[shorthand outlines]

(137)

....

318.

[shorthand outlines]

fu'el
safe'ty
vi'tal

[shorthand outline] (100)

319. Chuckle

[shorthand outline] (64)

Assignment 35

Principles

320. Word Beginnings Inter-, Intr-, Enter-, Entr-. The word beginnings *inter-, intr-, enter-, entr-* are represented by a disjoined *n*.

Inter-

Intr-

Enter-, Entr-

Interest, interested, interrupt, interval, interpret, intervene, interview, intercept.

Introduce, introduces, introduction, introductions, intricate, intricately, intrude.

Enter, entered, entertain, entertained, enterprise, enterprises, entrance, entrances.

321. Word Ending -ings. The word ending *-ings* is represented by a disjoined left *s*.

Openings, holdings, proceedings, clippings, meetings, evenings, outings.

322. Omission of Words in Phrases. It is often possible to omit one or more unimportant words in a shorthand phrase. In the phrase *one of the,* for example, the word *of* is omitted; we write *one the.* When transcribing, the stenographer will insert *of,* as the phrase would make no sense without that word.

One of the, one of them, some of our, many of the, will you please, in the world, up to date.

Building Transcription Skills

323. BUSINESS VOCABULARY BUILDER

payroll deductions   Money withheld from an employee's wages for such expenses as insurance, medical care, social security, and income tax.

comptroller (pronounced *kŏn·trōl'ẽr*)   The officer of a company who has the responsibility for accounting and financial operations.

interior   The inside.

324. SIMILAR-WORDS DRILL

Quite, quiet

   quite   Completely; entirely.

He was quite pleased with the articles.

   quiet   Not excited; calm; free of noise.

He is a quiet person who seldom has anything to say.

A quiet place to study is the library.

Remember that in *quiet* the *e* comes before the *t;* in *quite,* the *e* comes after the *t.* (Also, be careful of *quit,* in which there is no *e.*)

Reading and Writing Practice

325.   Phrase Letter.   This letter contains several illustrations of the omission of words in phrases.

of'fered
En·ter·pris'es

en·roll'ing
pur'pose

comp·trol'ler
fur'ther

(127)

....

326.

of'fer
in·tro·duc'to·ry

ap

30

ser

in·form'a·tive
ar'ti·cles

par

there'fore
prompt'ly (133)

································

327.

dif'fer·ence
Ceil'ings

e'co·nom'i·cal
in·stall'

(153)

....

328.

bul'le·tin
Fi·nan'cial

[Shorthand outline]

pur'chas·es
ex·am'ple

par

[Shorthand outline]

en'ter·tain'ing
prac'ti·cal

ser

[Shorthand outline]

(164)

····························

329. [Shorthand outline]

wel'come
stock'hold'ers

[Shorthand outline]

ser

[Shorthand outline]

an'nu·al
re·ceive'

[Shorthand outline]

(73)

Assignment 36 RECALL

Assignment 36 is once again a breather. In Assignment 36 you will find a chart that contains a review of the shorthand devices you studied in Assignments 1 through 35 and a Reading and Writing Practice that tells what businessmen think about their secretaries. It should give you food for thought!

330. Recall Chart. The following chart contains a review of the shorthand devices you studied in previous assignments. It contains 78 brief forms, words, and phrases. Can you read the entire chart in 5 minutes?

BRIEF FORMS

WORDS

PHRASES

12					
13					

Building Transcription Skills

331.   BUSINESS VOCABULARY BUILDER

comprehensive   Covering a wide range.

grooming   Neatness; tidiness of dress and appearance.

indispensable   Absolutely necessary or essential.

Reading and Writing Practice

X**332.   How Do You Look?**

un'der·took'
peeves

chews
mov'ing

ser

[Shorthand outlines]

match
col'ors
like'ly

busi'ness·man'
glam'our

groom'ing
choice
taste'ful

in'dis·pen'sa·ble
fac'tors

(222)

333. Courtesy

[Gregg shorthand outlines]

oc·ca'sion·al
min'i·mum

good will

greet
pleas'ant

par
ser

(155)

334.   Business Dress

clothes
ap·pro′pri·ate

dai′ly

ser

car′ried
fash′ion

(154)

335. Chuckle

(41)

STUDY-HABIT CHECK LIST

No doubt as a conscientious student you do your home assignments faithfully. Do you, however, derive the greatest benefit from the time you devote to practice?

You do if you practice in a quiet place that enables you to concentrate.

You don't if you practice with one eye on the television and the other on your practice work!

You do if, once you have started your assignment, you do not leave your desk or table until you have completed it.

You don't if you interrupt your practice from time to time to call a friend or raid the refrigerator!

What Does a Secretary Do?

The answer to the question, "What does a secretary do?" will be different for almost every secretary. Most people think of a secretary as one who merely takes dictation and transcribes it. The fact is that taking dictation and transcribing it <u>is</u> a highly important — if not the most important — part of the secretary's job. But it is only one of many things that occupy her time.

The business executive thinks of the secretary as his "strong right arm." She frees him of the details of his job so that he will have time for managing people and procedures. Besides taking his dictation and transcribing it into good-looking letters, memoranda, and reports, she keeps his appointment calendar, answers his telephone, meets callers who wish to see him, files his important papers, writes letters and short reports, takes care of his mail, and arranges his business-travel accommodations. She may also do his banking, keep his income tax records — she may even shop for him and his family. Each secretary has duties connected with her job that differ in some respects from those of another secretary, depending on the kind of work her boss is engaged in and his willingness to delegate details to her.

The secretary to an accountant, to a retail store owner, or to a company treasurer is likely to need to know bookkeeping. The secretary to a lawyer must know legal forms and terminology. The secretary to a doctor may be required to know something about medical laboratory procedures and medical record keeping; she most certainly will have to know medical terminology. The secretary to a dentist may double as a technician — preparing the dental equipment for use, sterilizing instruments, assisting the dentist with X rays, keeping his records, and following up on appointments.

No two secretarial jobs are alike. Each is different, and each has its interesting facets. But there is a common thread that runs through all of them — taking dictation and transcribing it quickly and accurately.

Chapter

7

Assignment 37

Principles

336. Word Ending -ingly. The word ending *-ingly* is represented by a disjoined *e* circle.

[shorthand outlines]

Accordingly, exceedingly, increasingly, willingly, surprisingly, knowingly, seemingly.

337. Word Beginnings Im-, Em- The word beginnings *im-, em-* are represented by *m*.

Im-

[shorthand outlines]

Em-

[shorthand outlines]

Import, impressed, impose, impossible, improve, improperly, imply. Employ, emphasis, embrace, embarrass, emphatically, empire.

338. Omission of Minor Vowel. When two vowel sounds come together, the minor vowel may be omitted.

[shorthand outlines]

Courteous, serious, genuine, period, theory, previously, union, ideal.

Building Transcription Skills

339. BUSINESS VOCABULARY BUILDER

progressive   Characterized by continuous improvement; accepting new ideas.

quarterly   Occurring four times a year.

imperative   Not to be avoided; compulsory.

340. PUNCTUATION PRACTICE

, if clause

One of the most frequent errors made by the beginning transcriber is the failure to make a complete sentence. In most cases the incomplete sentence is a dependent or subordinate clause introduced by *as, when,* or *if*. The dependent or subordinate clause deceives the transcriber because it is a complete sentence, except that it is introduced by a word such as *if*; therefore, it requires another clause to complete the thought.

The dependent or subordinate clause *often* signals the coming of the main clause by means of a subordinate conjunction. The commonest subordinating conjunctions are *if, as,* and *when*. Other subordinating conjunctions are *though, although, whether, unless, because, since, while, where, after, whenever, until, before,* and *now*. In this assignment you will consider clauses introduced by *if*.

A subordinate clause introduced by *if* and followed by the main clause is separated from the main clause by a comma.

> If you cannot be present, please notify me.
> If you finish before noon, you are free to go home.

Each time a subordinate clause beginning with *if* occurs in the Reading and Writing Practice, it will be indicated thus in the shorthand:

if

⊙

Reading and Writing Practice

341.

var'i·ous
gen'u·ine
weath'er

pro·gres'sive
so·lu'tion

par

los'ing
ex·treme'ly

if

sur·pris'ing·ly
in'ex·pen'sive
en·closed'

if

(162)

342. [shorthand outlines]

cour'te·ous
re·ceived'
em·ploy'ees

[shorthand outlines]

sug·ges'tions
fur'ther

[shorthand outlines] (136)

....

343. [shorthand outlines]

[Shorthand outlines]

fi·nan'cial
cit'y's

friend'ly
cor'dial
wel'come

(120)

....

344.

em·bar'rassed
an'swered

dis·cour'te·ous
mis·placed'

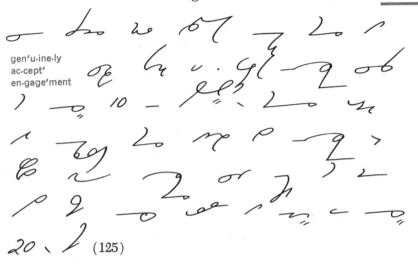

gen'u·ine·ly
ac·cept'
en·gage'ment

(125)

HOMEWORK CHECK LIST

When you do your homework assignment each day —

1. Do you study the Business Vocabulary Builder and the other transcription helps in the lesson before you start your work on the Reading and Writing Practice?

2. Do you read aloud each Reading and Writing Practice before copying it?

3. Do you spell each shorthand outline that you cannot immediately read? Remember, nothing builds shorthand speed more rapidly than the regular reading and writing of shorthand.

4. Do you note carefully the reason for the use of each comma that is encircled in the Reading and Writing Practice?

5. Do you spell aloud all the words given in the margins of the shorthand in the Reading and Writing Practice?

Assignment 38

Principles

345.   Word Ending -ship.   The word ending *-ship* is represented by a disjoined *sh*.

[shorthand outlines]

Steamship, friendship, membership, relationship, townships, scholarships.

346.   Word Beginning Sub-.   The word beginning *sub-* is represented by *s*.

[shorthand outlines]

Submit, subscribe, substantial, subdivide, subway, sublet, suburbs.

347.   Joining of Hook and Circle Vowels.   When a hook and a circle vowel come together, they are written in the order that they are pronounced.

[shorthand outlines]

Poem, poet, poetry, radio, folio, snowy.

Building Transcription Skills

348.   BUSINESS VOCABULARY BUILDER

> **substantially**   To a large extent.
>
> **jeopardizing**   Risking the loss of.
>
> **suburbs**   Residential areas on the outskirts of a city.
>
> **subdivided**   Broken up into small sections.

349. PUNCTUATION PRACTICE

, as clause

A subordinate clause introduced by *as* and followed by the main clause is separated from the main clause by a comma.

> As I am sure you are aware, the store closes at five.
> As I told you on the telephone, I cannot preside at the meeting.

Each time a subordinate clause beginning with *as* occurs in the Reading and Writing Practice, it will be indicated thus in the shorthand:

as

Reading and Writing Practice

350.

au·to·mat'i·cal·ly
sub·scrip'tion
bul'le·tin

en·closed'
an'nu·al

sub·stan'tial·ly
re·ceive'

(shorthand outlines) (127)

....

351. *(shorthand outlines)* 16 as

schol'ar·ships
un·u'su·al

(shorthand outlines) par

sen'iors
com·pete'

(shorthand outlines)

com'pe·ti'tion
sub·mit'ted

(shorthand outlines) if

(shorthand outlines) ap 10 as

(shorthand outlines)

par *(shorthand outlines)* (133)

....

352. *(shorthand outlines)* as

[Gregg shorthand outlines]

bal'ance
jeop'ard·iz·ing

par

per·suade'
pre·serve'

550/

(112)

・・・・・・・・・・・・・・・・・・・・・・・・・・・

353. as

sub'urbs
sub'di·vid'ed

15

sub·lease' par

5= 415

18 6

[shorthand outlines] (111)

∙∙∙∙∙∙∙∙∙∙∙∙∙∙∙∙∙∙∙∙∙∙∙∙∙∙∙∙∙∙

354. *[shorthand outlines]*

in·ter·rup′tion *[shorthand outlines]*

al·read′y
ca·pac′i·ty *[shorthand outlines]*

par *[shorthand outlines]*

[shorthand outlines] (108)

355.

sched'ule
an'nu·al

ap

ap

10

14

Sep·tem'ber
grad'u·al·ly

re·ceive'
an·nounce'ment

(100)

356. Chuckle

(50)

Assignment 39

Principles

357. Word Ending -rity. The word ending *-rity* is represented by a disjoined *r*.

Security, authorities, maturity, majority, sincerity, popularity, prosperity.

358. Word Ending -lity. The word ending *-lity* is represented by a disjoined *l*.

Ability, facilities, personality, possibility, reliability, qualities.

359. Word Ending -lty. The word ending *-lty* is also represented by a disjoined *l*.

Penalty, faculty, loyalty, royalty, casualty.

360. Word Endings -self, -selves. The word ending *-self* is represented by *s*; *-selves*, by *ses*.

Herself, himself, myself, itself, oneself, yourself, themselves, yourselves, ourselves.

Building Transcription Skills

361.   BUSINESS VOCABULARY BUILDER

mediocrity   Quality of being ordinary.

security   Freedom from anxiety or care.

prosperity   Financial success.

refunded   Given back.

362.   PUNCTUATION PRACTICE

, when clause

A subordinate clause introduced by *when* and followed by the main clause is separated from the main clause by a comma.

> When you finish the job, please let me know.
> When John arrives, ask him to see me.

Each time a subordinate clause beginning with *when* occurs in the Reading and Writing Practice, it will be indicated thus in the shorthand:

when

Reading and Writing Practice

363.

hap′pi·ness
me′di·oc′ri·ty   ser

sin·cer'i·ty
course

when

de·scribes'
fa·cil'i·ties

ap

ser

if

(134)

....

364.

due
in·teg'ri·ty

when

e·ven'tu·al·ly
sen'si·ble

par

(93)

365.

choice

when

ton'al
clar'i·ty

if

(127)

366.

ar'ti·cle
male
fam'i·ly

when

choose
in'di·vid'u·al'i·ty

ser

be·lieve'
traits

par

phas'es
ad'ver·tis'ing

(119)

367.

① ② ③

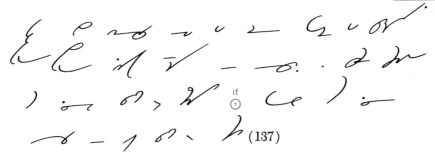

368. Chuckle

DID YOU KNOW THAT —

George Bernard Shaw did all his composing in short-hand and then had his secretary transcribe his notes?

James F. Byrnes used his shorthand regularly while he was a Supreme Court justice, a Secretary of State, and the Governor of South Carolina?

Assignment 40

Principles

369. Abbreviated Words — in Families. Many long words may be abbreviated in shorthand by dropping the endings. This device is also used in longhand, as *Jan.* for *January*. The extent to which you use this device will depend on your familiarity with the words and with the subject matter of the dictation. When in doubt, write it out! The ending of a word is not dropped when a special shorthand word-ending form has been provided, such as *-lity*.

Notice how many of the words written with this abbreviating device fall naturally into families of similar endings.

-tribute

-quent

-quire

-titute

-titude

Tribute, attribute, contribute, contributed, contribution, distribute, distributor.

Consequent-consequence, subsequent, subsequently, frequent, frequently, eloquent, delinquent.

Require, requirement, inquire, inquiry, inquiries, inquired, esquire.

Substitute, institute, constitute, substitution, institution, constitution, restitution.

Aptitude, latitude, gratitude, altitude, attitude.

Building Transcription Skills

370. BUSINESS VOCABULARY BUILDER

consequently   Therefore.

subsequently   Later.

delinquent   Behind in payment.

distributor   An agent for marketing goods.

aptitude tests   Tests that help to determine a person's suitability for a given line of work.

371. PUNCTUATION PRACTICE

, introductory

A comma is used to separate the subordinate clause from a following main clause. You have already studied the application of this rule to subordinate clauses introduced by *if*, *as*, and *when*. Here are additional examples:

> While I understand the statement, I do not agree with it.
> Although it was only three o'clock, he closed the office.
> Before you let out your next advertising contract, give us an opportunity to discuss it with you.

A comma is also used after introductory words or phrases such as *furthermore, on the contrary*, and *for instance*.

> Furthermore, you made a mistake in grammar.
> On the contrary, you are at fault.
> For your convenience in sending me the information I need, I am enclosing a stamped envelope.

Each time a subordinate (or introductory) word, phrase, or clause other than one beginning with *if, as,* or *when* occurs in the Reading and Writing Practice, it will be indicated thus in the shorthand.

intro

⊙

Note: If the subordinate clause or other introductory expression follows the main clause, the comma is usually not necessary.

I am enclosing a stamped envelope for your convenience
in sending me the information I need.

Reading and Writing Practice

372.

fu'el
coun'ty

intro

con'se·quent·ly
dis·trib'u·tors

suc·cess'
com·plete'ly

if

(117)

373.

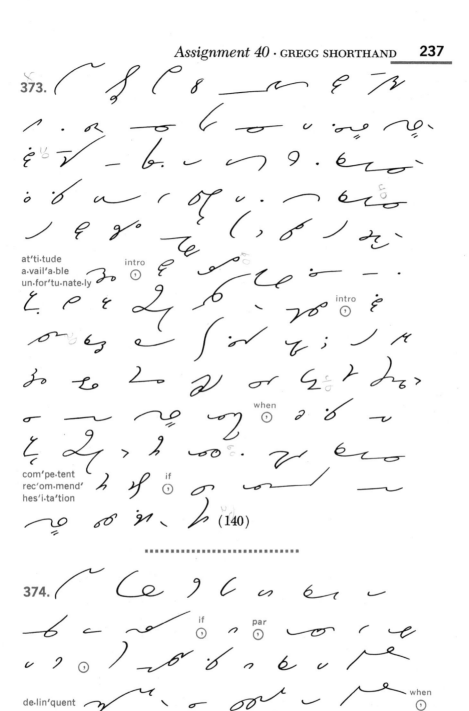

at'ti·tude
a·vail'a·ble
un·for'tu·nate·ly

intro

intro

when

com'pe·tent
rec'om·mend'
hes'i·ta'tion

(140)

....

374.

if
par

if

de·lin'quent

when

(shorthand outlines)

ap·pre'ci·ate
sat'is·fac'tion

intro

par

intro

par

pur'pose

(108)

· ·

375.

re·ceive'
in·quir'ies
ap'ti·tude

intro

intro

wheth'er
prac'ti·cal

as

sub·mit'ted

[Shorthand outlines]

re'con·sid'er
whole   intro

(123)

....

376.

too   intro

par   intro

in'voic·es

if   (101)

Assignment 41

Principles

377. Abbreviated Words — Not in Families. The ending may be omitted from some long words even though they do not fall into a family.

Convenient-convenience, memorandum, alphabet, equivalent, reluctant-reluctance, philosophy.

Privilege, privileges, privileged, significant-significance, arithmetic, atmosphere, anniversary.

378. Word Beginning Trans-. The word beginning *trans-* is expressed by a disjoined *t*.

Transacted, translate, transported, transferred, transplant, transcribe, transit.

379. Word Ending -ification. The word ending *-ification* is represented by a disjoined *f*.

Classification, justification, notification, modification, specifications, qualifications, verification.

Building Transcription Skills

380. BUSINESS VOCABULARY BUILDER

    transmitted   Sent; turned over to.

specifications A written description giving details of construction.

significant Important.

reluctant Unwilling.

facility Ease.

transcript A written or typewritten copy, as of short-hand notes.

381. **SIMILAR-WORDS DRILL**

There, their

their Belonging to them.

I cannot approve the plans in their present form.

there In or to that place.

I went there at his request.

(Also, watch out for *they're*, the contraction of *they are.*)

Reading and Writing Practice

382.

spec'i·fi·ca'tions
trans·mit'ted

ap
○

sig·nif'i·cant
knowl'edge

intro
○

[Gregg shorthand outlines]

intro ⓘ

con·ven'ient
dis·cuss'

(118)

··

383.

past   as ⓘ

18 25 > ②

③

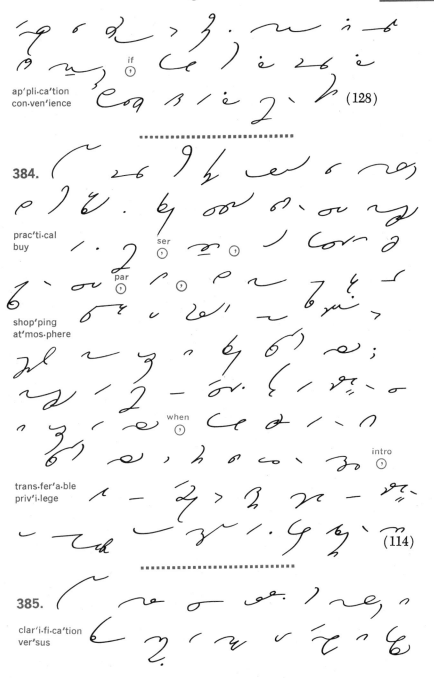

ap'pli·ca'tion
con·ven'ience

if

(128)

384.

prac'ti·cal
buy

ser

par

shop'ping
at'mos·phere

when

intro

trans·fer'a·ble
priv'i·lege

(114)

385.

clar'i·fi·ca'tion
ver'sus

Trans'con·ti·nen'tal
in'di·cate

(shorthand outlines)

par

(123)

....

386.

an'ni·ver'sa·ry
its

ap

10

growth
con'fi·dence

(95)

387.

[shorthand outlines]

lo'cal
sim'ply

[shorthand outlines]

(102)

388. Chuckle

[shorthand outlines]

(34)

Assignment 42 RECALL

There are no new shorthand devices for you to learn in Assignment 42. However, it does contain a review of the word beginnings and endings you have studied thus far and a Reading and Writing Practice that contains suggestions that you should heed carefully if you wish to get ahead in business.

389. Recall Chart. There are 84 word beginnings and endings in the following chart. Can you read them in 5 minutes?

WORD BEGINNINGS AND ENDINGS

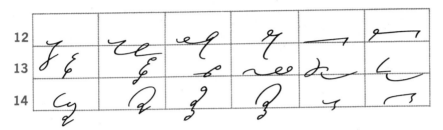

Building Transcription Skills

390. BUSINESS VOCABULARY BUILDER.

encounter To meet.

vaguely In an unclear manner; uncertainly.

compile To collect facts into a list or into a volume.

Reading and Writing Practice

Reading Scoreboard.   Twelve assignments have gone by since you last measured your reading speed. You have, of course, continued to do each Reading and Writing Practice faithfully; and, consequently, your reading speed will reflect this faithfulness! The following table will help you measure your reading speed on the *first reading* of Assignment 42.

Assignment 42 contains 528 words.

If you read Assignment 42 in	your reading rate is
15 MINUTES	35 WORDS A MINUTE
17 MINUTES	31 WORDS A MINUTE
19 MINUTES	28 WORDS A MINUTE
21 MINUTES	25 WORDS A MINUTE
23 MINUTES	23 WORDS A MINUTE
25 MINUTES	21 WORDS A MINUTE

If you can read Assignment 42 through the first time in less than 15 minutes, you are doing well. If you take considerably longer than 25 minutes, perhaps you should:

1. Pay closer attention in class while the shorthand devices are being presented to you.

2. Use the Key to Shorthand more efficiently.

3. Review, occasionally, all the brief forms you have studied through the chart on the inside back cover.

391. How Is Your Vocabulary?

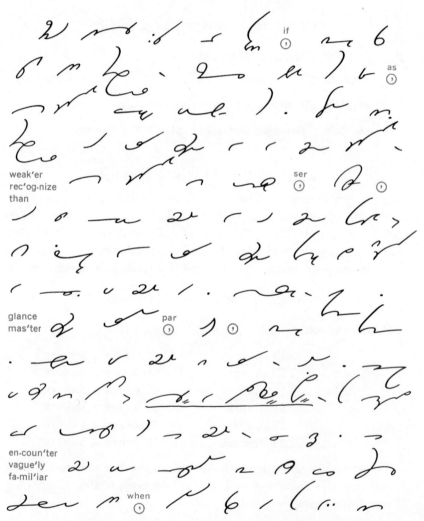

weak'er
rec'og·nize
than

ser

glance
mas'ter

par

en·coun'ter
vague'ly
fa·mil'iar

when

[Shorthand outlines]

ef·fi′cient·ly
a·cross′

if

when

par

lan′guage
u′su·al·ly
read′i·ly

intro

intro

lat′er

when

[shorthand outline] intro ⊙ *[shorthand outline]*

am·bi′tion
con′stant·ly

[shorthand outline] if ⊙ *[shorthand outline]*

[shorthand outline] (350)

392. Economy

[shorthand outlines]

stin′gi·ness
re′al·ly

[shorthand outlines] intro ⊙

intro ⊙ *[shorthand outlines]*

(shorthand outlines)

e·con'o·mize
ad·van'tage

intro

intro

intro

(178)

TRANSCRIPTION CHECK LIST

Are you getting the full benefit from the spelling and punctuation helps in the Reading and Writing Practice by —

1. Encircling all punctuation in your notes as you copy each Reading and Writing Practice?

2. Noting the reason for the use of each punctuation mark to be sure that you understand why it was used?

3. Spelling aloud at least once the spelling words given in the margin of the shorthand?

The Secretary Communicates

What is communication? In the office, communication refers to anything having to do with the written or spoken word. Most of what the secretary does in the office is concerned with communications in one form or another.

In the first place, she talks in person or by phone to many people outside the company for which she works — friends of her boss, customers, business executives, sales representatives, messengers, and various visitors. She talks with many people inside the company — her boss, other executives, secretaries, department heads, accountants, repairmen, receptionists, and janitors. She talks informally in groups and more formally in meetings. Oral communication goes on constantly — much of it highly important, some of it trivial. All of it, however, requires skill. Skill in "handling" people by means of the spoken word is vital to harmonious relations both inside and outside the company. The secretary's boss depends on her to say the right thing at the right time, because what she says and how she says it reflects on him.

The secretary needs skill in written communications, too. She must know how to write letters — letters asking for information, letters answering requests for information, and thank-you letters for favors received. She needs to know how to write interoffice memos— memos about meetings, about changes in procedures, or about routine matters of company business. She may write telegrams, minutes of meetings, and messages of various kinds.

The extent to which the secretary is given responsibility for written communications depends entirely on her own initiative and the willingness of her boss to delegate these details to her. In all cases, however, her shorthand comes in very handy. Shorthand is an ideal instrument for composing written communications of all kinds. It helps the writer to think through what he is going to say before he types it — he can revise to his heart's content without sacrificing too much time and energy. Form the habit now of using your shorthand for thinking through all your written work. It will stand you in good stead later.

Chapter
8

Assignment 43

Principles

393.   Word Ending -ulate.   The word ending *-ulate* is represented by a disjoined *oo* hook.

[shorthand outlines]

Accumulate, circulate, stipulate, congratulates, tabulator, regulated.

394.   Word Ending -ulation.   The word ending *-ulation* is represented by *oo-tion*.

[shorthand outlines]

Accumulation, population, circulation, calculation, stimulation, congratulations.

395.   Word Beginning Post-.   The word beginning *post-* is expressed by a disjoined *p*.

[shorthand outlines]

Postage, postman, post office, postmark, postpone, postponed, postponement.

396.   Word Beginning Super-.   The word beginning *super-* is expressed by a disjoined right *s*.

[shorthand outlines]

Supervise, supervisor, supersede, supervision, superintendent, superhuman, superior, superstition.

Building Transcription Skills

397. BUSINESS VOCABULARY BUILDER

circulation.   The total number of copies of a publication distributed each issue.

expenditures   Moneys paid out.

calculations   Figurings; computations.

398. PUNCTUATION PRACTICE

, conjunction

A comma is used to separate two independent clauses that are joined by one of the following conjunctions: *and, but, or, for, nor.*

An independent clause (sometimes called a main or a principal clause) is one that has a subject and predicate and that could stand alone as a complete sentence.

> The unit is one of the most dependable on the market, and it is economical to operate.

The first independent clause is:

> The unit is one of the most dependable on the market

and the second is:

> it is economical to operate

Both clauses could stand as separate sentences, with a period after each. Because the thoughts of the two clauses are closely related, however, the clauses were joined to form one sentence. Because the two independent clauses are connected by the co-ordinating conjunction *and,* a comma is used between them, before the conjunction.

Each time this use of the comma occurs in the Reading and Writing Practice, it will be indicated thus in the shorthand:

conj

⊙

Reading and Writing Practice

399.

be·lieve'
post·pone'
as·sist'ant

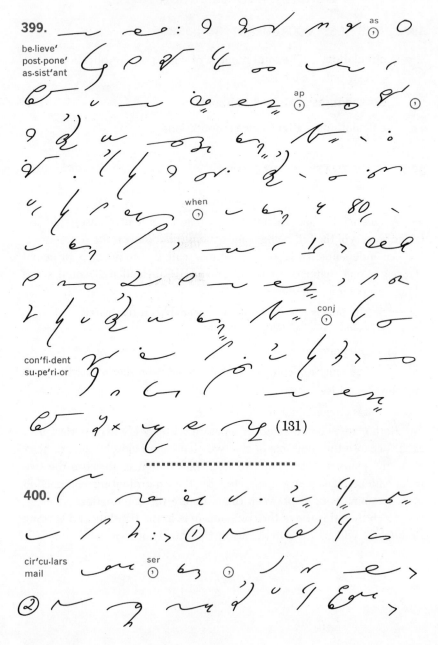

(131)

con'fi·dent
su·pe'ri·or

400.

cir'cu·lars
mail

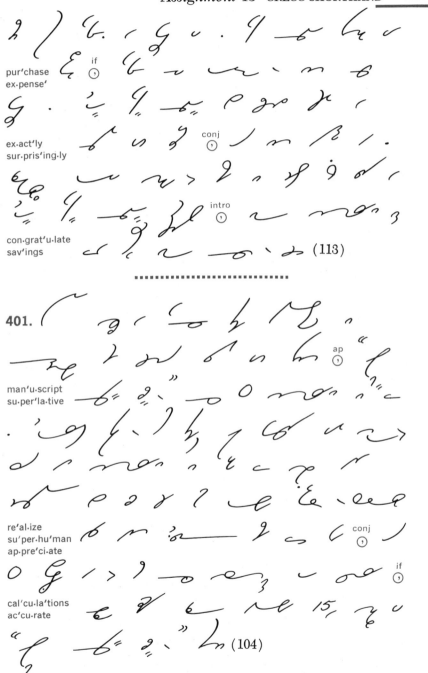

pur'chase
ex·pense'

ex·act'ly
sur·pris'ing·ly

con·grat'u·late
sav'ings

(113)

401.

man'u·script
su·per'la·tive

re'al·ize
su'per·hu'man
ap·pre'ci·ate

cal'cu·la'tions
ac'cu·rate

(104)

402.

sub·scrip′tion
Su′per·vi′sor's

(113)

....

403.

ed′i·tors
ac·cu′mu·late   *250*

[Gregg shorthand outlines]

re·ceiv'ing
cur'rent
af·fects'

if

(173)

....

404.

un·a'ble
sched'ule

par

(51)

Assignment 44

Principles

405. Word Ending -sume. The word ending -sume is represented by *s-m*.

Resume, consume, assume, presume, consumer, consumed.

406. Word Ending -sumption. The word ending *-sumption* is represented by *s-m-tion*.

Resumption, consumption, assumption, assumptions, presumption.

407. Word Beginning Self-. The word beginning *self-* is represented by a disjoined left *s*.

Self-confident, self-made, self-reliant, self-defense, selfish, selfishness, selfishly.

408. Word Beginning Circum-. The word beginning *circum-* is also represented by a disjoined left *s*.

Circumstance, circumstances, circumstantial, circumnavigate, circumvent, circumvented, circumvention.

Building Transcription Skills

409. BUSINESS VOCABULARY BUILDER

manuscript   Handwritten or typewritten copy prepared for publication.

submit   To send in; to turn over to.

contract   An agreement.

tedious   Tiresome.

resumption   Act of beginning again.

410. PUNCTUATION PRACTICE

, and omitted

When two or more adjectives modify the same noun, they are separated by commas.

He was a quiet, efficient worker.

However, the comma is not used if the first adjective modifies the combined idea of the second adjective plus the noun.

She wore a beautiful green dress.

Note: You can quickly determine whether to insert a comma between two consecutive adjectives by mentally placing *and* between them. If the sentence makes good sense with *and* inserted between the adjectives, then the comma is used. For example, the first illustration would make good sense if it read:

He was a quiet and efficient worker.

Each time this use of the comma occurs in the Reading and Writing Practice, it will be indicated thus in the shorthand:

and o

⊙

Reading and Writing Practice

411. *[shorthand outlines]*

man'u·script
en·ti'tled

when

and o

intro

wheth'er
au'thor's

par

(148)

....

412. *[shorthand outlines]*

ap

16 ·

ap

17×7

as·sump'tion
Par'lors

ser

if

intro

and o

prof'it·a·ble
well'·at·tend'ed
self'·ad·dressed'
con·ven'ience

and o

(98)

413.

if

as·sume'

o'ver·come'
fright

as

and o

te'di·ous
dif'fi·cult

(shorthand outlines) (124)

414.

re·sumed′
cit′ies

in′ter·rup′tion
be·yond′

re·sump′tion
sched′ules

(98)

415.

as·sist′ant
sub·scrip′tion

be·gin′ning
cur′rent

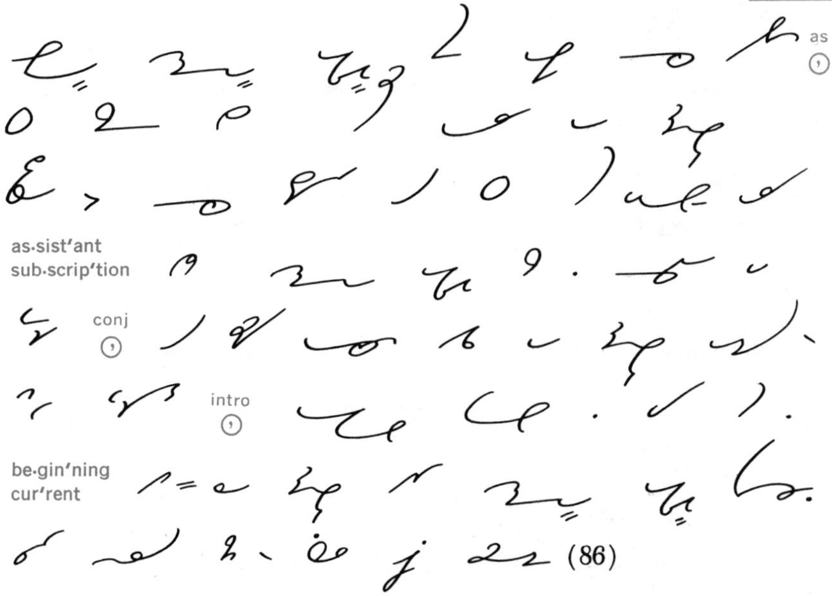
as
conj
intro
(86)

416.

re·mit′tance
out·stand′ing
al·read′y

intro
15
if
if
and o
(84)

Assignment 45

45

Principles

417. Word Ending -hood.   The word ending *-hood* is represented by a disjoined *d*.

Neighborhood, manhood, childhood, brotherhood, motherhood, likelihood.

418. Word Ending -ward.   The word ending *-ward* is also represented by a disjoined *d*.

Afterward, inward, outward, backward, onward, awkward, forward, forwarded.

419. Ul.   *Ul* is represented by *oo* when it precedes a forward or upward stroke.

Consult, result, insulted, adults, multiply, culminate.

420. Quantities and Amounts.   Here are a few more helpful abbreviations for quantities and amounts.

$500; 5,000,000; $5,000,000; 5,000,000,000; $5,000,000,000; a dollar: a million.

Several hundred, several hundred dollars, few hundred, few hundred dollars, a hundred, 4 pounds, 400 pounds, 8 feet, 200 feet.

Notice that the *m* for *million* is written beside the figure, as a positive distinction from *hundred,* in which the *n* is written underneath the figure.

266

Building Transcription Skills

421. BUSINESS VOCABULARY BUILDER

attorneys   Lawyers.

attribute (*verb*)   To assign as the reason or cause of.

depositors   Those who have money on deposit in a bank.

dividends   Profits of a corporation that are shared with stockholders.

422. SPELLING FAMILIES

An effective device to improve your ability to spell is to study words in related groups, or spelling families, in which all the words contain the same spelling problem; for example, words in which silent *e* is dropped before -*ing*.

To get the most benefit from these spelling families, practice them in this way:

1. Spell each word aloud, pausing slightly after each syllable.

2. Write the word once in longhand, spelling it aloud as you write it.

You will find several of the words in each spelling family used in the Reading and Writing Practice.

Words in Which Silent E Is Dropped Before -ing

a·chiev′ing	guid′ing	re·ceiv′ing
de·sir′ing	hous′ing	sav′ing
ex·am′in·ing	in·creas′ing	typ′ing
forc′ing	man′ag·ing	us′ing

Reading and Writing Practice

423.

awk'ward
sit'u·a'tion

intro

and o

pur'chas·es
seed

as

ser

won't

par

for'ward

and o

(140)

··································

424.

re·ward'ing
ex·pe'ri·ence

conj

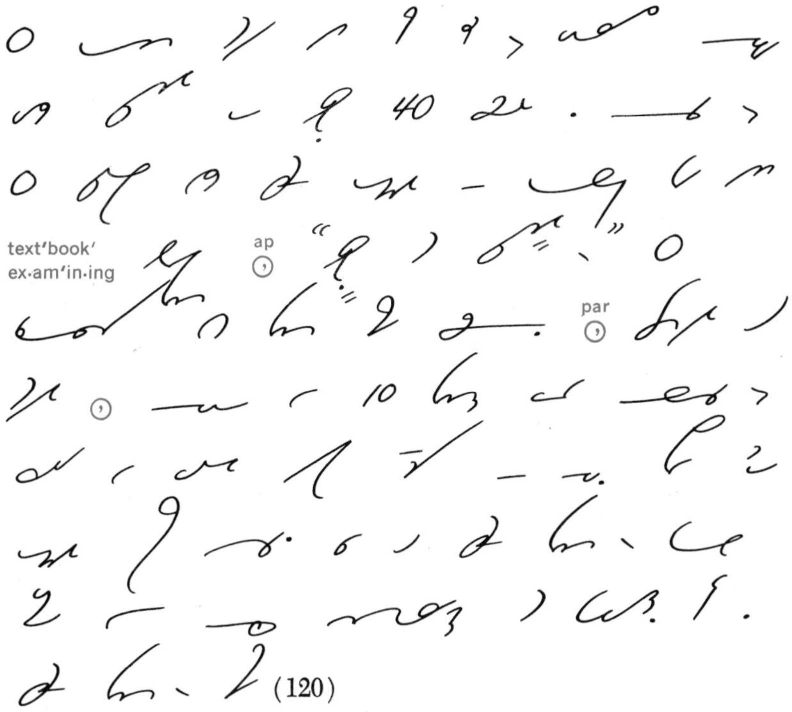
text'book'
ex·am'in·ing
ap
par
(120)

425.

intro
re·ceived'
div'i·dends
if

[Shorthand outlines]

of'fi·cers
sim'ple

when

(133)

....

426.

as

28

con'fi·dent
suit'a·ble

75/

if

(67)

427. Housing for the Future

when

a·chieve'
par'ent·hood

when

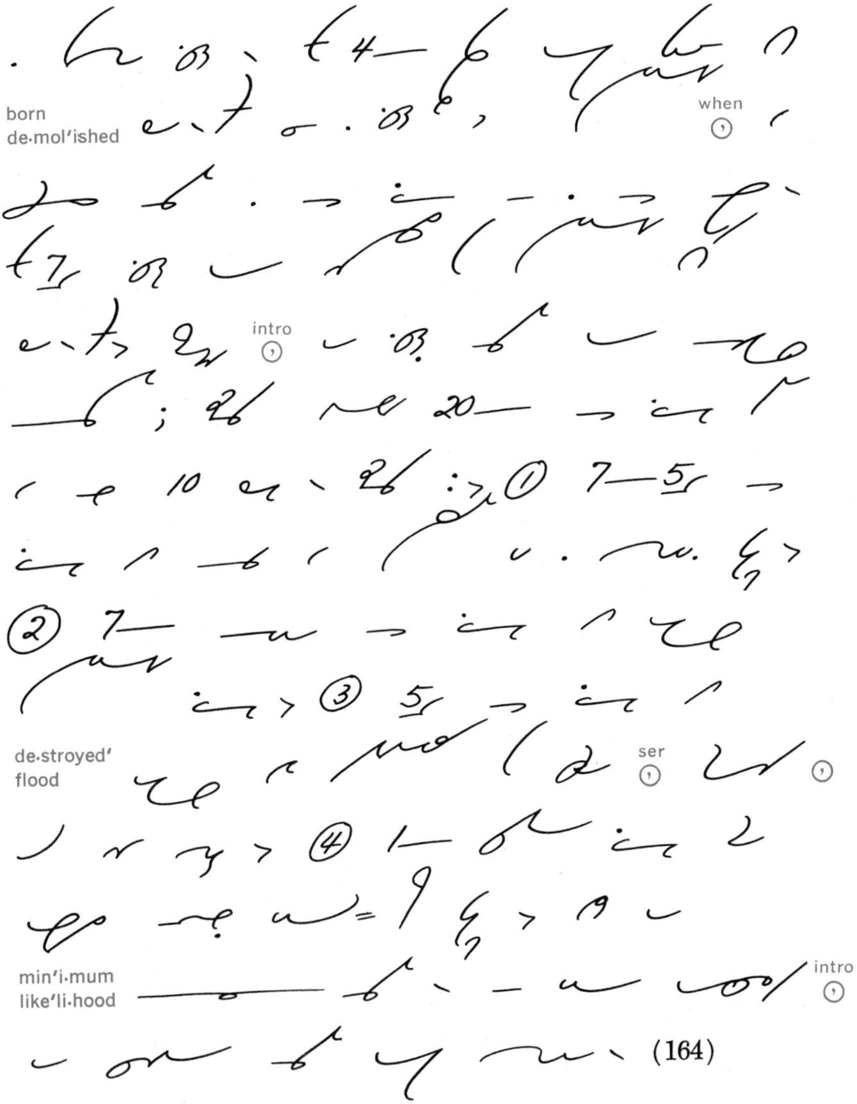
born
de·mol′ished
when
intro
de·stroyed′
flood
ser
min′i·mum
like′li·hood
intro
(164)

Assignment 46

Principles

428. Word Ending -gram. The word ending -*gram* is represented by a disjoined *g*.

[shorthand outlines]

Telegram, diagram, programs, cablegram, radiogram.

429. Word Beginning Electric. The word beginning *electric* is represented by a disjoined *el*.

[shorthand outlines]

Electric, electrical, electrically, electric fan, electric wire, electric motor.

430. Word Beginning Electr-. The word beginning *electr-* is also represented by a disjoined *el*.

[shorthand outlines]

Electronic, electrotype, electroplate, electrician, electricity, electrode.

431. Compounds. Most compound words are formed by simply joining the outlines for the words that make up the compound. In some words, however, it is desirable to modify the outline for one of the words in order to obtain a facile joining.

[shorthand outlines]

272

Anyhow, anybody, anywhere, someone, worthwhile, however, within; withstand.

Notwithstanding, somewhere, wherever, whenever, whatever, anyone, everywhere.

432.   Intersection.   Intersection, or the writing of one character through another, is sometimes useful for special phrases. You should not, however, attempt to memorize lists of such phrases; you should devise such phrases only when the constant repetition of certain phrases in your dictation makes it clearly worthwhile to form special outlines.

Vice versa, Chamber of Commerce, a.m., p.m.

Building Transcription Skills

433.   BUSINESS VOCABULARY BUILDER

> **alerted**   Warned to be ready; made aware; placed in readiness to act.
>
> **tenant**   An occupant.
>
> **menacing**   Threatening.

434.   SIMILAR-WORDS DRILL

Brought, bought

> **brought**   The past tense and past participle of *bring*.

John brought the book back after having read it.

> **bought**   Purchased.

His wife bought a new hat.

Reading and Writing Practice

435. *[shorthand outlines]*

e·lec′tri·cal
im·me′di·ate·ly

when

ser

intro

su′per·vi′sors
not′with·stand′ing
sac′ri·fice

as

breaks
trans·mis′sion

par

e·lec′tric′i·ty
brought

intro

grate′ful   and o
pa′tience

(140)

....

436. *[shorthand outlines]*

(shorthand outlines)

Guide
re·ceive′

worth′while′
com·plete′ly

if

(107)

....

437.

ap

conj

ef·fi′cient
re·sult′

(shorthand outlines)

intro ⊙

bear
re·pairs′

(shorthand outlines) (117)

· ·

438. *(shorthand outlines)*

for′ward
e·quip′ment

(shorthand outlines)

intro ⊙

di′a·gram
in′stal·la′tion

(shorthand outlines)

ap ⊙   ⊙

aj *(shorthand outlines)* (83)

· ·

439. *(shorthand outlines)*

intro ⊙

e·lec′tron′ics
mir′a·cle

(shorthand outlines)

al·read'y
tel'e·vi'sion

[Gregg shorthand outlines]

its
budg'et

[Gregg shorthand outlines]

(121)

440.　Chuckle

[Gregg shorthand outlines]

(41)

Assignment 47

Principles

441. Geographical Expressions. In geographical expressions, *-burg* is represented by *b*; *-ingham*, by a disjoined *m*; *ington*, by a disjoined *ten* blend; *-ville*, by *v*.

-burg

-ingham

-ington

-ville

Harrisburg, Pittsburgh, Plattsburg, Greensburg, Bloomsburg, Galesburg, Newburgh.

Buckingham, Cunningham, Framingham, Birmingham, Nottingham.

Lexington, Washington, Wilmington, Burlington, Huntington.

Jacksonville, Nashville, Evansville, Danville, Knoxville, Brownsville, Zanesville, Louisville.

Building Transcription Skills

442. BUSINESS VOCABULARY BUILDER

complicated   Hard to solve.

utmost   The most possible.

278

enviable   Desirable.

maintenance   Upkeep.

443.   GRAMMAR CHECKUP

Most businessmen have a good command of the English language. Some rarely make an error in grammar. There are times, though, when even the best dictators will perhaps use a plural verb with a singular noun or use the objective case when they should have used the nominative. They usually know better; but in concentrating intently on expressing a thought or idea, they occasionally suffer a grammatical lapse.

It will be your job, as a stenographer or secretary, to catch these occasional errors in grammar and correct them when you transcribe.

From time to time in the assignments ahead, you will be given an opportunity to brush up on some of the rules of grammar that are frequently violated.

Subject and Verb

A verb must agree with its subject in number.

> Our *representative is* looking forward to the pleasure of serving you.
> Your canceled *checks are* mailed to you each month.

The inclusion of a phrase such as *in addition to, as well as,* or *along with* after the subject does not affect the number of the verb. If the subject is singular, use a singular verb. If the subject is plural, use a plural verb.

> Our *representative,* as well as our managers, *is* looking forward to the pleasure of serving you.
> Your canceled *checks,* along with your statement, *are* mailed to you each month.

Reading and Writing Practice

444.

com·plete'ly
re·paved'

ser

com'pli·cat'ed
cus'tom·ers

conj

serv'ice
Pitts'burgh's

par

ap

(109)

· ·

445.

ar·range'ments
mov'ing

18

if

stor'age
en'vi·a·ble

and o

par

〔shorthand outline〕 (88)

· ·

446. 〔shorthand outlines〕

theft
car'ry·ing

〔shorthand outlines〕

main'te·nance
can'celed 〔shorthand outlines〕 25 〔outline〕 .

〔shorthand outlines〕 par ⊙

〔shorthand outlines〕 ⊙

neigh'bor·hood 〔shorthand outlines〕 when ⊙

con·ven'ient
mail 〔shorthand outlines〕 if ⊙

〔shorthand outlines〕 (108)

· ·

447. 〔shorthand outlines〕

〔shorthand outlines〕 conj ⊙

a·mong'
wel'come

[shorthand outlines]

as
(,)

[shorthand outlines]

par
(,)

op'por·tu'ni·ty
per'son·al·ly

par
(,)

(115)

....

448.

[shorthand outlines]

au'thor·ized
sea'son

[shorthand outlines] 9 . 2

[shorthand outlines] 20,

[Gregg shorthand outlines]

wheth'er
ac·cept'

conj

if

par

(138)

· ·

449.

re·leas'es
ma·te'ri·al
bright

ser

ser

du'pli·cat·ing
es·pe'cial·ly
sten'cil

(89)

Assignment 48 RECALL

In Assignment 47 you studied the last of the new shorthand devices of Gregg Shorthand. In this assignment you will find a Recall Chart that reviews all the word-building principles of Gregg Shorthand and a Reading and Writing Practice that contains some "food for thought."

450. Recall Chart. This chart contains one or more illustrations of every word-building and phrasing principle of Gregg Shorthand.

WORDS

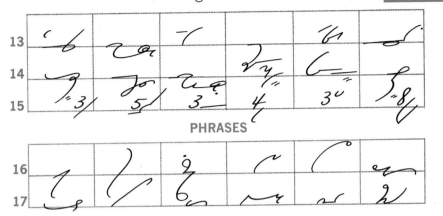

13						
14						
15						

PHRASES

| 16 | | | | | | |
| 17 | | | | | | |

Building Transcription Skills

451. BUSINESS VOCABULARY BUILDER

vital Necessary; essential.

humble Lowly.

productive Yielding results.

Reading and Writing Practice

452. Pride

re′al·ly
some′one′

ser
⊙

when
⊙

rise
ex·ec′u·tive

(shorthand outlines)

ser

their
sat′is·fac′to·ri·ly

intro

par

ex·am′ple
fac′to·ry

ser

intro

ser

stand′still′

if

when

par

em·ploy′ee
hum′ble

conj

(209)

453.   Self-Control

[Gregg shorthand outlines]

los'ing
theirs

intro

ex·am'ine
traits

if

calm'ly
per'son·al   intro

con'tra·ry   intro

(147)

454. Faithful Servant

[Shorthand outlines]

dai′ly
dis′tance

de·liv′er·y
minds

(161)

REINFORCEMENT

PART

2

The Secretary "Looks It Up"

Suppose a strange word is given to you in dictation. It sounds like "ingenuous." Or was it "ingenious"? Both are perfectly good words. But which is correct? You read your notes carefully and you look up these two words in the dictionary; then you make your choice. You are right, because you make sure the word fits the meaning your notes show was intended. The smart secretary doesn't guess — she looks it up.

"I don't expect my secretary to be a 'walking encyclopedia,' " says the executive, "but I do expect her to <u>know when she doesn't know</u> — and to know where to look things up."

Do you know when and where to look things up? Now is the time to begin forming the habit of looking things up when you aren't sure. Even the experienced secretary turns to several reference sources during the course of a day to make absolutely sure she is right. She may use the dictionary, a grammar handbook, a company style manual for typists and stenographers, an encyclopedia, a book on filing, a letter-writing handbook, and a book on etiquette. Nothing is left to chance. To be right is important. It's the smart secretary who <u>knows when she doesn't know</u>.

Do you know how to address a member of the clergy? a senator? Do you know how to write an acceptance to a formal invitation? Do you know the correct salutation when writing to a company composed entirely of women? Which is correct: "Whom are you expecting?" or "Who are you expecting?" How do you address a package to someone in a foreign country? What is meant by the Latin expression <u>sine qua non</u>? You may have to answer questions such as these every day. Of course, you aren't expected to know the answers to everything asked of you, but you <u>are</u> expected to know where to find the information you need.

It's smart to be right.

Chapter

9

Assignment 49

The ungraded practice material in this assignment concentrates on the shorthand principles you studied in Chapter 1.

455. BRIEF FORMS AND DERIVATIVES

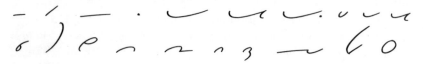

In-not, it-at, am, a-an, will-well, wills, willing, of, are-hour-our, ours. With, have, that, can, cannot, you-your, yours, Mr., but, I.

Building Transcription Skills

456. BUSINESS VOCABULARY BUILDER

vocation   Profession; line of work.

grasp   Understanding.

corrective measures   Steps to make a situation right.

Reading and Writing Practice

457.

ap·point'ed
ter'ri·to'ry

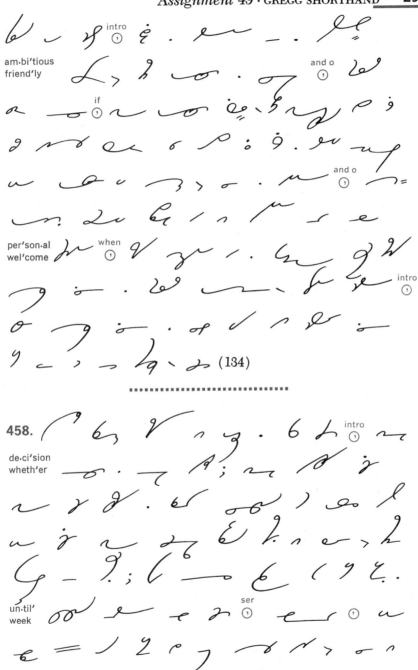

am·bi'tious
friend'ly

per'son·al
wel'come

(134)

458.

de·ci'sion
wheth'er

un·til'
week

re·ceive′
in′de·pend′ence

(shorthand outlines) (109)

....

459.

mer′chan·dise

(shorthand outlines)

clothes
of′fered

(shorthand outlines) (77)

....

460.

(shorthand outlines)

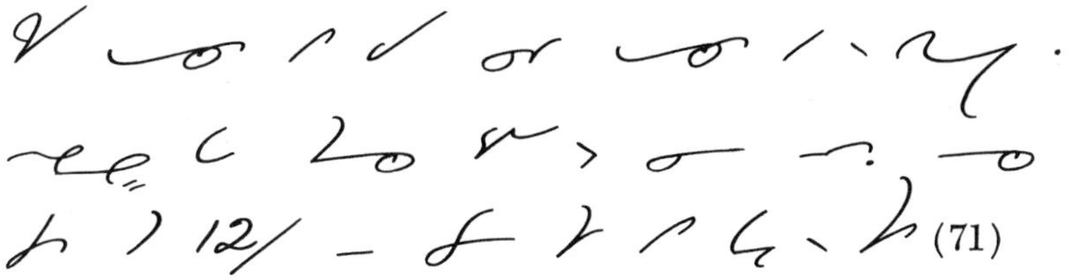
(71)

461.

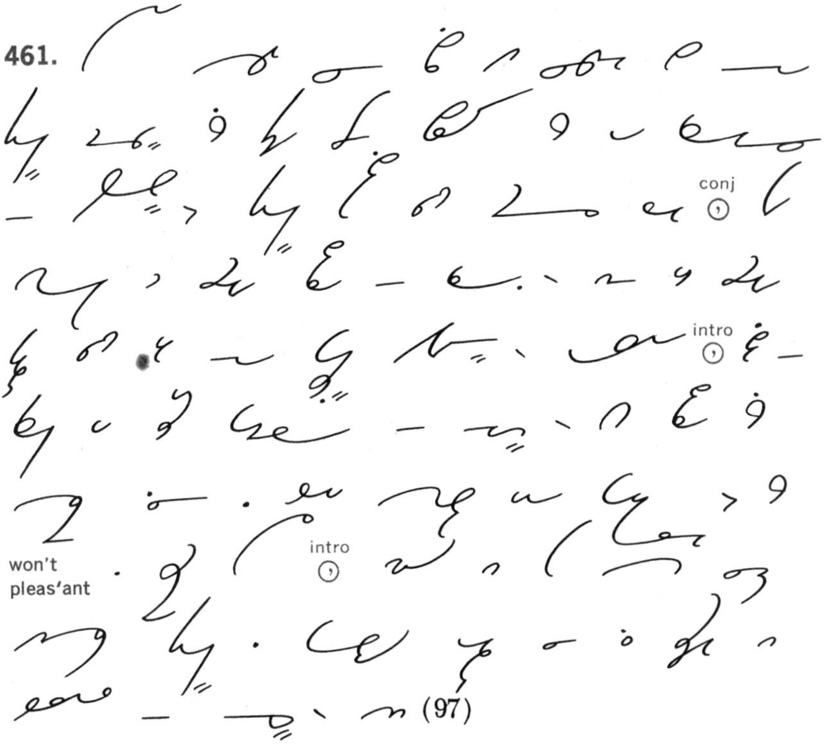
conj
intro
intro
(97)

won't
pleas'ant

462.

fourth
due

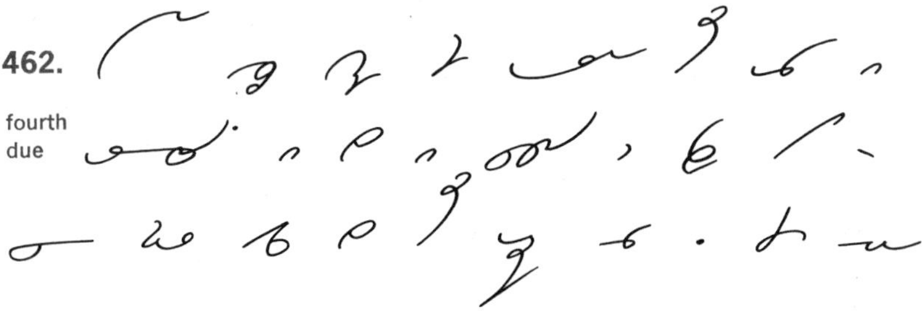

(shorthand outlines) as

Bu'reau
yours *(shorthand outlines)*

when *(shorthand outlines)*

3

par
2 *(shorthand outlines)*

vi'tal·ly *(shorthand outlines)* (122)

· ·

463. *(shorthand outlines)*

(shorthand outlines) 15 *(shorthand outline)* 150/

(shorthand outlines) 15 *(shorthand outline)* (67)

Assignment 50

The ungraded practice material in this assignment concentrates on the shorthand principles you studied in Chapter 2.

464. BRIEF FORMS AND DERIVATIVES

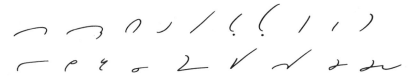

Good, goods, this, their-there, would, putting, being, which, shall, for. Them, they, was, when, from, should, could, send, sender.

Building Transcription Skills

465. BUSINESS VOCABULARY BUILDER

loath   Unhappy; reluctant.

mart   A market or store.

good will   Kindly feeling; well wishing.

Reading and Writing Practice

466.

sec're·tar'y
an'swer

297

(shorthand outlines)

par

a'gen·cy
loath

conj

15

15

150/

(114)

467.

as

20

conj

350/

if

par'tial
pre·serve'

(shorthand outlines) (101)

....

468. *(shorthand outlines)*

(shorthand outlines) (87)

....

469. *(shorthand outlines)*

cloth'ing
peak
choose

intro
①

(shorthand outlines)

[shorthand outline] *if* *[shorthand outline]* (87)

....

470. *[shorthand outline]* ... 1960.

[shorthand outline]

buy'er
lose *[shorthand outline]* *conj* *[shorthand outline]*

[shorthand outline] *par* *[shorthand outline]*

[shorthand outline] *intro* *[shorthand outline]*

[shorthand outline]

[shorthand outline] (99)

....

471. *[shorthand outline]*

16 *[shorthand outline]* 10/ *[shorthand outline]*

de·pos'it
Christ'mas *[shorthand outline]*

[shorthand outline]

[Shorthand outlines] (69)

---

472. *[Shorthand outlines]*

re·ceived′
cat′a·logue

[Shorthand outlines] 15.

if

con·ven′ient
sup·plies′

intro

[Shorthand outlines] (81)

---

473. *[Shorthand outlines]*

rea′son·a·ble *[Shorthand outlines]* (49)

Assignment 51

The ungraded practice material in this assignment concentrates on the shorthand principles you studied in Chapter 3.

474. BRIEF FORMS AND DERIVATIVES

Gladly, worker, yesterday, orders, thanks, very, soon, enclosed, years. Values, than, once, what, about, greater, businesses, why, thinking. Gentlemen, morning, important-importance, those, where, manufacture.

Building Transcription Skills

475. BUSINESS VOCABULARY BUILDER

offended   Displeased; angered.

statistics   Facts that can be expressed in numbers.

Reading and Writing Practice

476.

[Shorthand outlines]

wheth'er
right

if

as

bar'gains
racks

(101)

· ·

477. *[Shorthand outlines]*

15

fi·nan'cial
sta·tis'tics

as

if

3/

(93)

478. [shorthand outline]

intro
⊙

par
⊙

can'dies
at·trac'tive·ly
wrapped

as
⊙

par
⊙

if
⊙

(94)

••••••••••••••••••••••••••••

479. [shorthand outline]

their
bright

[Gregg shorthand outlines]

op′er·a′tor
cou′pon

(110)

. . . .

480.

shop′ping
mov′ie

when
①

[shorthand outlines] (97)

·······························

481. *[shorthand outlines]*

re'al·ize
yours *[shorthand outlines]* as

loss
re·spon'si·ble *[shorthand outlines]* if

par *[shorthand outlines]*

intro *[shorthand outlines]*

[shorthand outlines] (137)

Assignment 52

The ungraded practice material in this assignment concentrates on the shorthand principles you studied in Chapter 4.

482. BRIEF FORMS AND DERIVATIVES

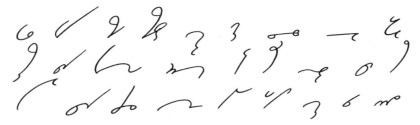

Presently, parted, after, advertises, companies, wishes, immediately, must, opportunities.

Advantages, used, bigger, suggestion, such, several, corresponds, how-out, ever-every.

Times, acknowledged, generally, gone, during, overdue, questions, yet, worthy.

Building Transcription Skills

483. BUSINESS VOCABULARY BUILDER

correspondent   A letter writer.

gratifying   Pleasing; satisfying.

pulling power   An advertising term indicating the effectiveness of an advertisement in persuading potential customers to react favorably.

rigid   Exacting; careful.

484. SPELLING FAMILIES

Words Ending in -tion

ac'tion	com·ple'tion	lo·ca'tion
ap'pli·ca'tion	con·nec'tion	mo'tion
cel'e·bra'tion	cor·rec'tion	ques'tion
col·lec'tion	il'lus·tra'tion	re·la'tion

Words Ending in -sion

con·clu'sion	di·vi'sion	pro·vi'sion
de·ci'sion	pen'sion	tel'e·vi'sion
de·pres'sion	per·sua'sion	ten'sion

Reading and Writing Practice

485.

Sep·tem'ber
cor're·spond'ent

(98)

486.

ad'ver·tis'ing
re'cent·ly

intro

re·plies'
grat'i·fy'ing

(120)

·····························

487.

conj

[Gregg shorthand outlines]

rig'id
fac'to·ry

if

(104)

· ·

488. *[Gregg shorthand outlines]* 1925

par

40

serv'ing
min'i·mum

intro

de·ci'sion
pur'chase 1960

when

(102)

489.

in·quir′ies
a·vail′a·ble

fa·mil′iar
pol′i·cies

intro

ser

intro

Christ′mas
ap·proach′ing

intro

(130)

·····························

490.

conj

(42)

Assignment 53

The ungraded practice material in this assignment concentrates on the shorthand principles you studied in Chapter 5.

491. BRIEF FORMS AND DERIVATIVES

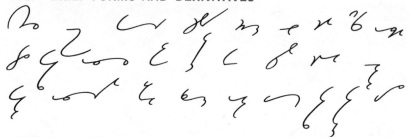

Difficulty, envelope, progressed, satisfied, successes, next, states, underpay, requests.

Particularly, probably, regularly, speaker, subjects, upon, ideas, streets, newspapers.

Purposes, regards, opinions, circulars, responsible, organization, publicly, publishes-publications, ordinarily.

Building Transcription Skills

492. BUSINESS VOCABULARY BUILDER

novel   New; different; unusual.

enhance   To make greater; to increase.

mailing department   A department in a large firm that handles incoming and outgoing mail.

Reading and Writing Practice

493.

col·lec'tion
sum'ma·rized

[shorthand outlines] (58)

494. *[shorthand outlines]* — 1910

pi'o·neer'
for'eign

[shorthand outlines]

if

writ'ing
prompt'ly

if

[shorthand outlines] (107)

495. *[shorthand outlines]*

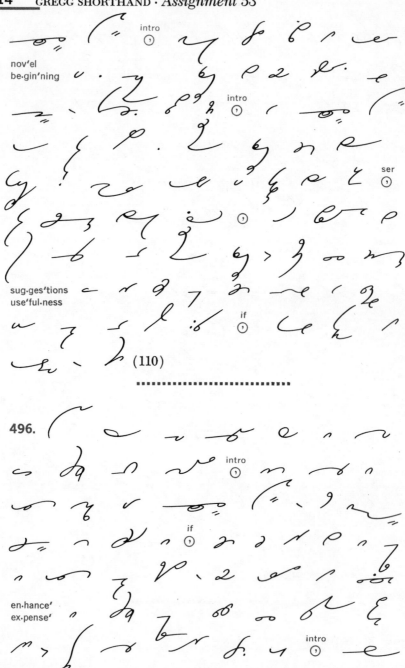

nov'el
be·gin'ning

sug·ges'tions
use'ful·ness

(110)

．．．．．．．．．．．．．．．．．．．．．．．．．．．．．．

496.

en·hance'
ex·pense'

[Gregg shorthand outlines] (94)

································

497. *[shorthand outlines]*

ex·pe′ri·enc·ing
dif′fi·cul·ty

[shorthand outlines] intro ⊙

[shorthand outlines] as ⊙

du′pli·cate *[shorthand outlines]* as ⊙

[shorthand outlines] conj ⊙

[shorthand outlines] (115)

································

498. *[shorthand outlines]*

(shorthand outlines)

piece
scratched

ap

intro

par

when

(97)

• •

499.

sub·scrip'tion
prompt'ly

(61)

Assignment 54

The ungraded practice material in this assignment concentrates on the shorthand principles you studied in Chapter 6.

500. BRIEF FORMS AND DERIVATIVES

Merchants, merchandise, recognized, never, experiences, between, quantities, situations.

Railroads, worlds, throughout, objected, characters, government, shortly.

Building Transcription Skills

501. BUSINESS VOCABULARY BUILDER

achieve   To obtain; to attain.

foremost   Most advanced; first in importance.

hazard   Danger.

refund   To repay.

502. SIMILAR-WORDS DRILL

Weather, whether

weather   State of the atmosphere with respect to wetness or dryness, cold or heat; climate.

You can take a good picture regardless of the weather.

The game was called because of the weather.

whether　Indicating a choice (often followed by *or*).
Also used to introduce an indirect question.

You can take a good picture whether the sun is shining or whether it is raining.

Let me know whether you will be free on Friday.

Reading and Writing Practice

503.

a·chieve′
peace

par

ex·pe′ri·ence
con′fi·dence

ser

ap

[shorthand outlines] (82)

··

504. *[shorthand outlines with annotations:]*

as

un·for'tu·nate·ly
traf'fic
haz'ard

par

per·mis'sion
ob·jec'tion

par

par

(111)

·······································

505. *[shorthand outlines with annotations:]*

Sam'u·els
re·ceived'

par

mer′chan·dise

par

fig′ures
im·me′di·ate·ly

par

(135)

∙∙∙∙∙∙∙∙∙∙∙∙∙∙∙∙∙∙∙∙∙∙∙∙∙∙∙

506.

prac′ti·cal
but′ton

intro

ser

beau′ti·ful
weath′er

[Gregg shorthand outlines]

in'doors'
out'doors'

cloud'y
re·ceive'
de·scrip'tive

ser

ap

(166)

507.   Chuckle

[Gregg shorthand outlines]

× (54)

Assignment 55

The practice material in this assignment concentrates on the shorthand principles you studied in Chapter 7.

508. BRIEF FORMS AND DERIVATIVES

Greater, sooner, bigger, shorter, worker, sender, manufacturer.
Particularly, successfully, timely, immediately, partly, presently, gladly, purposely.
Suggested, corresponded, timed, progressed, organized.

Building Transcription Skills

509. BUSINESS VOCABULARY BUILDER

clarity   Clearness.

convey   To tell; to impart.

aptitude   Natural ability.

510. GRAMMAR CHECKUP

The Infinitive   (The form of the verb usually introduced by *to — to see, to be, to have, to do.*)

Careful writers try to avoid "splitting" an infinitive; that is, inserting a word or phrase between *to* and the following word.

No

To properly do the job, you need better tools.

Yes

To do the job properly, you need better tools.

No

He was told to carefully prepare the report.

Yes

He was told to prepare the report carefully.

Reading and Writing Practice

511.   Your Telephone Voice

pleas′ant
im·pressed′

prob′a·bly
dif′fi·cult

con·vey′
clar′i·ty

[shorthand outlines]

soft′ly
choos′ing

ser

[shorthand outlines]

intro

[shorthand outlines] (168)

· ·

512. *[shorthand outlines]*

conj

intro

when

slop′py
im·pres′sion

intro

[shorthand outlines]

ap

(120)

··

513.

a·maz'ing·ly
Us'ing

ap

ser

pre'vi·ous
ap'ti·tude

dif'fi·cul·ty
de·scrip'tion

[shorthand outline] (130)

514. Chuckle

[shorthand outlines] (92)

SPELLING AND PUNCTUATION CHECK LIST

Are you careful to punctuate and spell correctly when —

1. You write your compositions in English?

2. Prepare your reports for your social studies classes?

3. Correspond with friends to whom you must write in longhand?

In short, are you making correct spelling and punctuation a habit in all the longhand writing or typing that you do?

Assignment 56

The practice material in this assignment concentrates on the shorthand principles you studied in Chapter 8.

515. BRIEF FORMS AND DERIVATIVES

Streets, objects, situations, merchants, regards, quantities, satisfies, newspapers.

Bigness, goodness, greatness, gladness, orderliness.

Government, apartment, departments, advertisement, acknowledgment, statement.

Building Transcription Skills

516. BUSINESS VOCABULARY BUILDER

executive A person charged with administrative work in a company.

simultaneously At the same time.

accrue To come (to someone) by way of increase or advantage.

ultimately Finally; in the end.

postage meter A machine that "prints" postage on envelopes automatically.

517. COMMON WORD ROOTS

Many English words are derived from the Greek and Latin. Consequently, an understanding of the meanings of Greek and Latin prefixes and suffixes will often give you a clue to the meaning of words with which you are unfamiliar.

Perhaps you never heard the word *posterity*. However, if you know that *post* means *after*, you will probably be able to figure out that *posterity* refers to those who come after, or descendants.

In each "Common Word Roots" exercise you will be given a common prefix or suffix, together with its meaning, and a list of words in which the prefix or suffix is used.

Read each definition carefully, and then study the illustrations that follow. A number of the illustrations are used in the Reading and Writing Practice.

Super-: *over, more than*

> **supervise**   To oversee.
>
> **supervisor**   One who oversees.
>
> **superior**   Over in rank; higher.
>
> **supertax**   A tax over and above a normal tax.

Building Transcription Skills

518.

suc·cess'ful
busi'ness·men'

ser

pat'tern
ex·ec'u·tive

par

self'-con'fi·dence

(Gregg shorthand outlines)

su′per·vi′sor
at·trac′tive

par

and o

when

(157)

519.

for′ward·ed
Main′te·nance

as

at·ten′tion
ben′e·fits
ac·crue′

re·duc'es
min'i·mum
ex·pense'

(shorthand outlines) (107)

....

520. *(shorthand outlines)*

ser

par

bur'den
fi·nanc'es

par

try'ing
past

(shorthand outlines) (102)

521.

av'er·age
mod'el — intro

loss
mis·use'

self'–in'ter·est — intro
neigh'bor·hood

(113)

....

522.

ten'ants
at·tend'ants

par

[Shorthand outlines]

in'stal·la'tion
new'er

(130)

· ·

523. *[Shorthand outlines]*

(57)

524. Chuckle

[Shorthand outlines]

(41)

SHORTHAND AND TRANSCRIPTION SKILL BUILDING

PART

3

Going Up?

The kind of job you will get and the progress you will make in it will depend almost entirely on you. Does this sound old-fashioned? Well, it is still true. Good looks and a sparkling personality are wonderful assets to anyone; and if you are blessed with these gifts, make the most of them. But they are by no means everything. They are merely "frosting on the cake." If you manage to use your head and make the most of the talents, looks, and abilities you do have, you will make the grade in fine style.

The business executive wants his secretary to have <u>interest</u> and <u>ability</u>. With those two qualities, she can lick the world. Of course, he expects her to look smart, neat, and clean. Note that we did not say he insists that she be a raving beauty. While he is not averse to a sparkling personality and good looks, he can't afford to let these qualities influence his decision in hiring and promoting.

In a secretarial position, the opportunity to learn is unlimited. You will have an orchestra seat to all the important goings-on in your executive's domain. It has happened many times that the secretary moved into the boss's shoes when he was promoted.

Even if you don't aspire to the boss's job, your future will depend on how well he does his job. Are you skeptical? Let's examine this statement. In a typical company there are many executive promotions every year. Those promotions go to the people who have proved to be outstanding in their jobs and who "have a future." An executive can hardly be outstanding if he is saddled with inefficient secretarial help. Usually, when he receives a promotion, his secretary gets one, too. Suppose he is a department head and is promoted to the position of vice-president. Automatically his salary is increased. And the secretary to a vice-president is a more important person than the secretary to a department manager; so, she generally gets a salary increase, too. If the secretary is really good, she moves right up the ladder with her boss.

You and your boss will be a team. Your success will depend on his success. It's that simple.

Chapter

10

Assignment 57

The practice material in this assignment is "loaded" with brief forms. If you gave proper attention to the brief forms as they were introduced, you should be able to complete this lesson in record time!

Building Transcription Skills

525. **BUSINESS VOCABULARY BUILDER**

speculates   Wonders; thinks.

identical   The same.

browse   To examine casually merchandise offered for sale.

time-payment plan   A charge plan offered by retail stores whereby customers may pay for merchandise in installments.

526. **SPELLING FAMILIES**

Words in Which Silent E Is Retained Before -ment

ad·vance'ment	en·gage'ment	re·tire'ment
ad·ver'tise·ment	man'age·ment	re·quire'ment
a·muse'ment	move'ment	state'ment
en·cour'age·ment	re·place'ment	

Words in Which Silent E Is Omitted Before -ment

ac·knowl'edg·ment	judg'ment	ar'gu·ment

Reading and Writing Practice

527.

[Gregg shorthand outlines]

sug·ges′tions
de·rive′

serv′ic·ing
lo′cal
judg′ment

par ⊙

when ⊙

intro ⊙

intro ⊙

(137)

. . . .

528.

yours
worn

if ⊙

worth'while'
var'i·ous

[shorthand outlines]

pur'chase
re·quire'ments

[shorthand outlines]

(114)

·····························

529.

[shorthand outlines]

some'how
dif'fer·ent

[shorthand outlines]

[Shorthand outlines]

prompt'ly
browse
e'qual·ly

conj

conj

intro

hard'ware'
fas'ci·nat'ing

par

(152)

530.

wheth'er
Man'u·al

if

par

(78)

531.

[shorthand outline]

in'di·ca'tion
suc·cess'
al·read'y

as

ser

(146)

532. TRANSCRIPTION QUIZ

Beginning with Assignment 57, you will have an opportunity to see how well you have mastered the nine uses of the comma that were introduced in Chapters 6, 7, and 8. Assignments 57–69 contain one letter each that is called a "Transcription Quiz." It contains several illustrations of the uses of the comma that you have studied. The commas, however, are not indicated in the printed shorthand. It will be your job, as you copy the letter in shorthand in your notebook, to insert the commas in the proper places and to give the reasons why the commas are used. The shorthand in your notebook should resemble the following example:

[shorthand outlines] when ...

Caution: Please do not make any marks in your shorthand textbook. If you do, you will destroy the value of these quizzes to anyone else who may use the book.

The correct punctuation of the following letter calls for 4 commas — 1 comma *as* clause, 2 commas parenthetical, 1 comma introductory.

[shorthand outlines]

(114)

Assignment 58

This assignment is designed to increase further your ability to use the frequent phrases of Gregg Shorthand. It contains several illustrations of all the phrasing principles.

Building Transcription Skills

533. BUSINESS VOCABULARY BUILDER

brochures   Pamphlets.

stationery   Writing supplies, such as paper, envelopes, pens, pencils, and so on. (Do not confuse with *stationary*, which means "fixed; not moving.")

confidential   Private.

credit card   A means of identification issued by business firms to their charge customers.

534. GRAMMAR CHECKUP

Sentence Structure

Parallel ideas should be expressed in parallel form.

No

I hope our relationship will be long, pleasant, and *of profit* to both of us.

Yes

I hope our relationship will be long, pleasant, and *profitable* to both of us.

No

As soon as we receive the necessary information, your account will be opened and *we will ship your order*.

Yes

As soon as we receive the necessary information, your account
   will be opened and *your order will be shipped.*

It is especially important to keep parallel all ideas in a tabulation.

No

Her main duties were:
   1. Taking dictation and transcribing
   2. Answering the telephone
   3. *To take care* of the files

Yes

Her main duties were:
   1. Taking dictation and transcribing
   2. Answering the telephone
   3. *Taking care* of the files

Reading and Writing Practice

535.

re·quest'ed
bro·chures'

intro

ap

ar·rives'
dis·cuss'

when

if

(110)

536.

ap·pre'ci·ate
sta'tion·er'y

ap

intro

par

par

be·gin'ning
pleas'ant

ser

(104)

....

537.

intro

ap·pre'ci·at'ed
past

par

ser

(84)

538.

[Gregg shorthand outlines]

shop'ping
cat'a·logue

as
⊙,

if
⊙,

intro
⊙,

sim'i·lar
mer'chan·dise

if
⊙,

intro
⊙,

(176)

539.

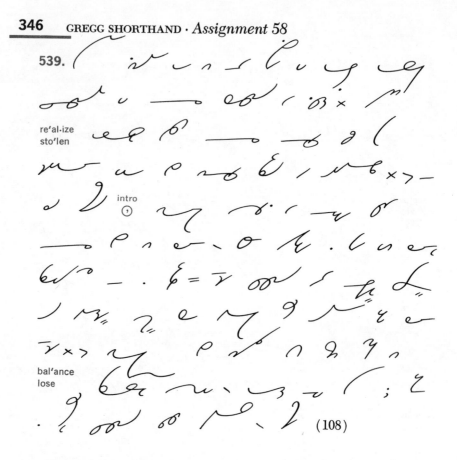

re'al·ize
sto'len

intro

bal'ance
lose

(108)

540. Transcription Quiz. To punctuate the following letter correctly, you must supply 5 commas — 1 comma conjunction, 2 commas series, 2 commas parenthetical.

No marks in the textbook, please!

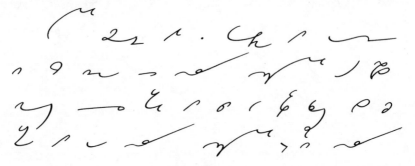

[Gregg shorthand outlines] (86)

541. Chuckle

[Gregg shorthand outlines] (62)

Assignment 59

Are some of the joined word beginnings still a little hazy in your mind? The practice material in this assignment will help fix all the joined word beginnings more firmly in your mind.

Building Transcription Skills

542. BUSINESS VOCABULARY BUILDER

> **financial statement** A statement prepared by a business firm showing its financial condition or progress.
>
> **via** By way of.
>
> **express** A method of shipping merchandise by rail, truck, and plane.
>
> **discount** An amount deducted from a customer's bill when prompt payment is made.
>
> **ensue** To follow.

543. SPELLING FAMILIES

Words Ending in -ence

com·mence′	ev′i·dence	neg′li·gence
con′fer·ence	ex′cel·lence	oc·cur′rence
con′fi·dence	ex·per′i·ence	ref′er·ence
dif′fer·ence	in′de·pend′ence	vi′o·lence

Words Ending in -ance

ac·cept′ance	bal′ance	in·sur′ance
al·low′ance	cir′cum·stance	per·form′ance
as·sist′ance	ig′no·rance	re·li′ance
as·sur′ance	in′stance	sub′stance

Reading and Writing Practice

544. *[Gregg shorthand outlines]*

vi'a
re·ceive'
week

as ⊙

conj ⊙

if ⊙

intro ⊙

ev'er·y·thing'
con'fi·dence

(117)

· ·

545. *[Gregg shorthand outlines]*

la'bels
un·for'tu·nate·ly

par ⊙

[Shorthand outlines]

ex′cel·lent
fi·nan′cial·ly   conj

un·doubt′ed·ly
im·me′di·ate·ly   intro

80

when   (138)

. . . .

546.   ap

for′mer
sub·mit′ted
ref′er·ence

ser

as·sist'ance
pro·spec'tive
em·ploy'ee

par

(120)

547.

ap·pre'ci·a'tion
re'cent

es·pe'cial·ly
com'pli·men'ta·ry
yours

conj

(101)

548.

sup·ply'ing
let'ter·heads'

[shorthand outlines] conj ⊙ *[shorthand outlines]* intro ⊙ *[shorthand outlines]*

[shorthand outlines]

[shorthand outlines]

conj ⊙ *[shorthand outlines]*

[shorthand outlines] (93)

··

549. *[shorthand outlines]*

[shorthand outlines]

[shorthand outlines]

[shorthand outlines] 250 *[shorthand outlines]*

priv'i·leg·es
sched'uled *[shorthand outlines]*

[shorthand outlines] 80 *[shorthand outlines]*

[shorthand outlines]

[shorthand outlines]

[shorthand outlines]

[shorthand outlines]

[shorthand outlines]

[shorthand outlines] intro ⊙ *[shorthand outlines]*

[Gregg shorthand outlines]

250/ (174)

550. Transcription Quiz.   The correct punctuation of the following letter calls for 8 commas — 1 comma conjunction, 2 commas series,
4 commas parenthetical, 1 comma *and* omitted.

[Gregg shorthand outlines]

(98)

Assignment 60

In this assignment you will "brush up" on joined word endings.

Building Transcription Skills

551. BUSINESS VOCABULARY BUILDER

> **bank statement**   A statement given by the bank to its depositors showing checks written, deposits made, and other information.
>
> **recur**   To happen again.
>
> **unprecedented**   Never having been done before.

552. COMMON WORD ROOTS

Re-: *again*

> **reprint**   To print again.
>
> **repeat**   To say again.
>
> **reconsider**   To take up again.
>
> **replenish**   To fill or supply again.

Reading and Writing Practice

Reading Scoreboard.   How much has your reading speed increased over your first score in Assignment 18? The table on the next page will help you determine your reading speed on Assignment 60.

Assignment 60 contains 834 words.

If you read Assignment 60 in	Your reading rate is
24 MINUTES	35 WORDS A MINUTE
26 MINUTES	32 WORDS A MINUTE
28 MINUTES	30 WORDS A MINUTE
30 MINUTES	28 WORDS A MINUTE
32 MINUTES	26 WORDS A MINUTE
34 MINUTES	24 WORDS A MINUTE
36 MINUTES	23 WORDS A MINUTE

553.

[shorthand outlines]

it·self′
pre·cau′tion
de·pos′i·tors

[shorthand outlines]

par

grate′ful
pa′tience

[shorthand outlines]

par

mis·take′
re·cur′

(113)

554.

ap

spe′cial
ef·fi′cien·cy

[shorthand outline] 15 *[shorthand]* 2 *[shorthand]* 50

[shorthand outlines]

10 *[shorthand outlines]* 12 *[shorthand outlines]*

[shorthand outlines]

[shorthand] when *[shorthand outlines]* 25

[shorthand] 25 *[shorthand outlines]*

at·tempt′ed
truck′men

[shorthand outlines]

[shorthand] conj *[shorthand outlines]*

[shorthand] when *[shorthand outlines]*

sit′u·a′tion
in′con·ven′ience

[shorthand] as *[shorthand outlines]*

[shorthand] par *[shorthand outlines]*

25 *[shorthand outlines]*

[shorthand outlines] (164)

·····························

555. *[shorthand outlines]* intro *[shorthand outlines]*

[shorthand outlines]

e·con′o·my
ef·fi′cient·ly *[shorthand outlines]*

[Shorthand outlines]

3 intro ⊙

[Shorthand outlines]

conj ⊙

① *[Shorthand outlines]*

② *[Shorthand outlines]* conj ⊙

③ *[Shorthand outlines]*

con·sump'tion
spe'cial

[Shorthand outlines]

5

(162)

•••••••••••••••••••••••••••••

556. *[Shorthand outlines]*

if ⊙

ap ⊙ *[Shorthand outlines]*

and o ⊙

ad·vice'
suc·cess'ful
in·i'tial

[Shorthand outlines]

[Shorthand outline]

(137)

....

557. [Shorthand outline]

ad·vise'
Gov'er·nors

(72)

558. Transcription Quiz. The correct punctuation of the following letter calls for 5 commas — 1 comma conjunction, 1 comma apposition, 1 comma *and* omitted, 2 commas series.

As you copy the letter in your notebook, be sure to insert the necessary commas at the proper points and to indicate the reason for the
punctuation.

[Shorthand outline]

[Gregg shorthand outlines] (142)

559. Chuckle

[Gregg shorthand outlines] (44)

Assignment 61

Disjoined word beginnings are given intensive treatment in this assignment.

Building Transcription Skills

560. BUSINESS VOCABULARY BUILDER

compelled   Forced.

enterprising   Venturesome; aggressive; imaginative.

561. GRAMMAR CHECKUP

Comparisons

The comparative degree of an adjective or adverb is used when reference is made to two objects; the superlative degree is used when reference is made to more than two objects.

Comparative

Of the two boys, Jim is the taller.
Which boy is more efficient, Jim or Harry?
Is Mr. Smith or Mr. Green better qualified to do the job?

Superlative

Of the three boys, Jim is the tallest.
Which of the boys is the most efficient, Jim, Harry, or John?
Is Mr. Smith, Mr. Green, or Mr. Brown the best qualified to do the job?

Reading and Writing Practice

562.

360

oc·ca'sions
al·ter'na·tive

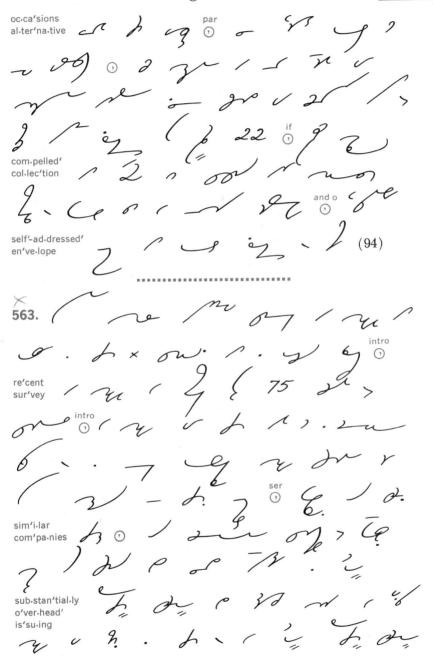

com·pelled'
col·lec'tion

self'-ad·dressed'
en've·lope

(94)

563.

re'cent
sur'vey

sim'i·lar
com'pa·nies

sub·stan'tial·ly
o'ver·head'
is'su·ing

[Shorthand outlines]

is'su·ance
safe'ty

intro

conj

and o   (159)

・・・・・・・・・・・・・・・・・・・・・・・・・・・

564.

ap

16

as

de·scribe'
ex·pe'ri·enc·es

fur'ther
as·sist'ance

if

(127)

565. *(shorthand outlines)*

en'vel·ope
post'mark'

par

theft
an'y·one

intro

if

(137)

566. *(shorthand outlines)*

con·sid'er·a·ble
ad'ver·tise'ment

site
ex·pan'sion

em·ploy'ing
sub·stan'tial

re·cruit'ed
a're·a

(121)

567.

re·ceived'
pos'si·ble

par

conj

(101)

568. **Transcription Quiz.** In the following letter you must supply 5 commas to punctuate it correctly — 1 comma *when* clause, 2 commas parenthetical, 2 commas series.

(126)

Assignment 62

Do you find that you don't know the disjoined word endings as well as you would like? Then practice this assignment carefully.

Building Transcription Skills

569. BUSINESS VOCABULARY BUILDER

> **tradition** A practice carried on over a period of years.
>
> **critical** Involving risk.
>
> **potential** In the making; possible.

570. SIMILAR-WORDS DRILL

Past, passed

> **past** (*noun*) A former time. (*Past* is also used as an adjective.)

The program has been very successful in the past.

Please take care of your past-due account.

> **passed** Moved along; went by; transferred.

I passed him on the street.

(shorthand outline)

Before many days had passed, he took care of his account.

(shorthand outline)

I passed the report on to him.

Reading and Writing Practice

571. *(shorthand outlines)*

typ'i·cal
pro·vid'ing

as

if

par

(115)

572.

for'ward·ed
spon'sor·ship
ra'di·o

a·vail'a·ble
ef·fect'

intro

fa·cil'i·ties
ad'ver·tis'ing

ap

ap

(158)

....

573.

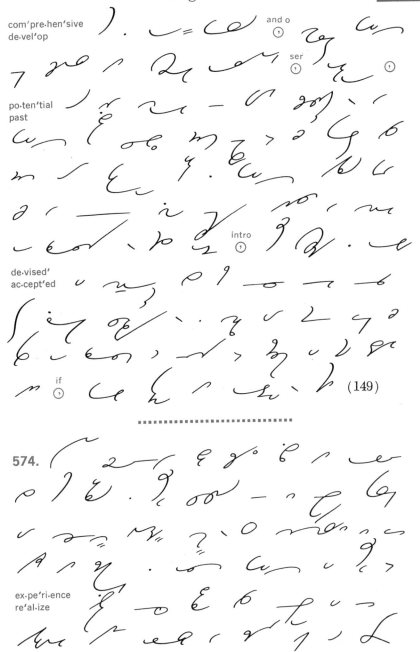

com'pre·hen'sive
de·vel'op

and o

ser

po·ten'tial
past

intro

de·vised'
ac·cept'ed

if

(149)

574.

ex·pe'ri·ence
re'al·ize

[shorthand outlines] intro ①

(118)

....

575. *[shorthand outlines]*

e·lec'tric'i·ty
an'y·bod'y

[shorthand outlines] intro ①

ad'ver·tised
ap·pli'anc·es   intro ①

and o ①

intro ①

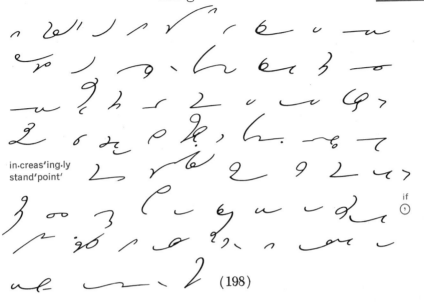

in·creas′ing·ly
stand′point′

(198)

576. Transcription Quiz.   The following letter calls for 4 commas — 1 comma introductory, 1 comma *when* clause, 2 commas parenthetical. Can you supply them?

(74)

Assignment 63

Blends form a very important part of Gregg Shorthand. Without them, Gregg Shorthand could not be written so easily and fluently. The material in this assignment reviews all the blends many times.

Building Transcription Skills

577. BUSINESS VOCABULARY BUILDER

unintentionally Without meaning to.

remedy To correct; to make right.

reciprocate To repay; to return in like measure.

net worth The difference between the total assets owned by a company and its total debts and obligations.

578. COMMON WORD ROOTS

Co-: *with, together, jointly*

co-operation The act of working together.

coeducation Joint education, especially of boys and girls in the same school.

co-ordinate To bring together.

coherence A sticking together.

Reading and Writing Practice

579.

de·light'ed
spe'cial·iz·ing

[shorthand outlines] conj ① [shorthand outlines] 1850 [shorthand outlines] and o ①

[shorthand outlines]

[shorthand outlines]

[shorthand outlines] intro ① [shorthand outlines]

[shorthand outlines] (92)

....

580. [shorthand outlines] as ①

[shorthand outlines]

[shorthand outlines] 30 [shorthand outline]

[shorthand outlines]

don't
nat'u·ral·ly [shorthand outlines] when ① [shorthand outlines]

[shorthand outlines]

un'in·ten'tion·al·ly
did'n't
rem'e·dy [shorthand outlines]

[shorthand outlines] if ① [shorthand outlines]

[shorthand outlines]

[shorthand outlines]

ones
treas'ure

(130)

....

581.

Tow'els
rea'son
be·lieve'

co-op'er·a'tion
as·sure'
re·cip'ro·cate

(117)

582. [shorthand outlines]

de·liv'er·y
min'i·mum

intro
⊙

(82)

....

583. [shorthand outlines]

slipped
re'al·ize

conj
⊙

if
⊙

[Gregg shorthand outlines]

ap·proach'ing
nov'el·ties

(170)

....

584.

re·ceived'
rea'sons
buy'ing

ser'i·ous
cor·rec'tive

[shorthand outline] (98)

585. Transcription Quiz. The following letter requires 7 commas to be punctuated correctly — 1 comma apposition, 2 commas conjunction, 2 commas parenthetical, 2 commas series.

[shorthand outline] 1950 *[shorthand outline]* 31 *[shorthand outline]* (124)

586. Chuckle

[shorthand outline] (31)

Assignment 64

As you learned during the early stages of your study of Gregg Shorthand, vowels are omitted in some words to help gain fluency of writing. In this assignment you will find many illustrations of words from which vowels are omitted.

Building Transcription Skills

587. BUSINESS VOCABULARY BUILDER

utilize To turn to profitable use; to make use of.

marketing The field of business concerned with distributing and selling goods and services.

complimentary Expressing approval or admiration; favorable.

588. SPELLING FAMILIES

Words Ending in -ary

an′ni·ver′sa·ry	el′e·men′ta·ry	sec′re·tar′y
com′pli·men′ta·ry	li′brar′y	sum′ma·ry
cus′tom·ar′y	nec′es·sar′y	tem′po·rar′y
dic′tion·ar′y	sec′ond·ar′y	vo·cab′u·lar′y

Words Ending in -ery

bind′er·y	mas′ter·y	re·fin′er·y
dis·cov′er·y	re·cov′er·y	scen′er·y

Words Ending in -ory

di·rec′to·ry	his′to·ry	ter′ri·to′ry
fac′to·ry	in′ven·to′ry	vic′to·ry

Reading and Writing Practice

589.
sum'ma·ry
per'son·al
ca·reer'

gen'u·ine·ly
u'ti·lize

ser

mean'while'
com'pli·men'ta·ry

if
par

intro

(107)

590.
pre·scrip'tion
ton'ic

and o

[shorthand outline] ser
[shorthand outlines]

bask
scen'er·y
fa'vor·ite

[shorthand outlines] ap

[shorthand outlines] conj

re·ceive'
heart'y

[shorthand outlines]

(116)

....

591. *[shorthand outlines]*

[shorthand outlines] when

[shorthand outlines] conj

past
col'umns
for'eign

[shorthand outlines]

[shorthand outlines] intro

[shorthand outlines] intro

[shorthand outlines]

9.

Christ'mas
i·de'al

(109)

·······························

592.

hap'pi·er
rea'son

com'fort·a·ble
se'ri·ous

se·cu'ri·ty
mind

intro

(shorthand outlines)

(192)

·····························

593. *(shorthand outlines)*

priv'i·lege
stand'ards

if

intro

ex·ec'u·tive
per'son·al

(145)

594. Transcription Quiz. For you to supply: 5 commas — 4 commas introductory, 1 comma parenthetical.

(121)

Assignment 65

You will frequently have to write numbers in business dictation. Because of the tremendous importance of accuracy in transcribing numbers, you must take special care to write numbers legibly in your notes. The following material will help you fix more firmly in your mind the various devices for expressing amounts and quantities in Gregg Shorthand.

Building Transcription Skills

595. BUSINESS VOCABULARY BUILDER

juvenile   Pertaining to or suitable for youth.

analyzing   Examining carefully.

manually   By hand.

overhead   Rent, taxes, lighting, and other expenses necessary to the operation of a business.

596. SIMILAR-WORDS DRILL

Country, county

country   A nation.

He joined the armed forces of our country.

county   A political division of a state.

Westchester County, in New York State, has many beautiful parks.

Reading and Writing Practice

597. America's Cultural Growth

rise
past

sym'pho·ny
or'ches·tra

pho'no·graph
an'nu·al·ly

(156)

598.

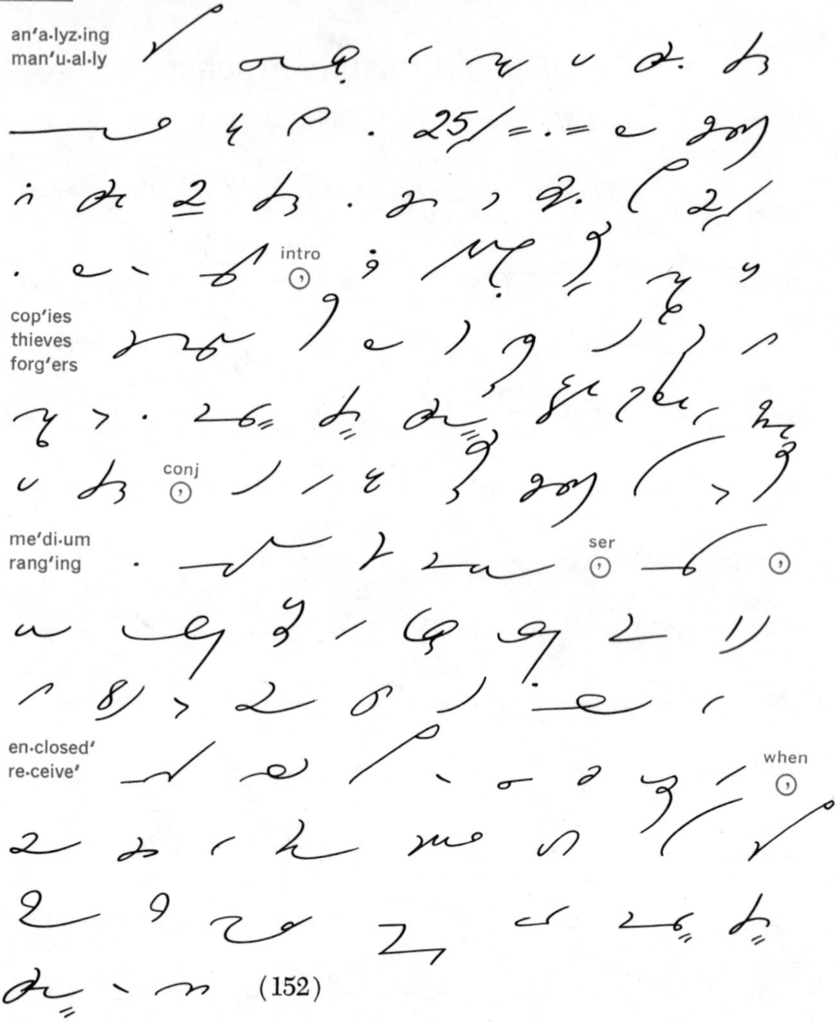

an'a·lyz·ing
man'u·al·ly

[Gregg shorthand outlines]

cop'ies
thieves
forg'ers

[Gregg shorthand outlines]

me'di·um
rang'ing

[Gregg shorthand outlines]

en·closed'
re·ceive'

[Gregg shorthand outlines]

(152)

- -

599. *[Gregg shorthand outlines]*

[Gregg shorthand outlines]

un·nec'es·sar'y
in'stal·la'tion

fa·cil'i·ties
wheth'er

intro

o'ver·head'
de·scribes'

ap

if

(127)

∙∙∙∙∙∙∙∙∙∙∙∙∙∙∙∙∙∙∙∙∙∙∙∙∙∙∙∙∙∙

600.

suf·fi'cient
Christ'mas

mer'ri·est
sim'ply

intro

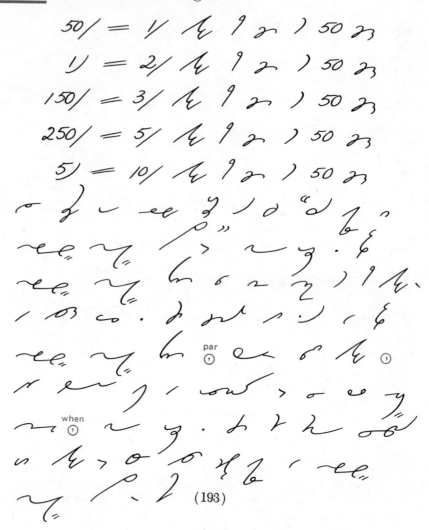

(193)

601. Transcription Quiz. To punctuate the following letter correctly, you must supply 8 commas—4 commas parenthetical, 1 comma introductory, 1 comma *and* omitted, 1 comma *if* clause, 1 comma apposition.

[Shorthand outlines] (155)

PERSONAL-USE CHECK LIST

Do you substitute shorthand for longhand wherever possible when you —

1. Take down your daily assignments?
2. Correspond with your friends who know shorthand?
3. Draft compositions and reports?
4. Make notes to yourself on things to do, people to see, appointments to keep, etc.?

Assignment 66

This is another assignment that concentrates on brief forms.

Building Transcription Skills

602. BUSINESS VOCABULARY BUILDER

remiss   Careless; negligent.

capacity   Position; job.

air freight   A method of shipping merchandise, usually heavy and bulky articles, by air.

603. COMMON WORD ROOTS

Un-: *not*

unsatisfied   Not satisfied.

unnecessary   Not needed.

unhappy   Not happy; sad.

uncertain   Not sure.

Reading and Writing Practice

604.

al'ways
wel'come

conj

390

mind
wheth'er
ab'sence

par

intro

ap·pre'ci·ate
won't

en·closed'
en've·lope

and o

(139)

....

605.

stor'age
un·nec'es·sar'y

if

ad'ver·tise
col'umns

ap

[Shorthand outlines]

conj

con'fi·dent
re·sponse'

par

(122)

• •

606.

conj

of'fered
for'mer

intro

par

[shorthand outlines] (148)

••••••••••••••••••••••••••••••

607. *[shorthand outlines]*

ex·pe'ri·enced
per'son·nel'
ac·cept'

[shorthand outlines] (104)

••••••••••••••••••••••••••••••

608. *[shorthand outlines]*

suc·ceed'ed
in·crease'

[shorthand outlines]

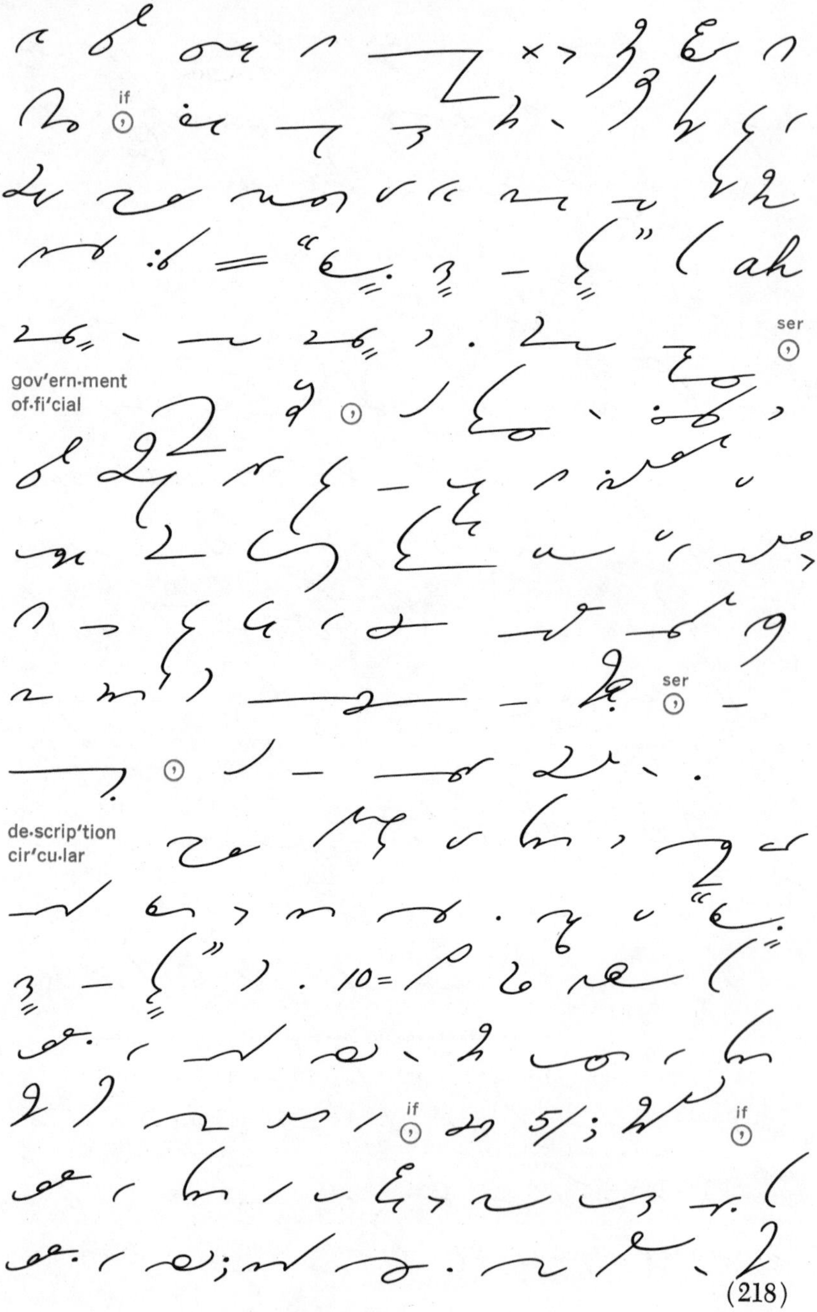
if
ser
gov'ern·ment
of·fi'cial
ser
de·scrip'tion
cir'cu·lar
if
if

(218)

609.   Transcription Quiz.   For you to supply: 5 commas — 2 commas introductory, 1 comma *when* clause, 2 commas series.

(130)

DICTATION CHECK LIST

When you take dictation, do you —

1. Make every effort to keep up with the dictator?

2. Refer to your textbook whenever you are in doubt about the outline for a word or phrase?

3. Insert periods and question marks in your shorthand notes?

4. Make a real effort to observe good proportion as you write — making large circles large, small circles small, etc.?

Assignment 67

In this assignment you will have another opportunity to check up on your phrasing skill.

Building Transcription Skills

610. BUSINESS VOCABULARY BUILDER

franchise An arrangement whereby a distributor is given an exclusive right to handle a manufacturer's products and services in a given locality.

considerate Showing thoughtfulness.

harassing Worrying.

investigate To look into.

611. GRAMMAR CHECKUP

Verbs — with "one of"

1. In most cases, the expression *one of* takes a singular verb, which agrees with the subject *one*.

> *One* of the men on the staff *is* ill.
> *One* of our typewriters *does not* work.

2. When *one of* is part of an expression such as *one of those who* or *one of the things that,* a plural verb is used to agree with its antecedent in number.

> He solved one of the *problems* that *have been* annoying businessmen for years.
> He is one of the *men* who *drive* to work.

Reading and Writing Practice

612. *[shorthand outlines]*

o'ver·due'
pa'tient

[shorthand outlines with annotations: par, conj, par]

(82)

• •

613. *[shorthand outlines]*

sea'son
ap·proach'es
be·half'

[shorthand outlines with annotation: as]

[shorthand outlines with annotation: as]

past
ma·te'ri·als

[shorthand outlines with annotation: conj]

[shorthand outlines]

[Gregg shorthand outlines]

Christ'mas
pros'per·ous

and o

(111)

614.

in'voic·es
sten'cils

ser

intro

ma'jor
har'ass·ing

at·tached'
de·tails'

if

par

(113)

615.

intro

ap

when

ap

ap·peared'
ap·prov'al

(120)

616.

as

par

lose
los'ing

if

ac·com'plish
in'con·ven'ient

if

[shorthand outline] **(132)**

● ●

617. *[shorthand outline]* **(55)**

618. Transcription Quiz. For you to supply: 5 commas — 2 commas introductory, 1 comma *as* clause, 2 commas parenthetical.

[shorthand outline]

[Gregg shorthand outlines] (108)

619. Chuckle

[Gregg shorthand outlines] (73)

Assignment 68

This assignment contains a general review of the major principles of Gregg Shorthand.

Building Transcription Skills

620. BUSINESS VOCABULARY BUILDER

compensate To pay.

divulge To reveal; to disclose.

proficient Skillful; able.

standard This term, when referring to typewriters, means "manual" (non-electric).

621. SIMILAR-WORDS DRILL

Assistance, assistants

   assistance Help.

If we can be of assistance to you in any way, please write us.

   assistants Helpers.

He is so busy that he needs two additional assistants to take care of the work.

Reading and Writing Practice

622.

ex·pressed′
su′per·vi′sors

ad·vice′
di·vulge′

in′di·vid′u·al
vi′o·lat′ing
em·ploy′ees

(130)

....

623.

switch′ing
e·lec′trics

[shorthand outlines]

intro ①

stud′ies
op′er·a′tor
par ③

and o ①

③

self′–ad·dressed′
con·ven′ience

(147)

· ·

624. *[shorthand outlines]*

15

par ③

for′ward
sub·stan′tial

and o ①

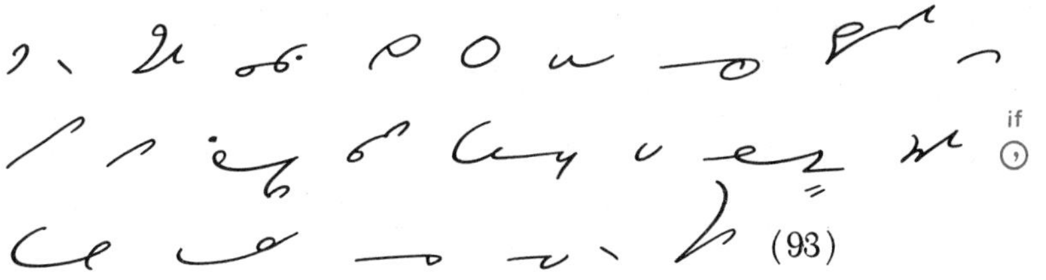

625. 

per'son·al
can'celed

626. 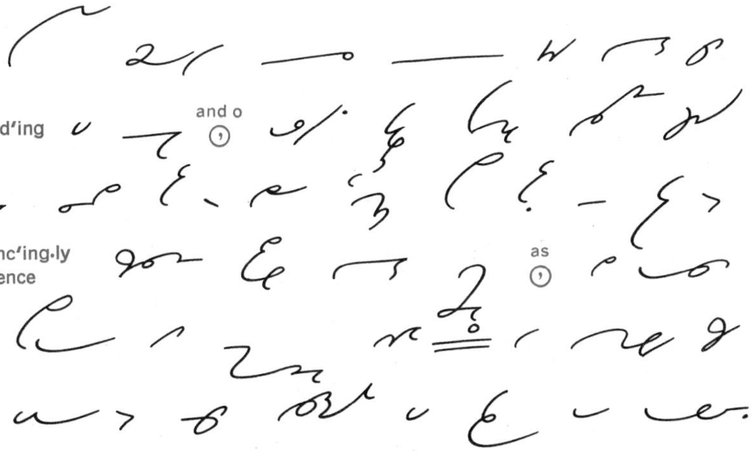

re·ward'ing

con·vinc'ing·ly
in'flu·ence

[Shorthand outlines]

prac′ti·cal
pre·dict′

and o
Ⓞ

fas′ci·nat′ing
de·scribes′

if
Ⓞ

(156)

627.   Transcription Quiz.   For you to supply: 5 commas — 1 comma conjunction, 2 commas series, 1 comma introductory, 1 comma *when* clause.

[Shorthand outlines]

(130)

628. Chuckle

(104)

Assignment 69

You won't be able to refrain from chuckling as you read the Reading and Writing Practice of this assignment. It concerns an exchange of letters between a hotel manager and a guest.

Building Transcription Skills

629. BUSINESS VOCABULARY BUILDER

customary   Usual.

desolated   Sad; unhappy; disappointed.

establishment   A place of business.

630. COMMON WORD ROOTS

Pre-: *before, beforehand*

predict   To tell beforehand; to prophesy.

preliminary   Coming before the main business.

premature   Happening before the proper time.

prearrange   To arrange beforehand.

Reading and Writing Practice

631.

cus'tom·ar'y
house'keep'er
wool'en

intro
①

par
①

408

[shorthand outlines]

lug'gage
guests
un·know'ing·ly

[shorthand outlines]

par

(93)

· ·

632. [shorthand outlines]

slight
sou've·nirs'

[shorthand outlines]

vis'i·tor
con·ceiv'a·bly

[Gregg shorthand outlines]

par

as

conj

5^{50}

intro

intro

lat'er
maid

and o

gen'tle·man·ly
lan'guage

if

[shorthand outline] (257)

633. Transcription Quiz. 6 commas — 2 commas series, 1 comma introductory, 1 comma conjunction, 2 commas parenthetical.

[shorthand outlines] (154)

634.

[Gregg shorthand outlines]

typ'i·cal
dai'ly

intro
①

seize
won'der·ful

conj
①

(166)

635. Chuckle

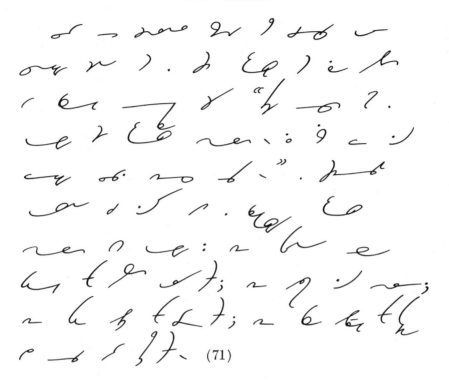

(71)

VOCABULARY CHECK LIST

Has your command of words improved since you began your study of Gregg Shorthand? It has if you —

1. Studied all the words in the Business Vocabulary Builders and added them to your everyday vocabulary.

2. Paid careful attention to the Similar Words Drills, so that you know the difference between *addition, edition; past, passed,* etc.

3. Learned the meanings of the common word roots presented in a number of the lessons of your textbook.

Assignment 70

The articles in this assignment contain information that will be of great help to you when you enter the business world. Read and study the articles carefully.

Building Transcription Skills

636. BUSINESS VOCABULARY BUILDER

    exerting   Putting forth.

    habitually   Usually; by force of habit.

    likelihood   Chance; possibility.

    motives   Aims; objectives.

637. SPELLING FAMILIES

Past Tenses in Which R Is Doubled

blurred	**de·ferred'**	**pre·ferred'**
con·curred'	**in·ferred'**	**re·ferred'**
con·ferred'	**oc·curred'**	**trans·ferred'**

Past Tenses in Which R Is Not Doubled

cov'ered	**ma'jored**	**hon'ored**
dif'fered	**of'fered**	**suf'fered**

Reading and Writing Practice

Reading Scoreboard.   Now that you are on the last assignment, you are no doubt very much interested in your final shorthand reading rate. If you have followed the practice suggestions you received early

414

in the course, your shorthand reading rate at this time should be a source of pride to you.

To get a real picture of how much your shorthand reading rate has increased with practice, compare it with your reading rate in Assignment 18, the first time you measured it.

The following table will help you determine your rate on the *first reading.*

Assignment 70 contains 698 words.

If you read Assignment 70 in	your reading rate is
14 MINUTES	50 WORDS A MINUTE
16 MINUTES	43 WORDS A MINUTE
18 MINUTES	39 WORDS A MINUTE
20 MINUTES	35 WORDS A MINUTE
22 MINUTES	32 WORDS A MINUTE
24 MINUTES	29 WORDS A MINUTE
26 MINUTES	27 WORDS A MINUTE

638. Names

un·for'tu·nate·ly
o'ver·come'

par

ser

re'al·ly
sim'ply

intro

(Gregg shorthand outlines)

some'one'
for·gets'

when

care'ful
at·ten'tion

when

if

as·so'ci·ate
au'to·mat'i·cal·ly

ap

gen'u·ine·ly
ex·treme'ly

conj

(257)

639. Loyalty

fair
def'i·ni'tion

conj

conj

par

an'y·one
re·ferred'

pos·sess'es
trait

(shorthand outlines)

ser

(shorthand outlines)

(196)

640.   Judgment

mere'ly
de·cid'ing

(shorthand outlines)

conj

(shorthand outlines)

be·gin'ning
ex'er·cise
nev'er·the·less'

(shorthand outlines)

intro

(shorthand outlines)

in·val'u·a·ble
de·ci'sion

(shorthand outlines)

weighed
rea'son·ing

im'pulse
ax'i·om

(245)

APPENDIX

State Abbreviations

The abbreviations used by the Post Office Department:

Ala.		La.		Ohio	
Alas.		Maine		Okla.	
Ariz.		Md.		Oreg.	
Ark.		Mass.		Pa.	
Calif.		Mich.		R. I.	
Colo.		Minn.		S. C.	
Conn.		Miss.		S. Dak.	
Del.		Mo.		Tenn.	
Fla.		Mont.		Tex.	
Ga.		Nebr.		Utah	
Hawaii		Nev.		Vt.	
Idaho		N. H.		Va.	
Ill.		N. J.		Wash.	
Ind.		N. Mex.		W. Va.	
Iowa		N. Y.		Wis.	
Kans.		N. C.		Wyo.	
Ky.		N. Dak.			

Principal Cities of the United States

Akron	Denver	Long Beach
Albany	Des Moines	Los Angeles
Atlanta	Detroit	Louisville
Baltimore	Duluth	Lowell
Birmingham	Elizabeth	Memphis
Boston	Erie	Miami
Bridgeport	Fall River	Milwaukee
Buffalo	Flint	Minneapolis
Cambridge	Fort Wayne	Nashville
Camden	Fort Worth	Newark
Canton	Gary	New Bedford
Charlotte	Grand Rapids	New Haven
Chattanooga	Hartford	New Orleans
Chicago	Houston	New York
Cincinnati	Indianapolis	Norfolk
Cleveland	Jacksonville	Oakland
Columbus	Jersey City	Oklahoma City
Dallas	Kansas City	Omaha
Dayton	Knoxville	Paterson

424

Peoria	Salt Lake City	Tacoma
Philadelphia	San Antonio	Tampa
Pittsburgh	San Diego	Toledo
Portland	San Francisco	Trenton
Providence	Scranton	Tulsa
Reading	Seattle	Utica
Richmond	Somerville	Washington
Rochester	South Bend	Wichita
Sacramento	Spokane	Wilmington
St. Louis	Springfield	Worcester
St. Paul	Syracuse	Yonkers

Common Geographical Abbreviations

America	England	Canada
American	English	Canadian
United States	Great Britain	Puerto Rico

Recall Drills

LIST OF JOINED WORD ENDINGS

1. -ment

2. -tion

3. -tial

4. -ly

5. -ily

6. -ful

7. -sume, -sumption

8. -ble

9. -ther

10. -ual

11. -ure

12. -self, -selves

13. -ort

14. -tain

15. -cient, -ciency

LIST OF DISJOINED WORD ENDINGS

16. -hood

17.   -ward

18.   -ship

19.   -cle, -cal

20.   -ulate

21.   -ingly

22.   -ings

23.   -gram

24.   -ification

25.   -lity

26. -Ity

27. -rity

LIST OF JOINED WORD BEGINNINGS

28. Per-, Pur-

29. Em-

30. Im-

31. In-

32. En-

33. Un-

34. Re-

35. Be-

36. De-, Dĭ-

37. Dis-, Des-

38. Mis-

39. Ex-

40. Com-

41. Con-

42. Sub-

43. Al-

44.   For-, Fore-

45.   Fur-

46.   Tern-, Etc.

47.   UI

LIST OF DISJOINED WORD BEGINNINGS

48.   Inter-, Intr-, Enter-, Entr-

49.   Electr-, Electric

50.   Post-

51.   Super-

52. Circum-

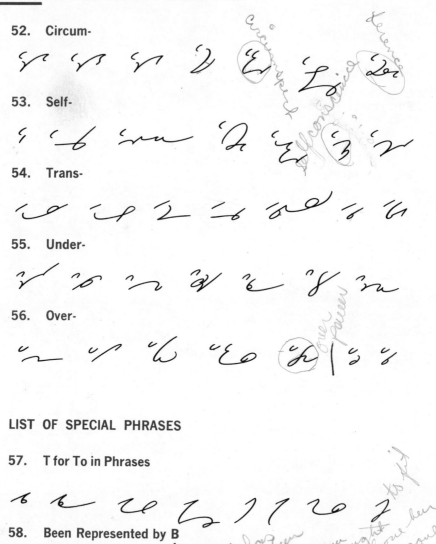

53. Self-

54. Trans-

55. Under-

56. Over-

LIST OF SPECIAL PHRASES

57. T for To in Phrases

58. Been Represented by B

59. Able Represented by A

60.   Want Preceded by Pronoun

61.   Ago Represented by G

62.   To Omitted in Phrases

63.   The Omitted in Phrases

64.   Of Omitted in Phrases

65.   A Omitted in Phrases

66.   Intersected Phrases

67.   Special Phrases

Key to Shorthand

(The material is counted in groups of 20 standard words or 28 syllables for convenience in timing the reading or dictation.)

CHAPTER 1

Assignment 3

Group A

1. Dale reads at least an hour a day.
2. Mr. Stone will not buy our stove at our price.
3. My neighbor, Mr. Peters, knows Mary[1] well.
4. I will read my evening paper at home at night.
5. I have not made my will.
6. I will not drive late at night;[2] I have no spare tire.
7. I am writing a story in my spare hours. (52)

Group B

8. I hear Mr. Bates will open a retail store in Erie.
9. Please see me at my home at eight.
10. Our sales in our Erie[1] store are high; our sales in our Reno store are low.
11. I have a pain in my ear; I may stay home.
12. Our plane will not[2] leave Moline at nine at night; it will leave at ten.
13. My niece will meet our plane in Mobile.

14. He drove at least 60 miles[3] an hour. (61)

Group C

15. I need more filing space; I need at least four more files.
16. Mr. Ray owns a typewriter; he types well.
17. Peter's neighbor[1] plays polo well.
18. Mary typed my brief in an hour.
19. Ray will not eat here; he will eat at home later. (38)

Assignment 4

Group A

1. I am taking my two girls skating. My niece will go, too.
2. I feel Mary's grades are too low; Mr. James shares my feeling.[1]
3. Jane Drew will reach age sixty-five in June. She will have to retire in June.
4. Jane showed me a speech she wrote. I liked[2] Jane's speech.
5. At my age, I am not able to eat fried foods. (50)

Group B

6. I am teaching typing to my

niece, who likes to type. She types four pages in an hour.

7. I am not able to locate[1] our keys.

8. Kate Gray will fly home. She will change planes in Reno.

9. Whose keys are in my safe?

10. I am flying to Rome in[2] May. My plane will reach Rome in eight hours. (47)

Group C

11. Mr. James will teach in Rome.

12. I do not know who will drive to Erie. Mr. James wrote me a note saying he will[1] not drive.

13. I like to go sailing in my sailboat.

14. Please shine my riding boots.

15. I do not like to drive at night. (38)

Group D

16. Please do not phone me at home at night.

17. Most retail chain stores in Mobile close at nine.

18. It will take me at least an hour[1] to read my paper.

19. He will provide two more chairs. (28)

Assignment 5

28. Mrs. Keith: I am happy to write you that your niece Mary passed her history test; in fact, she passed the test with[1] a grade of 85. Her teacher, Mr. Drew, is pleased with her, too. He said that she made the best mark in his class.

I cannot[2] give you Mary's French grade; but her French teacher feels that she passed that test, too. Dean Harry H. James (58)

29. Mrs. Gates: I have your letter asking me to act as chairman of your meeting in March. I am afraid, though, that[1] I cannot do so. In March I have arranged to give a series of five speeches in Dallas. I can cancel three[2] of these speeches, but two I cannot cancel.

Mrs. Church is not busy in March. You might arrange with her to act[3] as chairman. A. H. Smith (64)

30. Dear Fred: Did you know that Mrs. Baker is planning to retire as dean at the close of the semester? She tells me[1] that in June she will reach the age of sixty-five but that she will not leave her post as dean till July 31.[2]

Please see that the rest of your staff is notified of Mrs. Baker's plans to retire. C. H. Knight (57)

31. Mr. Case: I have read the lease you left with me last evening, but I cannot sign it as it is. Your girl made two[1] typing errors in the last line. These typing errors change the meaning of the lease.

The lease is attached. Harvey Smith[2] (40)

Assignment 6

32. *Recall Chart*

1. Act, acts, acting; late, later, latest.

2. Change, changes, changed; keep, keeps, kept.

3. Ship, shipping, shipped; notify, notifies, notified.

4. Throw, throws, thrown; approach, approached, approaches.

5. Move, moves, moved; rule, ruling, ruler.

6. Face, faced; brace, braced; grow, grows.

7. I, are-our-hour, am, is-his, can, with.

8. Mrs., will-well, it-at, the, have, but.

9. Your-you, a-an, in-not, that, of, Mr.

10. I will, I can, I am; he will, he can, he may.

11. You will, you can, you are; of the, of our, of your.

12. In the, in that, in these; at the, at that, at least.

13. It will, it will not; he is, he is not; it is, here is.

14. With the, with our, with him; to the, to that, to get.

33. Mr. Gray: Attached is the first draft of our latest price list. I am well pleased with the plan of the price list, but I[1] am not happy with its size. It is too large. I feel that 64 pages are ample.

Please go through the draft of[2] the price list; then let me know if you agree with me. James Green (51)

34. Mrs. Stone: As you know, our firm is opening a branch in Dallas. I am to take charge of that branch in May. My plans[1] are to move to Dallas late in March.

As you are a native of Dallas, you may know of an agency in that[2] city that can help me locate a home. If you do know of an agency, please phone me collect at Main 4-1212[3]. Henry J. Lee (64)

35. Mr. Day: Last evening at home, I read the series of sales letters that Mr. Smith is planning to mail to your[1] list of food dealers in the East. I am well pleased with the letters. I like Mr. Smith's style of writing. I did not[2] realize that he wrote so well.

I feel, though, that he can omit the two letters I have checked with blue pencil; these letters[3] are not too clear. Bill Green (65)

36. Mr. Mead: I notice that the sales in Harry's territory have slipped again in March.

Harry is a fine chap,[1] but I am afraid that he is not a salesman. I have to admit that I made an error in hiring him in the[2] first place. I will write him to notify him of his release, effective May 15.

Do you have a man who can[3] take Harry's territory starting the middle of May? Allen G. Bates (73)

37. Mr. Smith: My secretary,

Miss Green, is taking a course in letter writing at the Baker School at night. I[1] have asked her to take the course, as it is my plan to let her answer most of my routine letters.

She has paid the[2] fees with her own check; but as she is taking the course to help me, may I have her charge the fees to the firm? A. R.[3] Farmer (61)

CHAPTER 2

Assignment 7

41. Dear Tom: I am mailing to your daughter Pauline a copy of the Red River College catalogue.

I realize[1] that Pauline has her heart set on our school, but I have a feeling that Red River College will not admit her in[2] the fall semester; her grades are too low.

As bursar of the college, I will do all I can to help Pauline. As[3] you know, Pauline is a favorite of mine. Sincerely yours, (71)

42. Dear Paul: On July 15 my private secretary, Mrs. Small, is leaving to take a promising job with[1] a travel agency abroad.

Is your daughter ready to take a job as a private secretary? If she[2] is, ask her to call at my office on June 30 or July 1. My office is in Room 16 on the[3] first floor. Very truly yours, (65)

43. Dear Sir: The Model 16 office desk I bought at your store on March 20 arrived last evening. I am sorry[1] to write you, though, that it arrived with two deep scratches on the top. I cannot accept the desk as it is.

Please[2] have your man call to take the desk back to your factory. Yours truly, (53)

44. Dear Tom: As I ran to catch my train last night, I lost the key to the school gym. I may have dropped it in Room 14[1] or Room 15 on the first floor.

If you locate the key, please leave it in the top drawer of my desk in my office.[2] Yours very truly, (44)

45. Mr. Shelley: I am attaching a draft of a letter I plan to mail to all the typing teachers on our[1] college mailing list. You will note that I am offering to mail to each typing teacher a set of our typing[2] charts at cost price. With the letter, I plan to mail a copy of our latest catalogue of supplies.

Please read the[3] draft with care. Make all your changes in red or blue pencil. James J. Sharp (73)

46. Dear Paul: I am afraid I have to call off our April 30 golf date. Our golf date on May 15, though, is[1] still on! Sincerely yours, (24)

Assignment 8

51. Dear Jack: There is a fairly

good chance that I shall be in Dallas early in July for a sales meeting, which will[1] take place in the Hotel Green. This meeting will last two days.

If I can arrange the trip, I earnestly hope that you[2] can spare an hour or so to take me through your main office. I am most eager to observe the billing machines you[3] have put in.

Would you please let me know by June 15 if you can do this for me. Sincerely yours, (77)

52. To all Dealers: As you may know, the cost of paper has risen nearly 15 per cent since last April; but the[1] price of our note pads has risen only 5 per cent.

To take care of these rising costs properly, I shall have to[2] raise the price of our whole line of pads; therefore, the following price changes will be put in effect on July 5:[3]

Style 16 pads will sell for $110 a gross.

Style 17 pads will sell for $115[4] a gross.

Style 18 pads will sell for $120.50 a gross.

I sincerely hope[5] that this price change will be the last. Harry S. James (109)

53. Dear Professor Smith: On April 2 I shipped to you 500 of the 1,000 copies of our leaflet,[1] "The Jet Age," for which you asked in your letter of March 30. The rest will be shipped on April 10.

There will be[2] no charge for this service.

If you would like more of these leaflets, please do not hesitate to write me. Yours very truly,[3] (61)

54. Mrs. James: I finally had a chance to read thoroughly the 100 pages of typed copy for our[1] catalogue that you put on my desk early in July. There are only four or five minor changes that I would make.[2] I have marked these changes in the margins in blue pencil.

All in all, I feel this is a good job. Harry J. Smith[3] (60)

55. Mr. Bates: At six o'clock last night I talked briefly with Harry Smith, whom you picked for the job as head of our shipping[1] room.

I am as highly pleased with him as you are. I sincerely feel that this man would do a good job as head[2] of our shipping room. I am highly pleased, too, with the fact that he will take $7,000 to start.

Please put his[3] name on the payroll as of May 15. James R. Baker (70)

56. Dear Sir: I have a typing job for a girl who can type rapidly. This job, which will take four or five days, calls for the[1] typing of labels for the 5,000 to 6,000 names on our mailing list of dealers. The pay is[2] good—$2.50 an hour.

If you have in your files the name of a girl who can type rapidly, please ask her to[3] call me.

Very truly yours, (65)

57. Dear Salesman: Suppose you are caught in a snow or ice storm. Will you have to "call it a day"? You will not have to if[1] you carry a set of Thomas Tire Chains in your car.

Thomas Tire Chains will enable you to drive your car in safety[2] on icy roads. Yours very truly, (47)

Assignment 9

63. Dear Sir: On my last visit to Fresno, I saw an efficient ranch-type home that I know you will like. It is on[1] a half-acre plot in an especially fine section of the city.

The owners are asking $12,000[2] for it, but there is a chance that you can get it for $10,000 or less. Even at $12,000,[3] though, it would still be a good bargain.

If you would care to see the place, I shall be happy to show it to you.[4] Yours truly, (82)

64. Mr. Baker: An official of the National Clothing Corporation has applied for a special loan of[1] $3,000. Before I can take efficient action on this loan, I shall have to have more data on the[2] financial position of the National Clothing Corporation.

Can you collect these essential data for me[3] on or before March 16? Harry J. Barnes (68)

65. Mr. Hall: My physician tells me that I shall have to have an operation to remove the bone chips in my[1] right elbow. I shall, therefore, have the operation at ten o'clock on June 15 at the National Hospital.[2] This is only a minor operation, but I shall have to stay at the National Hospital as a[3] patient till June 20 for special observation. I know that I can rely on you to see that the[4] office operates with efficiency in my absence.

If all goes well, I plan to be back at my desk on June[5] 21. James Green (103)

66. Dear Keith: As our factory is finally operating with a high degree of efficiency, I am[1] going to fly to Dallas to see my daughter. This will be my first vacation since 1960.

Will you[2] be free to play a little golf with me on July 15 or 16? As I recall, I have not played golf with[3] you since 1959. If you will not be free to play golf, I sincerely hope that you will save an evening[4] to visit with me. It will be good to see you again. Sincerely yours, (94)

67. Mr. Rich: Please make a special trip to see Mr. Smith of the National Paper Corporation in Mobile.[1] Mr. Smith has not paid his July bills in spite of the four collection letters that I wrote him.

May I caution[2] you to be patient but firm with him. It is essential that you get his check for $950 but[3] keep his good will.

I sincerely hope that I   shall

not have to take legal action against him. A. B. Teller (79)

68. To the Staff: It is official that the financial section will be moved to the first floor. The day set for the move[1] is June 5. It is essential, therefore, that all preparations for moving be made on or before June 4, as[2] the movers will arrive at nine o'clock on June 5.

If the staff of the financial section will take special care[3] to see that all desks are clear at five o'clock on June 4, this move will take place smoothly.

If no problems arise, the[4] office will be operating with normal efficiency by June 6 or 7. James R. Harper (98)

Assignment 10

73. To the Staff: This evening I learned with regret that Mr. Trent will be leaving our firm on April 10 to take[1] the position of financial secretary of the National Paint Corporation in Flint. I know that all[2] of you will be as sorry to have Mr. Trent leave as I am.

A tea is being planned in Mr. Trent's honor[3] on April 6 at three o'clock in the Hotel Francis. I sincerely hope that you can arrange to be there. James[4] R. Baker (82)

74. Mr. Strand: On March 15 our binder, Mr. Bond, phoned me

to say that our stock of the initial printing of[1] "The Nurse's Guide" is low; in fact, he says that there are only 5,000 copies in the bindery. At the current[2] rate of sale, the chances are that these 5,000 copies will not last through July. Who would have imagined last[3] fall that "The Nurse's Guide" would sell half so well?

Please start the ball rolling for a second printing of 50,000[4] copies. James R. Smith (84)

75. Dear Sir: My sister said that she left her reading glasses in the center drawer of the desk in Room 25 on[1] the second floor of your premises. Would you please check to see if the glasses are there.

If the glasses are there, please[2] phone me at Main 4-5112. I shall then arrange to call for the glasses before your office closes at[3] five o'clock. Sincerely yours, (65)

76. Dear Sir: In talking to my friend Mrs. Harry Bond, in Akron, I learned that:

1. Your cottage on Grand Island is[1] for rent this July.

2. The rental is $120.

3. You would be willing to vacate the cottage[2] on June 28 if necessary.

If these facts are correct, can you arrange to take me through the cottage[3] on April 10 or 12? Very truly yours, (67)

77. Dear Ted: I am attaching two copies of the leases for the premises that you agreed to rent in Atlanta.[1] The leases are signed by the owner's agent.

Please sign the leases in the places I have marked with blue pencil[2] crosses.

Keep the carbons for your files. The agent will call at your offices to get the originals on March[3] 15 or 16. Sincerely yours, (67)

78. Mr. Baker: I find on checking through our central file of current magazines that the copy of the June Printer's[1] Guide is missing. Did you borrow it, or do you know who did?

The June Printer's Guide has a list of the printing[2] firms in the East to whom I am planning to mail our latest catalogue. Bob Smith (54)

79. Mr. Crandall: I am sorry to say that I am not entirely pleased with the sale of our mattresses in our[1] Atlanta store. In April, the Atlanta store had a decrease of 10 per cent; in May, the decrease is even[2] larger—12 per cent.

These decreases are causing me to lose a good deal of sleep!

Can you arrange to take a trip[3] to Atlanta to see if you can find an answer to these losses in sales? A. H. Davis (77)

Assignment 11

86. Mr. Fields: When I was in Garden City on May 10, I called on the owners of the Garden City Children's[1] Shop. They told me that they have not been pleased with the service they have been getting from our local salesman, Mr. Shields.[2] In fact, he has not been in to see them since March. Nor did he send them the catalogues for which they asked.

I told them[3] that I was sorry they felt they had been ignored and that I should be happy to check into the matter.

Could you[4] check the facts for me so that I can take the necessary steps to see that they get the service to which they are[5] entitled. James R. Mild (104)

87. Dear Dad: On July 15 our chief record clerk retired, and I have been offered his job. I was told that I would[1] be given a nice raise in salary.

Would you say that a record-keeping job could be a stepping-stone to a[2] higher position, and do you feel that I should accept it? As you know, I trained to be a secretary; and[3] I am not especially fond of record keeping.

Please let me have your advice. Your daughter, Mary (78)

88. Dear Fred: I have finally been able to locate the address of Doctor Baird, who retired last July. I learned[1] from an old patient of his that Doctor Baird is living with his oldest daughter at 4 Garden Lane, in Dallas.[2] I sincerely hope that when you visit Dallas again you will be able to stop in to see him. I know that[3] he will be happy to see you.

I am sending him a small gift as a token of my affection. Very truly[4] yours, (81)

89. Dear Sir: On April 12 I bought an airplane ticket from Dallas to Mobile at your ticket office in Dallas.[1] I bought the ticket with my air-travel card. Since then, I have not been able to find my card.

Could I have left the[2] card on the desk in your office? If you find it, please send it to my home at 4 Orchard Lane, in Dallas. Sincerely[3] yours, (61)

90. Mr. Golden: On June 30 I heard of a two-story building in Plainfield that is for sale for[1] $100,000. I called the building agent; and from the facts he gave me, I have a feeling that this building[2] is the answer to your storage problems. It is an old building, but it is in good shape and should serve your storage-space[3] needs nicely.

The agent offered to take me through the building on July 5. Will you be able to spare an[4] hour or two on July 5 to see the building with me? I. R. Moses (93)

91. Dear Fred: When I was in Toledo, I heard Mrs. Ellen Fields make two speeches on hobbies for children that I[1] feel should be printed in our magazine, Child Care. When I asked Mrs. Fields for copies of her speeches, she was

flattered[2] and said she would send me the originals.

You should be able to print the first speech in June and the second[3] in July. Sincerely yours, (64)

Assignment 12

92. *Recall Chart*

1. Send, could, should, from, when, was.

2. They, them, and, good, this, their-there.

3. Would, put, be-by, which, shall, for.

4. Hard, harder, hardly; fold, folder, folded.

5. Patient, patients, patiently; proficient, proficiently, proficiency.

6. Initial, initially, initialed; brand, brands, branded.

7. Rent, rented, rental; arise, arising, arises.

8. Neat, neatly, neatness; cause, caused, causes.

9. Change, changes, changed; cool, cools, cooled.

10. Throw, throwing, threw; thick, thicker, thickness.

11. Go, goes, going; share, shares, shared.

12. To put, to be, to have, to pay, to see, to blame.

13. Had been, have been, has been, I should be able, I have not been able, he will be able.

14. Sincerely yours, Yours very truly, Very truly yours, Yours truly,

Dear Sir, Dear Madam.

15. $4; 400; 400,000; $400,000; 5 per cent; six o'clock.

94. Dear Sir: The four lamps that you sent me from your factory arrived on April 16, but two of the shades have been[1] torn so badly that I am not able to accept them. I am sending the two torn shades back to you by parcel[2] post.

If you have two similar shades in stock in your Garden City store, let me know and I shall have my daughter[3] call for them. Very truly yours, (66)

95. Dear George: I have the two tickets you asked me to get for you for the ball game on July 15. The seats are in[1] the third row of Section 16. They are good seats, and you should be able to see well from them.

Should I send the tickets[2] to you by mail, or would you prefer to have me hold them till I see you on July 10? Sincerely yours, (59)

96. Mr. Macy: I have been asked by our salesman in Charlotte to send to Doctor E. H. Moses, who teaches at[1] the Charlotte College for Teachers, 100 copies of our pamphlet on child care. He asks that I send them free[2] of charge.

As you know, our offices have been charging 10 cents apiece for these pamphlets. Should I send these copies free of[3] charge as a token of good will, or should I write our salesman that I shall have to bill Doctor Moses for this service?[4] Harry Fields (83)

97. Dear Fred: I am sending you by parcel post a package of special records that I bought as Christmas gifts for your[1] children. Please let me know when the records arrive. I sincerely hope that the children will like them.

I had planned to[2] be with you and your children this Christmas, but I am afraid I shall have to change my plans. I was asked by an official[3] of our firm to sail for Paris five or six days before Christmas to check on our foreign operations.[4]

May you have the merriest and happiest of Christmases. Sincerely yours, (94)

98. Dear Bob: When I was in Little Rock, I ran into Harry Fields in the lobby of the Bates Hotel and had a[1] pleasant visit with him. He told me that he is married and has two children. He has been selling building supplies[2] since he left our Toledo office and is doing well. He asked me to say hello to you for him.

If you would[3] like to write Harry a note, his address is 14 Old Mill Road, Little Rock 16. Sincerely yours, (78)

99. Dear Sir: On your bill for July, I was charged $30 for a fishing rod and reel that I bought in[1] your store on April 15. I paid this bill by check on June 15; in fact, I have the canceled check in my[2] possession.

Please correct your records so that I will not be billed for the fishing rod and reel again. Yours truly, (59)

100. Dear Sir: You will find attached the gas bill for my cottage on Crystal Lake. You will notice that the bill is for $15.[1] Apparently, you have made an error on this bill.

I was in Mobile most of July visiting[2] friends, and my cottage was vacant for all but five or six days. Therefore, my bill for $15 cannot be correct.[3] Yours very truly, (64)

CHAPTER 3

Assignment 13

105. Dear Madam: Thank you for the order for a half dozen of our Number 16 wool sweaters that you gave to Mrs.[1] Woods of our Park Lane store. The sweaters were shipped yesterday and should reach you soon.

I am enclosing a copy[2] of our catalogue, which lists our full line of ladies' wearing apparel. You will be very glad to learn that this[3] year's prices are the lowest in our history. We have worked hard to keep them in line.

It is our earnest hope that[4] you will visit us again soon. Yours truly, (88)

106. Dear Bud: Thank you for the help you gave Mrs. Cook and me yesterday in planning our vacation for this year. We[1] were very glad that we stopped in to see you.

My wife and I have finally made up our minds to take a two-week[2] cruise to the Virgin Islands — the last week in June and the first week in July. We can hardly wait, as this will be[3] our first vacation from work in eight years. I shall stop at your office soon to plan the entire trip.

Again, thank you[4] for your help. Sincerely yours, (85)

107. Dear Sir: We were sorry to learn from your letter that we made an error in shipping your April 10 order for[1] 100 copies of Mrs. Sweet's "Cooking Is Not Work."

The order was properly marked that the cookbooks should be[2] sent to the Wood School and the bill mailed to your home address. Apparently, our billing clerk did not see this note on[3] the order and sent both books and bill to your home address.

Let me assure you that we shall take steps to see that this[4] error does not occur again.

Thank you for your patience with us. Sincerely yours, (94)

108. Dear Sir: This is just a note to thank you for the chance you gave me yesterday to show you samples of the work that[1] we did this year.

As I told you, we shall be very glad to help you plan booklets like the copy enclosed. We make[2] no charge for the services of our specialists, who will be only too glad to assist you.

I sincerely hope that[3] you will give us a chance to serve you soon. **Sincerely yours,** (70)

109. Mrs. Wall: I learned yesterday that we shall soon lose the services of our bookkeeper, Mrs. West. Mrs. West[1] is leaving at the end of the year to take care of her sister, who is ill. I shall be very sorry to lose[2] her, as she has been a most efficient worker.

Do you have a girl on your list who will be able to handle[3] the job? If you do, I shall be glad to talk to her — and the sooner the better. A. H. Sweet (76)

110. Dear Sir: Are you planning to place an order for a car soon? If you are, be sure to look into our financing[1] plan, which has been in operation for the past five years.

The people on our staff will be glad to assist you in[2] adapting the plan to your special needs. You will find them friendly and ready to serve you.

Stop in soon and talk to[3] them. Yours very truly, (64)

Assignment 14

116. Dear Doctor White: Buying tickets for flights on our airline is quick and very simple when you have our air-service[1] credit card. All you need do is phone our office at Broadway 4-5151, tell the clerk your needs, and give him[2] your credit-card number. Your tickets will be sent to you by mail the same day. Hundreds of firms have adopted this[3] quick and easy process of ticket buying.

Take steps today to get your airservice credit card. Just fill in and[4] mail the enclosed card. We will take care of all details. Yours very truly, (93)

117. Mr. Irwin: While you were on vacation, the auditor visited our offices twice. On his last visit[1] he said that he needed more detailed data on our credit policies before he would be able to give us[2] a clean bill of health. I told him that you headed our credit section and that you were the only man qualified to[3] answer his queries on credit policies.

He will call you in a week or so. When he calls, give him all the detailed[4] data for which he asks. Jack Dwight (87)

118. Mr. Baldwin: Today I visited the Broadway Office Machines Shop on Broadway and Russell Square and selected[1] a mail meter that should meet our special needs very nicely. The salesman quoted me a price of $250[2] on the model that I selected.

Would you like to see the meter in operation before[3] I place an order for it? James B. Green (67)

119. Dear Friend: The auditors are in our office for their yearly audit of our books, and they are criticizing our[1] credit practices severely.

They tell us that we should take firm steps to collect the $1,000 that you[2] owe us.

We have waited patiently for your check, but we have waited in vain.

Won't you send us your check for $1,000[3] or for at least a portion of it today. This will show us that the faith we have always had in you[4] has been justified. Sincerely yours, (87)

120. Mr. White: I have just finished a detailed study of our sales records for the past three years. This study indicates[1] that our sales of hardware always drop sharply in June and July. This fact is both surprising and alarming.[2] Please study the whole matter and let me know the steps we should take to build up our sales of hardware in June and July[3] this year.

We should take positive action quickly. Harry P. Macy (73)

121. Dear Mary: It is a pleasure to write you that you have been accepted into the freshman class of Baldwin College.[1]

You have been assigned to Dwight Hall, in which you will share a room with Helen Green, whom you met when you visited[2] us last April.

It is our sincere hope that you will be happy with your studies and your social life at Baldwin.[3] Sincerely yours, (63)

122. Dear Fred: I read in the financial section of the Evening Star of your promotion to the position of secretary[1] of the Peerless Tire Corporation.

Needless to say, I am pleased at your promotion to this high official[2] post. Sincerely yours, (45)

Assignment 15

128. Dear Sir: If you were to ask a businessman what the most valuable asset of his business is, I think he[1] would reply, "A good credit rating." Your fine bill-paying habits through the years have won you a very favorable[2] credit rating with us; but you are about to lose that rating — and for only $150,[3] which you have owed us for more than 90 days.

I am sure you realize that, once you lose your good credit position,[4] your business will be in great financial trouble.

If it is not possible for you to pay the entire[5] $150, at least tell us the reason why. Of one thing you may always be sure: You will find us patient[6] and reasonable. Sincerely yours, (127)

129. Mr. White: I am enclosing the following:

1. A letter I received from our salesman, Mr. Mild, giving the[1]

reasons why he is about to resign.

2. My reply urging him to change his mind.

3. His reply to my letter[2] saying that nothing can possibly make him change his mind.

As you know, Mr. Mild has been a valuable man[3] for more than twenty years; and his leaving would be a great loss to the business.

I think it would be advisable[4] for you to write Mr. Mild one more letter. What do you think? A. H. Green (93)

130. Dear Fred: I have checked and rechecked our files for the receipt you said you mailed me on July 15, but I have not[1] been able to find it. Is it possible that the receipt may still be on a desk in your mailing room?

Please check[2] once more to see if you can locate the receipt in your office.

I need this receipt very badly as our[3] auditors will be in my office in about a week to check our records. Sincerely yours, (76)

131. Dear Sir: Recently we hired two reliable, capable mechanics for our night staff; therefore, we can make all[1] types of repairs at all hours of the day or night.

Think of what this means for your business. If one of your trucks has motor[2] trouble in the daylight hours, we shall be able to take care of all necessary repairs at night. In that[3] way, your truck will be available again for service the following day.

This repair service costs no more than[4] our day service.

It is our earnest hope that you will give us a chance to take care of your repair needs soon. Yours very[5] truly, (102)

132. Dear James: Will it be possible for you to replace me as a referee at the basketball game at the High[1] School on April 15? I think the game starts about eight o'clock in the evening.

Yesterday I received a cable[2] from my sister that she is arriving from France on April 15, and she has asked me to meet her at the[3] pier.

If you can do this for me, you will be doing me a great favor. Sincerely yours, (76)

133. *Chuckle*

One day the head of a great boarding school noticed a lad wiping his knife on the tablecloth; the man made up his[1] mind to correct the lad then and there.

"Is that what you do at home?" he asked severely. "Oh, no," replied the lad quickly.[2] "At home we have clean knives." (44)

Assignment 16

139. Dear Sir: For five minutes make believe that you are the credit manager of the Detroit Oil Corporation. The[1] Doyle Shop has owed you $25 for oil for many months. What would you do? I believe you would take all[2] possible measures to collect the money because that was your job.

That is why, as credit manager of our firm,[3] I am writing you this letter — to collect our money.

Do not let this small bill spoil our friendly and profitable[4] business relations. Yours very truly, (88)

140. Mr. Doyle: Because of the affection all of us have held for John Francis, we are planning to have a special[1] 30-minute memorial service for him. This memorial service will take place on May 10 in the main[2] assembly room beginning at ten o'clock.

I believe that many members of the office staff, as well as the[3] salesmen, will want to be there.

Please make it a point to see that all your people are notified of this memorial[4] service. James Royal (84)

141. To the Members of the Staff: As I believe you all know, last month John H. Royal became the treasurer of the[1] Women's Magazine, succeeding Mr. Harry Joyce, who retired. This left vacant Mr. Royal's old position[2] as sales manager.

It is a pleasure for me to write you that we have just appointed Mr. A. H. Quill as[3] sales manager.

Mr. Quill joined our firm as a member of the Detroit sales staff. Because of his fine sales record,[4] he was later appointed manager of the Detroit office.

I think you will agree that we have made a wise[5] choice in the selection of a sales manager. James R. Davis (112)

142. Dear Sir: For many years I was with the Troy Men's Shop, but in July I left to join the staff of the Royal Clothing[1] Stores. At the beginning of the year I became manager of their Troy store.

Won't you make it a point to stop[2] in to see me and let me show you the choice values we have on our racks. I firmly believe you will be pleased with[3] our styles and our prices.

It is my hope that you will be able to call soon. You will not be sorry that you[4] did. Sincerely yours, (84)

143. Miss Smith: Please write to the Hotel Royal in Memphis to reserve a double room for my boy and me for one week[1] beginning July 15. Be sure to ask for a room at the minimum rate.

I am taking my boy with me[2] on a brief vacation. I believe he will benefit by a week's rest following his recent illness.

While I[3] am in Memphis, please take care of my mail. H. A. Joyce (70)

150. Gentlemen: Your financial and personnel records are of great importance to the operation of your[1] manufacturing plant. If you came to work one morning and learned that those important records had been burned in a fire,[2] you would have cause to worry because you might not be able to open your doors again.

One way to be sure that[3] those important records are well guarded is to place them in a Smith Safe, where they will be protected from the most[4] severe fire.

Do not delay; decide to take action today to guard those important records properly.

If you[5] will mail the enclosed card, we shall be delighted to send you the full story of our safes. Yours very truly, (119)

151. Mr. Fields: This morning I received the cover design for our book, "Great Debates in History," by H. R. Baker.[1] It's a fine piece of work for which the designer, Mr. Hart, deserves a great deal of credit.

I am delighted[2] that you have persuaded Mr. Hart to join our staff permanently. You made a wise decision in hiring him.[3] A. B. Wayne (62)

152. Dear Sir: Perhaps one day soon you will make the important decision to purchase a car. When you do decide to[1] buy, proceed

with caution. Before you make any decision, visit your local Baker dealer and ask him to[2] take you for a drive in our latest model.

In a matter of minutes you will learn that the Baker is the finest[3] car manufactured today and that its operating efficiency leaves nothing to be desired.

We[4] assure you that your visit to your local Baker dealer will be a profitable and memorable one.[5] Very truly yours, (104)

153. To the Staff: On April 10 I sent each of you a letter offering you a chance to purchase stock in the White[1] Manufacturing Corporation. In that letter, I listed the provisions of that offer.

This letter is[2] to remind you that, if you desire to purchase stock in accordance with those provisions, it is important that[3] you do not delay filing the necessary papers.

We have to have your decision no later than ten o'clock[4] on the morning of June 10.

It is my hope that no member of the staff will be deprived of this chance merely[5] because he did not act soon enough. John R. Parker (110)

154. Gentlemen: Perhaps there is a perfectly good reason why you have not paid us for the work we did for you on[1] June 16, but there cannot be any good reason why you have not at least answered our friendly letters.

Where do[2] we go from here? The decision is up to you.

Surely it is not your desire to have us refer the matter[3] to a collection agency. The credit rating of a manufacturer in your position is too important.[4]

Why not send us your check for $150 today, or at least give us a date on which we may[5] hope to receive it. Yours very truly, (107)

155. *Chuckle*

One morning two golfers, slicing their drives into the rough, went in search of their golf balls. They searched and searched for those balls,[1] but in vain. A perfectly charming old lady watched them with kind and friendly eyes.

When the search had proceeded for[2] half an hour, she approached them and said: "Gentlemen, I do not want to hold you up, but would it be cheating if I[3] told you where they are?" (64)

Assignment 18

156. *Recall Chart*

1. Were-year, enclose, order, soon, thank, work.

2. Glad, very, business, why, thing-think, great.

3. About, what, than, value, won-one, yesterday.

4. Gentlemen, morning, those, important-importance, where,

manufactured.

5. Color, colors, colored; want, wants, wanted.

6. Quote, quoting, quoted; deduct, deducts, deductions.

7. Boil, boiler, boiled; memorize, memorizing, memorized.

8. Salesmen, freshmen, women; begin, begins, beginner.

9. Person, personal, personally; persist, persists, persisted.

10. Desire, desired, desirable; repeat, repeated, repeatedly.

11. Proficient, proficiently, proficiency; hard, harder, hardly.

12. Special, specially, specialist; age, agent, agency.

13. Throw, throws, throwing; land, landing, landed.

14. To beat, to break, to plan, have been, I have been, I have not been.

15. 500; $3; six o'clock; $8,000; $150,000; 800,000.

158. *Desirable Traits*

A businessman whose secretary has been with him for many years was asked what traits he especially admires about[1] her. Here is his reply:

1. She likes her work. She approaches her job each morning as a fresh challenge.

2. She[2] likes people. She finds it easy to talk with people; and, even more important, she is a good listener.

3.[3] She is loyal. She takes pride in the fact that she is a trusted member of the firm. She does not gossip with[4] anybody about its affairs, not even with her closest friends.

4. She is poised. She does not let anything rattle[5] her. She believes in keeping cool, even when nothing seems to be going right.

5. She knows that office production[6] calls for teamwork. She cooperates with all the members of the office team for the good of the firm. She does[7] not look for personal glory.

When you are hired for your first job, will your boss find these desirable traits in you?[8] (161)

159. *Good Health*

Do you realize that good health is your greatest and most valuable asset? Good health can help you earn promotions,[1] or it can cause you to fail in business. You should, therefore, do all you can to protect your health.

Health is a[2] personal thing. Learn what is necessary for you to keep in good health. If you can honestly say that you do the[3] following, your chances of keeping your health are very good:

1. Do you get sufficient sleep each day?

2. Do you[4] eat what is good for you and not just what you like to eat?

3. Do you see your doctor about once a year for a checkup?[5]

4. Do you have a hobby from which you derive pleasure?

If your answer to any of the queries listed[6] above is "no," it is of great importance that you give earnest thought to the following:

1. Make it a point[7] to get a minimum of eight hours of sleep each day.

2. Learn what foods are essential for good health, and learn to like[8] them.

3. Decide to try a number of hobbies, and select the one that appeals to you most.

Remember, no person[9] can do his best work who does not possess reasonably good health. (192)

160. *The Power of a Smile*

All of us like the person who has a smile on his face. It is so easy to smile. A smile costs us nothing, but it[1] is our most valuable asset.

We all like to meet a person who greets us with a smile. We feel better at[2] once for having met him. This feeling remains with us, and we pass it on to our friends and fellow workers.

There are[3] people who rarely let a smile reach their lips. Life seems to have little in the way of pleasure and happiness for[4] them. If these people would learn to smile, many of their troubles would not be so hard to bear.

No matter what line of[5] work you may choose when you finish school, you will find that a pleasant smile will be an asset. (116)

CHAPTER 4

Assignment 19

165. Gentlemen: I must take this opportunity to write you about the effectiveness of our advertisement[1] in the Tribune in helping the Sales Department of our company locate capable office-equipment salesmen.[2]

Early in June our Sales Department needed two salesmen to represent us in Utica. We placed a small[3] advertisement in the June 18 Tribune and the following morning had six applicants, two of whom we[4] hired immediately.

I wish all our advertising could be as effective. Hereafter, when we need salesmen[5] quickly, you may be sure that we shall advertise for them in the Tribune. Yours very truly, (117)

166. Dear Sir: I wish you could change places with me for the present.

If you had my job as credit manager of the[1] United Advertising Company, you would want to be paid for the advertisement that you ran in the Tribune[2] for the Hughes Fuel Company.

If I were in your place, I believe I would say: "It is too bad we kept the[3] United Advertising Company waiting. After all, we owe them the money. I must see what I can do[4] for them immediately."

Then I would send a check for $102 if it were humanly possible[5] or make at least a partial payment.

Finally, I would take the opportunity to write them a letter[6] making arrangements for the settlement of the balance.

Won't you let me hear from you soon. Yours very truly, (139)

167. Dear Sir: I was sorry to learn from your letter of March 30 that our March 2 shipment of watches has[1] not arrived. Our receipt shows that the shipment was placed in the hands of the United Trucking Company on the[2] afternoon of March 2, which means that you should have had the shipment by perhaps March 8.

We are putting a tracer[3] on the shipment immediately.

It is our sincere hope that the shipment will soon be located as a[4] few of the units cannot be replaced. Yours very truly, (91)

168. Mr. Hughes: In view of our recent decision to move our office-equipment factory to Utica, do[1] you think it might be wise to review our decision to replace our present heating unit? It is my feeling[2] that we should try to repair our present unit. With a few adjustments I think the present unit will hold up[3] for at least two years.

After you have had an opportunity to think about this matter, please let me know your[4] wishes. A. H. Hugo (84)

169. To the Members of the Staff: If you wish an advance on your salary before you leave on your vacation, you[1] must take the following steps:

1. Fill in the attached sheet indicating your department, the date on which you are[2] leaving, and the number of vacation days for which you wish to be paid.

2. After you have filled in the sheet, have[3] your department head sign it.

3. Present the sheet to the company Payroll Department two weeks before you wish[4] to leave on your vacation. E. R. Doyle (87)

170. Dear Madam: This is a note to tell you that we were happy to have the opportunity to serve you in our[1] Jewelry Department recently. We are sure that the watch you purchased for your nephew as a Christmas present[2] will give him many years of fine service. If it does not, we urge your nephew to write us.

It is our hope that[3] you will visit us again when you need anything in the jewelry line.

Our catalogue is enclosed. Yours very[4] truly, (82)

171. *Chuckle*

While a third-grade class was in session one day, a bad storm came up. The teacher, wishing to lessen the fright of the[1] children, thought this would be a good opportunity to tell them about the wonders of the elements. After a[2] few minutes of this, she asked Jimmy, "Can you tell me why it is that lightning does not strike twice in the same place?"

"Because,"[3] Jimmy replied immediately, "after it hits once, the same place isn't there any more!" (74)

Assignment 20

176. Dear Sir: We note with considerable regret that for many months we have not had an opportunity to[1] serve you in the leather goods department of our South Bend store. This is a matter of concern to all of us here.[2] As we have always been proud to have you as a special friend of our store, we wonder whether our service has failed[3] you in any way.

Won't you take a moment now to comment on the back of this letter whether we have failed you[4] or whether there are other reasons why we have not heard from you. If we have failed you, I have no doubt that we can[5] make an adjustment that will please you completely. Sincerely yours, (112)

177. Miss Smith: I have finally been able to convince my mother and father to take a trip to South Bend to see[1] the flower show. My father will combine business and pleasure by visiting a few leather dealers while he is[2] in South Bend.

Would you be good enough to reserve a double room for my mother and father at the Hotel

South[3] Bend for the week of July 18. If the South Bend cannot accommodate them, perhaps the Hotel Brown can. Please[4] ask the hotel to confirm the reservation.

As this will be the first vacation my mother and father will[5] have together since more than a decade, I sincerely hope that the weather will be good. A. B. Doyle (118)

178. Mr. House: As you know, you and a number of other salesmen have sent us complaints from dealers in connection[1] with our ball-point pens. You will be glad to learn that our Production Committee has just concluded a series of[2] conferences with the manufacturer to see whether we could eliminate the causes of the complaints.

We[3] accomplished a great deal; in fact, there is now no doubt in my mind that we shall have a pen that compares favorably[4] with our competitor's product and that we can be proud to sell. A. B. Crowley (95)

179. Dear Sir: Contrary to any comments you may have heard, the contract for the construction of the Girl Scout house has[1] not been assigned to any builder. Our Building Committee is now considering bids from a number of builders[2] and hopes to complete its work by the middle of June.

The moment the Committee has reached a decision, we[3] will send you an announcement. Yours very truly, (69)

180. Dear Sir: The Building Committee, which has been considering bids for the construction of the Girl Scout house, reached its[1] decision on May 10. The Committee has decided to give the contract to the Powers Construction Company[2] of South Orange. While your bid was a fair one, it was considerably higher than that of the Powers[3] Construction Company. Yours very truly, (67)

181. *Chuckle*

Mr. Brown, a grouchy old soul, was very fussy about the way his hair was cut; in fact, he was a source of[1] concern and bother to all the barbers in the village in which he lived. He shattered their nerves with a steady flow[2] of complaints as they cut his hair. The other day, though, he met his match. After a series of complaints, Mr. Brown[3] ended with, "And I wish to have my hair parted in the middle!" "I can't do it sir," answered the barber. "Now that[4] is silly! Why can't you do it?" Mr. Brown shouted in a loud, complaining voice. "Because there is an odd number,[5] sir." (101)

Assignment 21

187. Dear Sir: Every month we send out a unique correspondence bulletin designed to help correspondents write[1] effective, friendly letters. Each bulletin contains several samples of good letters as well as suggestions on[2] how to write letters. These suggestions can be used to advantage whenever you have to compose letters of your[3] own.

This correspondence bulletin is written by James Fenton, an outstanding author in the field of letter[4] writing. Mr. Fenton's comments are of such value that he has built up a big following of businessmen,[5] correspondents, and others who must write letters.

If you would like to obtain complimentary copies of this[6] correspondence bulletin every month, I suggest that you fill out and mail the enclosed card. Yours truly, (138)

188. Dear Madam: We have written you several letters asking for payment for the six cotton dresses you purchased[1] at our Troy store on July 15. Evidently these letters have escaped your attention, because we have[2] not heard from you.

If you are not happy with these dresses or cannot use them for any reason, I suggest that[3] you write us immediately. Sincerely yours, (69)

189. Dear Sir: Would you like to learn how easy it is to build such pieces as cabinets, coffee tables, and bookcases[1] for your home? If you would, send for a copy of our book, "Using Your Hands."

This 400-page book is written[2] in a style that is easy to read. You need no special training whatever to follow the directions and[3] suggestions it contains.

Why not send for a copy of "Using Your Hands" today. It sells for only $4. Very[4] truly yours, (83)

190. Dear Mary: You cannot know how proud I was to learn that you have been elected president of the school council[1] at Trenton College. This is a big honor, and I am certain that you will do everything you can to justify[2] the confidence your classmates have shown in you. Your Dad, (50)

191. Mr. Green: I am afraid that I shall not be able to attend the dinner in honor of Mr. Brandon,[1] who is retiring as president of Smith and Company. I have been detained in Trenton and cannot leave till[2] I straighten out several matters of importance. John H. Baker (53)

192. Dear Captain Green: On July 18 our correspondent, Mr. Fenton, had a bad auto accident and will[1] be out for several months. It is the president's suggestion that I take charge of the Correspondence Department[2] till Mr. Fenton recovers.

This is a big job, and it means that I shall have to work nights for at least ten[3] days. Therefore, my wife and I shall have to abandon our plans to have dinner with you at your cabin on July[4] 22.

It is our sincere hope that you

will ask us again. Sincerely yours, (94)

193. Gentlemen: One of your salesmen told me recently that you occasionally permit high school classes to go[1] through your manufacturing plant in Detroit. Would you be willing to permit a class of 25 boys to go[2] through your plant any weekday in May? A morning visit would be best for us.

May I have your decision soon so[3] that I can make the necessary plans here at school. Sincerely yours, (73)

Assignment 22

201. Dear Mrs. Quill: We were sorry to learn that the vase you bought from us on Friday, September 5, was damaged when[1] it arrived. You will be glad to know that we have found another one just like it on our shelves, and it will be shipped[2] to you tomorrow. You should receive it by Monday or Tuesday.

Please send the damaged vase back to me collect.

I[3] assure you, Mrs. Quill, that it is a pleasure to have you as a customer. Cordially yours, (78)

202. Dear Mr. Baker: In the months of October, November, and December, I have had referred to me by our[1] salesmen no fewer than 15 complaints from customers to the effect that our pens scratch. On Friday, January[2] 4, I tested a dozen pens selected at random from our stock; and I find that the complaints are justified.[3]

Please check with the Production Department and attempt to get to the bottom of the trouble. If the cause of[4] these complaints is not eliminated immediately, we may lose many good customers in our domestic[5] market.

Can you stop in to see me on Monday, January 8, or on Wednesday, January 10, to[6] decide what we should do? Very cordially yours, (130)

203. Dear Miss Temple: The second printing of our book, "The Voice of Freedom," has been delayed because the press on which the[1] book is printed was damaged by a fire on Tuesday, August 30. The damage has been repaired, but the printer[2] estimates that it will be the last week of September or the first week of October before we can have[3] copies. We shall ship your copy the moment we receive stock.

I regret this delay, Miss Temple, but I know you[4] will agree with us that it was beyond our control.

I am confident that after you have read "The Voice of Freedom"[5] you will be glad you waited for it. Very cordially yours, (112)

204. Dear Mr. Gray: Do you have trouble keeping the rooms in your house warm in the cold months of December, January,[1] and February? If so, you will be glad to know that we have the answer to your problem — the efficient[2] Temple Automatic Heating System. A Temple Automatic Heating System keeps your house warm no matter[3] how cold the weather is outside.

If you will mail the enclosed card, which is addressed to me personally, I shall[4] be glad to make special arrangements to have our salesman call to demonstrate how easy it is to have freedom[5] from heating worries. If you wish, he will prepare for you an estimate of the cost.

It will be a pleasure to[6] have you as a customer. Very cordially yours, (130)

205. Dear Mr. Hughes: We learned with sorrow of the damage that your automobile repair shop suffered from the floods on[1] Saturday, August 31, and Sunday, September 1.

May we assure you that, as an old customer of[2] ours, we are ready to help you. Here is what we will do:

1. We will hold your bills for the automobile parts you[3] purchased in July till you feel you can spare the cash to pay them.

2. We will replace your damaged stock immediately[4] if you will send to me a list of the items you need.

Simply write your answer at the bottom of this[5] letter and mail it back to me; we will do the rest.

Very cordially yours, (113)

Assignment 23

212. Mr. Newton: Please pardon my delay in acknowledging receipt of the plan you developed during the month[1] of April for producing new sales volume for our division. I have been devoting most of my time to solving[2] numerous problems and answering questions that could not wait.

I have gone over the complete plan several[3] times; and, in general, it appeals to me. I think it has advantages over the plan that I devised and[4] is definitely worth considering.

I have a number of questions that I should like to talk to you about.[5] If you have not yet made any definite appointments for Monday evening, perhaps we can go over these questions[6] at that time. H. A. Doyle (126)

213. Mr. Green: I am happy to announce that on Friday, April 16, I offered the position of general[1] manager of our New-Products Division to Mr. A. R. Newman, and he accepted. Mr. Newman[2] recently resigned as chief financial officer of the Fifth Avenue Development Corporation.

Mr.[3] Newman will devote his entire time to the New-Products Division, thus freeing me for more urgent duties.[4]

When you have met Mr. Newman, I know you will agree with me that his appointment as general manager[5] is a definite move in the right direction. C. A. Smith. (111)

214. Dear Mr. Barnes: It is a pleasure to acknowledge receipt of your two-year renewal to Time Magazine. We[1] are very happy that you have decided to continue to receive Time Magazine, and it is our earnest[2] hope that you will find all issues well worth reading.

Nobody knows what news Time Magazine will carry during the[3] months before us, but you may be sure that the news will be told as clearly and vividly as we know how to tell[4] it. Very truly yours, (84)

215. Dear Mr. Parson: We have written you numerous letters during March and April about your overdue bill[1] dating back to January 4. As yet, we have not received your remittance; nor have we received an acknowledgment[2] of our letters.

I have gone over the question of your overdue bill with the manager of our Credit[3] Division, and he feels definitely that we should take legal steps to collect the $150[4] you owe us.

As a general rule, we do not like to sue a customer for payment of an overdue[5] bill because both of us lose. We lose you as a friend; you lose the advantages of a good credit standing.

I[6] shall, therefore, defer taking action for one week with the hope that by the end of that time we shall have your check. Very[7] truly yours, (143)

216. Dear Friend: For over two years we have been sending you each month a copy of the National Amusement Magazine.[1] During that time you have, no doubt, derived considerable pleasure from the pages devoted to stories,[2] new and different puzzles, and games.

We have just gone over our general mailing list and find that the February[3] issue will be the last one you will receive. We have not yet received a renewal from you, and we cannot[4] continue sending the magazine after February.

Why not take a little time from your busy day[5] to mail us the enclosed renewal. Take advantage of the definite saving you can make by renewing for[6] two years. Cordially yours, (124)

217. *Chuckle*

Two Navy veterans devised a system to help each other during a college quiz. Each time one came to a[1] tough question, he would tap out in code with his pencil the number of that question. The other would casually[2] tap back the answer.

They thought that everything had gone smoothly; but when the quiz was over, they were startled to[3] hear the professor tap out on his desk: "I was in the Navy, too. You both just earned a zero!" (77)

Assignment 24

218. *Recall Chart*

1. Replaced, replaceable, replacement; unite, uniting, united.

2. Amount, amounts, amounted; bother, bothering, bothered.

3. Consist, consisted, consistent; complain, complained-complaint, complaining.

4. Evidence, evident, evidently; damage, damaged, damages.

5. Estimate, estimates, estimated; devote, devoted, devotion.

6. Define, defines, defined; new, renew, renewed.

7. Memory, memorize, remember; boil, boiler, boiled.

8. Believe, believed, believing; proficient, efficient, deficient.

9. January, September, December; Monday, Thursday, Saturday.

10. Opportunity, must, immediate, wish, company, advertise.

11. After, part, present, correspond-correspondence, several, such.

12. Ever-every, big, use, advantage, how-out, suggest.

13. Time, acknowledge, gone, general, over, during.

14. Question, yet, worth; to me, to make, to know.

220. *Check Your Study Habits*

Do you get the most from the time you devote to studying from a book? In order to learn from a book, you must[1] know how to use it properly. A book will teach you little if you do not have a plan for reading, because active[2] participation on your part is necessary if you wish to remember what you read.

In order to[3] comprehend and remember the contents of a book, you must do more than read. You must actively recite, question,[4] and review the material you have read.

Here are a few suggestions that will help you study from a book most[5] effectively.

1. Skim through the assigned reading so that you will know what it is you are to study.

2. Concentrate[6] on what the author has to say. Remember, too, that many new and important points are presented in graphs,[7] charts, and maps. Do not overlook them.

3. As you read, stop occasionally and recite mentally the important[8] points you have read.

4. If the book is your personal property, make brief notes in the margins of the points you[9] feel are important. These notes will serve as cues when you review the material later.

5. Review the material[10] from

time to time after you have read it and immediately before you must take a test on it. These[11] reviews will pay big dividends in better grades.

6. Relate what you are reading to what you have learned in the classroom.[12]

7. Keep a good set of notes. A good, legible set of notes will be worth a great deal to you. Good notes will[13] help you learn more and learn it quickly. They will help you remember what you have read. (274)

221. *A Race with the Clock*

Recently I heard a prominent businessman make a talk entitled "A Race with the Clock." He said he attended[1] a track meet in which all the contestants in the race had their eyes on a huge clock. They realized the value[2] of time, and their goal was to save a fraction of a second.

He said this brought home the fact that time once lost cannot[3] be recovered. Minutes are as precious as pearls, but many people do not seem to mind wasting time.

Each one of[4] us has the same number of hours at his command, but one man can accomplish more in those hours than his neighbor.

Time[5] is truly a daily wonder. You wake up in the morning with twenty-four hours of time. It is yours. If you do[6] not use it, you will be the loser.

Life has a great deal in store for us. There are so many things that we would like[7] to accomplish but cannot because enough time is not available. (153)

222. *Chuckle*

A partner in a big advertising company was suffering from a severe cold. He finally called a[1] well-known doctor and told his secretary that he wished to make an appointment. After a few moments, the[2] secretary said, "Certainly, but the first definite appointment I can give you is in three weeks."

"Three weeks!" the man[3] cried. "I may be dead by that time!"

"Oh," said the secretary, "you can always cancel the appointment." (78)

CHAPTER 5

Assignment 25

227. Mr. Hughes: I have just looked over the sales record of Mr. E. H. Underwood, who represents us in the[1] state of California. I must confess that I am not completely satisfied with the progress he is making.[2] His lack of success in selling our products is difficult for me to understand.

I have written Mr.[3] Underwood requesting him to meet me next week in Los Angeles, at which time I hope to be able to get[4] a satisfactory answer to the problem.

If I should find it necessary to replace Mr. Underwood,[5] can you suggest a dependable man for his position?

Please let me have your answer as soon as possible[6]—by next Saturday, if you can.

A stamped envelope is enclosed for your answer. A. R. Green (137)

228. Dear Mr. Powell: Thank you for your order for 100 gross of our No. 16 Manila envelopes[1] that you gave to our traveler, Mr. Smith. In view of the fact that this was your first order for our envelopes,[2] it was a source of special satisfaction to him and to us.

The envelopes were shipped to your New York office;[3] but as you requested, our statement will be sent to your Chicago office.

We hope that you will be pleased with our[4] envelopes as well as with our service. Yours very truly, (91)

229. Mr. Baker: This is just a brief note to tell you that the business trip that I undertook at your request was[1] a very satisfactory one.

In Los Angeles, I met, quite by accident, the president of the Los[2] Angeles Envelope Company, with whom we have been having difficulty in recent months. I feel I made[3] a great deal of progress with him; in fact, he asked me to spend a few days as a guest at his estate on my next[4] visit to Los Angeles, which I plan to do.

I shall, of course, give you a complete statement of my activities[5] as soon as I have a few moments to spare.

I think I can say that my trip was a definite success. Harry[6] H. Coyne (122)

230. Dear Miss Green: Thank you for your check for $16.30.

It is difficult for us to understand why[1] your August statement did not reach you, because it was addressed to you correctly at 415 South Michigan[2] Avenue, Chicago 16, Illinois. Perhaps, it was lost in the mail.

We can, of course, understand your request[3] to have your statements mailed in an envelope. Other customers have made similar requests; and, of course, we[4] wish we could grant them. Under our present system of billing, though, the use of envelopes is not satisfactory.[5]

As I am sure you realize, we have thousands of bills and statements to send out each month. The use of a card[6] makes it possible for us to complete the task quickly, efficiently, and at low cost.

We hope that you have no[7] difficulty receiving your next statement. Sincerely yours, (151)

231. Gentlemen: Thank you for your order for eight leather traveling bags. On your order you request that three bags be[1] shipped to your office in Los Angeles, one to your office in New York, and four to your office in St. Louis.[2] We shall, of course, be glad to do this. The bags will go out as soon as the proper initials have been stamped on them.[3]

We hope that your men will derive many years of service and satisfaction from these bags. We hope, too, that you will[4] let us serve you whenever you need leather goods of any kind.

Once again, thank you for your order. Very truly[5] yours, (101)

232. Mr. Duffy: I have had no success in convincing Jim Smith to join our staff as credit manager of the New York office.[1] It seems that he has made very satisfactory progress in his present company, and I understand that[2] he is in line for a fine promotion next year.

I should like to fill this job as soon as possible; it is a[3] source of concern to me. Do you have anyone to suggest for the position? F. A. Burns (77)

Assignment 26

237. Dear Mr. Ryan: Machines have been invented for just about everything, but no one has yet been able[1] to invent a suitable machine for collecting money.

I am inclined to believe, though, that if such a machine[2] were invented it would be unsatisfactory. It would not have that friendly appeal that you and I know[3] is so

important.

Therefore, until we can find a better method, we shall have to ask you in the old-fashioned way[4] for your check for $1,000 to take care of your unpaid invoice covering the piano you ordered[5] last September from our Miami store.

Won't you endeavor to mail it today. We shall greatly appreciate[6] it. Yours very truly, (124)

238. Dear Mr. Myers: We have written you several times endeavoring to collect your unpaid invoice No.[1] 198 covering home appliances purchased by you and your associates during the month of July.[2] To date, we have had no reply to our letters asking for payment.

Of course, we do not like to suggest unpleasant[3] methods to collect unpaid invoices. We feel, though, that we have been more than patient. Unless we have immediate[4] payment, we intend to engage a competent lawyer to take appropriate action to collect our[5] money.

Won't you please mail us your check for $166 without delay. In that way, we shall both[6] continue to enjoy the fine relations that we have enjoyed in past years. Very truly yours, (137)

239. Dear Mr. Lyons: We understand that your boy is studying drawing at the School of Engineering in[1] Peoria, Illinois. Undoubtedly, he will soon be faced with the problem of purchasing an appropriate[2] set of drawing instruments. This is important indeed, because a person seldom purchases more than one set[3] of instruments during his lifetime.

If the set he purchases is a good one, like the Ryan, he will appreciate[4] and enjoy it the rest of his life.

Why not encourage your boy to visit our store to inspect a set[5] of Ryan instruments the next time he is home from engineering school. We are confident that once he has given[6] them a trial, he will not want to part with them. Sincerely yours, (132)

240. Dear Fred: I have recently been engaged as manager of the Miami office of the National Insurance[1] Association. The Association's clients in the Miami area have been increasing[2] rapidly in recent years, and the Association has opened this new branch in order to serve their needs more[3] efficiently.

My new position creates a problem for me, with which I should appreciate your help.

I am not[4] familiar with the Miami area, and, therefore, do not know where to look for a home. As you have been in[5] the home-appliance business in Miami for many years, you undoubtedly know the area well. May I[6] have your suggestions. Sincerely yours, (127)

241. Mr. Lyons: As you undoubtedly know, we have had an encouraging increase in the sales of our home[1] appliances, especially dryers, in the Miami area in the last three months. Perhaps I was unduly[2] concerned about the reception our new line would receive when we unveiled it last January.

I sincerely[3] appreciate the part you played in making this encouraging increase in sales possible. James Dwyer (79)

242. *Chuckle*

A question included in a test given to a class of science students read, "Which are the last teeth to appear[1] in the mouth?"

One girl's terse answer was, "False." (27)

Assignment 27

248. Mr. Lord: I have an idea that you will receive a special invitation to speak at the regular[1] spring meeting of the National Newspapermen's Association upon a subject of your choice. The meeting[2] will be held this year at the Hotel King on Franklin Street in Bangor on Saturday, April 16, and will[3] probably be followed by a banquet in the evening.

I am particularly anxious to have you accept this[4] invitation when you receive it. It will provide a fine opportunity for you to give these newspaper[5] people an idea of how our company operates.

If you cannot accept the invitation, please let me[6] know immediately. Frank H. Strong (129)

249. Mr. Strong: You will be happy to know that the invitation to speak at the regular spring meeting of the[1] National Newspapermen's Association arrived the other day. As you will see from the attached letter,[2] I have, in addition, been invited to be the speaker at the banquet. I shall, of course, accept both assignments.[3]

I decided upon "The Obligation of Business to Education" as my subject for the general[4] meeting.

Is there any particular subject that you would like me to take up in my banquet talk? I shall[5] be glad to have your ideas on this matter. B. A. Lord (111)

250. Dear Mr. Lang: As you have probably read in the late edition of yesterday's newspaper, we have just opened[1] a new drive-in branch of our bank opposite the King Street Station. In our estimation, these additional[2] accommodations will enable us to render even more efficient service to our customers.

The next[3] time you are in the vicinity of the King Street Station, why not stop in and speak to Mr. G. A. Frank,[4] manager of the new branch. He will be delighted to tell you how we can serve your banking needs. We have an idea[5] that you will enjoy doing business with a bank of our reputation. Sincerely yours, (116)

251. Dear Mr. Banker: A man is inclined to be particularly proud of his home because he owns it. Perhaps[1] you would like to own your own home.

Once you have talked with an officer of our bank, you will probably be surprised[2] to find how little it is going to cost for you to own your own home. He will tell you about our regular[3] low-cost loans and attractive conditions of repayment that we can arrange for you.

Stop in at the Spring Street[4] Branch of our bank the next time you have a few minutes to spare; that is all that will be necessary for us to give you[5] an idea of the way our different plans operate. Very truly yours, (115)

252. *Chuckle*

"Miss King," said the boss quietly, "I must say that you are probably the prettiest girl in the office." "Really!"[1] said the young typist.

"You dress well, and you speak nicely. In addition, your attendance has been regular; and I[2] can say without hesitation that your conduct is beyond reproach."

"You must not pay me so many compliments,"[3] she protested.

"Oh, that's all right! I only wanted to put you in a pleasant frame of mind before I take up[4] the subjects of grammar and spelling." (87)

Assignment 28

258. Dear Mrs. Yates: If you owed us $2,000, we know you would arrange some way to pay it without delay.[1]

Of course, we are aware that you do not owe us that amount. The balance is only $8.60, the[2] price of the mixer you purchased on October 18. Yes, this is a very small balance; but there is just as[3] much work and detail involved as though it were many times that sum.

We are sure, Mrs. Yates, that you did not look at[4] the matter in that light. You would not make us wait for a much larger sum; therefore, why make us wait for this small unpaid[5] balance?

Won't you please rush your check to us right away. We shall await it eagerly. Sincerely yours, (118)

259. To the Staff: On January 1 Mr. John L. Fox joined the Nelson Textile Company as tax director.[1] In this newly created post, Mr. Fox will devote all his time to company tax matters.

Mr. Fox received[2] his bachelor's degree from Yale in 1955. After serving as a captain in the Air Corps, he[3] continued his studies at Yale, where he obtained his law degree in the summer of 1958.[4] Approximately two years later, he joined the law firm of Knox and Brush, where he specialized in tax

work.

It is a pleasure[5] to welcome Mr. Fox to our staff. I know that you join me in this welcome. A. R. Dexter (117)

260. Mr. Young: You will be glad to know that our book on guns has just come off the press — approximately ten days ahead[1] of time.

Judging by what I have seen, this book on guns will sell much more rapidly than the other books we[2] have done for the Christmas trade. My son has finished the book and tells me he enjoyed it; it is fun to read. I[3] think the book will yield us a handsome profit.

When you receive a copy, you will notice that it has a flexible[4] yellow cloth cover. I am aware that we originally decided to use some shade of blue; but while you[5] were away, the author frankly told us that he did not like blue. Therefore, it was necessary for us to change[6] it to yellow. B. C. Rush (125)

261. Dear Mr. Yale: Is your home much too cold in the winter and much too hot in the summer? If it is, you need a[1] Johnson Air Conditioner, which both heats and cools.

A Johnson Air Conditioner will save you as much as 40[2] per cent of your fuel budget. It will help to keep your house warm in the winter and nicely cool in the summer.[3]

For a welcome solution to a perplexing weather problem, install a Johnson Air Conditioner without[4] delay. By planning ahead, we can arrange to have it installed while you are away on your vacation this spring.[5] It will take us a maximum of four days to complete the installation. Yours very truly, (117)

262. Dear Miss Hardy: The clock that you shipped us on April 16 has been received and inspected by our Repair[1] Department. We find that the clock will have to have considerable work done on it. Judging from the condition of[2] the clock, it has apparently been dropped from a high place or hit with a heavy instrument.

We estimate that[3] the cost of repairs will be approximately $15.20. Because you asked us to get in touch[4] with you before going ahead if the cost was more than $10, we shall await your instructions as to whether[5] we should make the repairs or send the clock back to you. Very truly yours, (114)

263. *Chuckle*

A café in Paris always served rabbit pie for lunch even when rabbits were scarce. An old customer questioned[1] the proprietor. "Now come, John, you put something beside rabbit in that pie!" he teased him.

"Yes," admitted the[2] proprietor, after a moment's hesitation, "sometimes I do put in just a bit of horse-meat." "I thought so," said[3] the customer. "And in approximately what proportion?"

"Oh," answered the proprietor, "50-50—one[4] horse to one rabbit." (84)

Assignment 29

270. To the Staff: The attached bulletin and circular were recently mailed to all authors of our publications.[1] The purpose of this material is to keep our authors in touch with the ordinary operations of[2] our organization. We are publishing this bulletin at the suggestion of several of our executives[3] who feel that we should do more in the way of public relations with our authors. For the present, I shall[4] be responsible for the editing of the bulletin.

Your opinion in regard to the content of this[5] initial issue will be welcomed. I shall be extremely grateful for all helpful suggestions. Please send them along[6] promptly. F. R. Yale (124)

271. Dear Mr. Knox: So many exciting and delightful books are being published these days that it is extremely[1] difficult for the ordinary person to examine and read them all.

To be sure that you are reading the best[2] books, you should have an expert's careful opinion of what the best books are. You should, in addition, have a helpful[3] list of new publications from which to choose.

This careful opinion and the helpful list are yours if you read the[4] "Reader's Magazine" faithfully. The purpose of this magazine is to give you a helpful preview of the latest[5] editions of books that have been released during the week by the major publishing organizations of[6] the country.

Why not take advantage promptly of the special offer that is explained on the enclosed circular.[7] Yours very truly, (144)

272. Dear Mr. Brown: Please pardon me for not writing you more promptly in regard to your request for my opinion[1] of Jane Frank. Ordinarily, I would have answered your letter immediately; but for the past three weeks[2] I have been overwhelmed with business problems.

For five years Miss Frank was my executive assistant in the Publications[3] Division of our organization. I regarded her as a cheerful, thoughtful, and responsible[4] person who organized her work carefully. My opinion of Miss Frank is confirmed by several of the[5] executives in the Publications Division with whom she came in contact.

Miss Frank seemed to enjoy working with[6] us but decided to leave for the purpose of taking care of her ailing mother. I was extremely sorry[7] to lose her, as she

was very valuable to me. Yours very truly, (154)

273. Dear Mr. Knox: It is not too early to start thinking about making those fall repairs to your home so that you[1] will be ready for the winter that will soon be here.

Under the helpful Home-Repair Plan that is carefully explained[2] in the enclosed circular, we are able to extend to you a loan that you can take as long as thirty-six months[3] to repay.

We are purposely making these loans available only to responsible persons who have an[4] excellent record for prompt payment of their obligations. We are happy to number you among them.

We should[5] appreciate an opportunity to explain this inexpensive plan to you in detail. Won't you drop in[6] the next time you are in this area. Yours very truly, (131)

274. Dear Mrs. Underwood: Haven't you often begged your husband to relax more? Perhaps he won't pay any attention[1] to you; but we think he will to Frank Strong after he has read his book, "Enjoy Your Leisure."

Frank Strong has written[2] a book that is designed to make a man relax. The illustrations make him laugh, which is good for everybody.[3]

"Enjoy Your Leisure" was originally published for doctors. Many doctors, though, complained that patients were[4] walking away with copies. Therefore, we decided to make the book available to people *before* they became[5] patients.

The enclosed circular provides a full explanation of the book.

You can get a copy of "Enjoy[6] Your Leisure" for your husband by using the enclosed stamped envelope to send in your order. When the book arrives,[7] you, too, will probably want to read it. In our opinion, you will like Mr. Strong's delightful treatment of[8] the subject of relaxation. Very truly yours, (170)

Assignment 30

275. *Recall Chart*

1. Ordinary, regard, opinion, circular, responsible, organize.

2. Public, publish-publication, purpose, newspaper, street, particular.

3. Upon, subject, idea, speak, regular, probable.

4. Request, under, state, next, success, satisfy-satisfactory.

5. Satisfied, progress, progressive, envelope, difficult, difficulty.

6. Explain, explanation, explained; prompt, promptness, promptly.

7. Dial, dials, dialed; create, created, creation.

8. Income, become, outcome;

invoice, invoices, invoiced.

9. Endeavor, endeavors, endeavored; bank, banker, banquet.

10. King, kings, kingdom; yield, yields, yielded.

11. Award, awards, awarded; hold, holds, holding.

12. Index, indexing, indexes; doubt, doubtful, undoubtedly.

13. Compliment, compliments, complimentary; continue, debate, ahead.

14. Review, reviews, reviewed; mother, memorable, credentials.

277. *Conversation Check List*

Do people enjoy conversing with you? They will if you follow these suggestions:

(1) *Listen carefully.* Many[1] of us are so concerned with what we plan to say next that we don't really hear what the other person is saying.[2] If you listen actively to other people, they will pay closer attention when *you* speak.

(2) *Avoid tiresome[3] details.* A famous man once said: "The secret of being tiresome is in telling *everything.*" We all know[4] the person who digresses and insists on giving you every detail, no matter how minute. "It was Saturday;[5] no, it was Sunday. Yes, it must have been Sunday because I remember reading the comics. It was ten o'clock,[6] or was it eleven o'clock? No, it was ten o'clock." As though it made any difference! The listener[7] is worn out long before the

speaker reaches his point.

(3) *Beware of trite expressions.* Nothing is more irritating[8] to a listener than to hear repeated over and over again such trite expressions as "You can say[9] that again," "It's simply divine," and "Fabulous!"

No doubt you are familiar with persons who in every second[10] sentence punctuate their conversation with "You know," and "I mean." These expressions add nothing to the conversation.[11]

(4) *Ask the right questions.* A question properly placed and stated helps to make the other person "open[12] up." It indicates a genuine regard for his opinions. A simple question, like "Don't you think?" or "How do[13] you feel about that point?" will often keep the other fellow talking and keep *you* from talking too much!

(5) *Praise the[14] other fellow whenever you can.* Your conversation will be richer if you learn how to pay an occasional[15] compliment — provided you do so sincerely. When you hear a person give a fine talk, tell him you enjoyed[16] it. When a classmate makes the honor roll, pat him on the back; he will then be more likely to pay you a compliment[17] when you have earned it — and we all thrive on well-deserved praise!

If you follow these suggestions thoughtfully, they[18] will help to make your conversation more meaningful and enable you to enlarge your circle of friends. (378)

278. *Nine Lessons in Living*

Learn to laugh. A good laugh is better than medicine.

Learn to attend strictly to your own business.

Learn to tell a[1] good story. A well-told story is as welcome as a sunbeam in a sickroom.

Learn the art of saying kind and[2] encouraging things.

Learn to avoid making unkind remarks that may cause friction.

Learn not to talk about your troubles.[3] Everyone has his own troubles to worry about without being burdened by yours.

Learn to stop grumbling.[4] If you cannot see something good in anything or anyone, at least keep quiet.

Learn to hide your aches and pains[5] under a pleasant smile. No one cares whether you have an earache, a headache, or rheumatism.

Learn to greet people[6] with a smile. They carry too many frowns in their own hearts to be burdened with any of yours. (136)

CHAPTER 6

Assignment 31

284. Dear Mr. Gray: I am sure that you, as a successful merchant, recognize the fact that it is never a pleasant[1] experience to try to collect very small unpaid bills. If you were in my situation, Mr. Gray,[2] I know you would be as unhappy as I am to have to write this letter asking for settlement of an[3] overdue account amounting to only $12.50. That is, as you know, the sum you owe us for[4] quantities of merchandise you purchased between April 10 and April 15.

I know, of course, that your failure to[5] pay is not intentional and that you eventually will pay us. It will be helpful, though, if you would do[6] so now.

May we expect your check shortly? Yours very truly, (131)

285. Mr. Brown: The account of the Harper Picture Company, amounting to $8,000, is now more than[1] ninety days overdue. I am, naturally, quite concerned about the situation. I am sure that something[2] is wrong, because the Harper Picture Company has never been behind in its payments before. Actually,[3] they have often paid their bills ahead of time.

I suggest, therefore, that you make a special trip to see them between[4] now and May 15 to get the answer.

I need not remind you, I am sure, to use extreme tact in handling this[5] situation, as the Harper Picture Company is a very important account. Harry G. Knox (118)

286. Mr. Gates: The attached sales figures provide a revealing picture of the accomplishments of Frank Brown as a[1] salesman. The figures show definitely that as a salesman he is a failure.

I knew, of course, that he had no[2] sales experience when I engaged him. He seemed to me, though, to be a natural salesman who would sell large[3] quantities of our merchandise. I am sorry to say that the attached figures prove that he cannot sell.

I am very[4] much afraid that we shall eventually have to let him go. B. C. Baker (95)

287. Dear Mr. Davis: This letter announces the publication shortly of three valuable lectures that[1] every merchant should read. These lectures were delivered before the National Merchants' Association by[2] experienced businessmen who are recognized leaders in the field of merchandising. These lectures take up the[3] following topics:

1. How to set up an accounting system.

2. How to prepare a sales manual.

3. How to[4] handle difficult sales situations.

A copy of these lectures is yours with our compliments, Mr. Davis,[5] if we receive your renewal to the Merchandising Magazine between now and June 1. Very truly yours,[6] (120)

294. Dear Mr. Morris: Thank you for the opportunity to tell you about our latest product, the Graham Fireplace.[1] The models that we can install for you are described in detail in our booklet, "Gracious Living."

Why not look[2] through the enclosed descriptive booklet and select the fireplace you would like. Then permit our representative in[3] the Albany area, Mr. Green, to visit your home and discuss with you the cost of installation. You[4] will, of course, be under no obligation.

After you and your family have enjoyed a Graham Fireplace for[5] a week or so, you will speedily discover why people consider it an investment in happy living.[6]

You will make no mistake, Mr. Morris, when you install a Graham Fireplace. Yours very truly, (137)

295. Mr. Dwyer: I am afraid I have some disappointing and disturbing news to give you. We have decided[1] to discontinue publication of our magazine, Family Life, on Friday, December 31. We[2] shall also close the Albany office on that date. It was a hard, but necessary, decision to make.

As[3] you know, for almost three years Family Life has been steadily in the red. We are now, in fact, heavily in[4] debt to our bank, The Albany Trust Company. Altogether, we owe the bank almost $50,-000.[5] You can readily see, therefore, why we had no other choice but to discontinue publication.

So that there[6] will be no misconception or misunderstanding in the minds of the members of the staff, please be careful not[7] to mention this matter to anyone until we are ready to make an official announcement. Rex Smith (159)

296. Mr. Smith: I was naturally sorry to receive your discouraging note of Monday, November 16,[1] telling me of the discontinuance of the publication of our magazine, Family Life.

Looking back[2] now, I can see that it was definitely a mistake to bring out this magazine at all, although at the time[3] it seemed like an extremely profitable idea.

I am temporarily keeping the present staff on the[4] payroll, although I hope that eventually everyone will be assigned to other departments in[5] Chicago, Illinois. Frank Dwyer (106)

297. Dear Mr. Hughes: Would you like to dispose of your Christmas shopping problem speedily and easily? Then just make[1] up a list of your friends, both young and old, who enjoy a good mystery and send them each month for a full year the[2] selections of the Mystery Book Club. By doing this, you will discover that you will not only dispose of[3] your Christmas shopping problem, but you will also save a good deal of money.

Very truly yours, (77)

298. *Chuckle*

Billie had reached school age, and his mother managed to make him enthusiastic about the idea of going[1] to school. She bought the young man new clothes, told him about the other children he would meet, and got him so sold on[2] the project that he eagerly went off to school the first day. He came back with some fine things to say about school.

Next[3] morning his mother went into his bedroom and said he had to get up.

"What for?"

"You have to go to school."

"What, again?"[4] asked Billy. (83)

Assignment 33

305. Gentlemen: I am happy to be a character reference for Mr. Franklin G. Brown, my former assistant,[1] who is applying for a Government position in which he will travel throughout the world for the State[2] Department.

When I was a district foreman with the Central Railroad some years ago, Mr. Brown worked closely with me.[3] He was a hard-working, faithful, and efficient worker who never objected to taking on new duties.[4] Furthermore, he was always eager to learn.

When I retired from the Central Railroad two years ago, he succeeded[5] me as foreman.

If there is any other information I can furnish you regarding Mr. Brown's character,[6] training, or work habits, please write me. Yours very truly, (131)

306. Dear Hugh: Several days ago I was asked to assist the Central Railroad in its efforts to collect from the[1] Government a tax overpayment that the Railroad claims it made two years ago. I formally accepted[2] the assignment yesterday.

This means that I shall have to devote all my time to the case throughout the months of March, April,[3] and part of May. Unfortunately, therefore, I cannot keep my fishing engagement with you on April 10.[4] If you have no objection, perhaps we can arrange to go fishing sometime in June. By that time, Hugh, I hope I[5] shall have completed my work for the Railroad. Sincerely, (110)

307. Dear Mr. Ferris: Vacation time is here. Perhaps you, like many other people, are already pouring over[1] railroad, bus, and airplane timetables, making your annual vacation plans. There is a strange thing about[2] vacations: they cause people to become forgetful in their hurried efforts to get away.

They forget to stop[3] delivery on the milk or the paper. Some forget

- Assignment 34 · KEY TO SHORTHAND

to shut off the furnace.

In their haste, a few of our customers[4] overlook bills that they would normally take care of as a matter of routine.

The object of this letter, Mr.[5] Ferris, is to remind you that there is a small balance of $60 on your account that was due several[6] weeks ago. Your vacation will be more enjoyable if you know that you have paid it. May we have your check[7] soon. Yours very truly, (144)

308. Dear Mr. Brown: About a week ago we sent you the Friday, December 15, issue of our magazine,[1] World and Government News. This is the third copy we have sent you beyond your expiration date. I felt you would[2] not want to miss this issue, with its wealth of information on events that are taking place throughout the world today.[3]

Unfortunately, though, we cannot afford to send you further copies without your authorization. As[4] you know, your renewal was due three weeks ago.

Please send us your OK on the enclosed form before you misplace[5] it. We shall then be able to continue sending you World and Government News regularly.

You need not send[6] any money at this time, Mr. Brown. We will bill you later. Cordially yours, (134)

309. Dear Mrs. Smith:

Throughout the week of April 15, the Johnson Furniture exhibit on Fourth Street and Railroad[1] Avenue will be open to the public. In this furniture exhibit you will find fifty complete rooms furnished[2] with furniture from many parts of the world. The planning for this furniture exhibit began more than three[3] years ago, and many famous designers are represented in it.

If you prefer furniture that has[4] character, grace, and charm, you cannot afford to miss this exhibit. We are sure that you will find many objects that[5] you will want to consider for your own home.

We hope to see you during the week of April 15. Very truly[6] yours, (121)

Assignment 34

315. Dear Mr. Knox: Do you want a wide assortment of patterns from which to choose your sports clothes? Do you want a practical[1] suit that will fit you like a glove? Then Stern Brothers, Des Moines' leading men's shop, is the logical, economical[2] place to shop.

That is where the men of Des Moines who are determined to get the best in sports clothes do their shopping.[3] These men know that at Stern Brothers they can get just what they want at the price they want to pay.

Come in, Mr. Knox, and[4] let us show you the wide assortment of patterns from which you can choose. Yours very truly,

P.S. You can, if you[5] wish, take advantage of our liberal credit terms. (110)

316. Dear Mr. Turner: Today it is a common sight to see a company-owned plane land at an airport and[1] discharge several of the company's top men. There was a time, of course, when that sight caused quite a stir around an airport.[2] That was before company-owned planes proved to be so practical and economical.

At the present time[3] hundreds of companies maintain one or more planes for the routine use of their technical, sales, and executive[4] staffs. These companies have determined that it pays off in terms of higher efficiency, in time saved, and in travel[5] costs.

If you want a report on how little it costs to own our modern plane, just return the enclosed card. Yours[6] very truly, (123)

317. To the Staff: It is with regret that I must report that John S. Stern, editor of our Chemical and Medical[1] Division, has decided to retire. Mr. Stern personally organized our Chemical and Medical[2] Division only eight years ago.

He has had a distinguished career in chemical and medical[3] publishing. He has written many practical articles that have ap-peared in leading medical journals.

I must[4] also report that Don Lyons, sales manager of the Export Division, has resigned. He will return to his[5] former position as a professor of modern languages at Northern State College.

I want to assure you[6] that both these men leave with our best wishes for a happy and successful future. A. B. Smith (137)

318. Dear Mr. Farmer: Safety comes first with the gas industry. Year after year, national fire protection records[1] show that gas causes fewer fires than any other fuel.

Safety is a vital part of your gas service. The[2] gas industry has taken the lead over the years in the development of safety standards.

Our gas ranges[3] are tested and retested to comply with the highest standards of safe operation.

You will be making a[4] smart move if you visit our showrooms when you are thinking of replacing your present range. Very truly yours,[5] (100)

319. *Chuckle*

Little Mary, who was six years old, proudly went off to school, looking very grown-up in a new skirt and sports jacket.[1] When she came home, her mother asked if anyone had liked her outfit. "Yes, the teacher did," said Mary.

"Oh, she[2] did not!" teased her father.

"She did, too!" retorted Mary. "She said as long as I was dressed like a lady, why didn't[3] I act like one." (64)

Assignment 35

325. To the Staff: Two or three weeks ago, you will recall, I offered to the men and women of the International[1] Division of Jennings Enterprises an opportunity to buy stock in our company and pay for[2] it from their earnings through payroll deductions.

I am glad to say that during the past week many of the members[3] of the International Division have enrolled in the plan, and more are enrolling every day.

The purpose[4] of this note is to remind you that the offer expires in a few days. If you are interested in[5] enrolling but have not done so, will you please fill out the enclosed form and return it to Mr. Frank, our comptroller,[6] without further delay. Frank H. Cummings (127)

326. Dear Mrs. Cummings: We are happy at this time to be able to offer you two years of the Home Magazine[1] at the special introductory price of $6.40. This special introductory offer[2] will expire on Friday, August 30.

We know that you will be quite pleased when you read the interesting fiction[3] and the entertaining, informative, and helpful articles in the Home Magazine.

To get the first issue[4] of the Home Magazine, just fill out and return the enclosed card. We will enter your order and charge your account[5] in the amount of $6.40.

Remember, though, that this introductory offer expires on[6] Friday, August 30. You must, therefore, act promptly. Yours very truly, (133)

327. Dear Mr. Jennings: Will you take a few moments to try an interesting experiment with us? Just put your[1] fingers in your ears for two or three seconds. Notice how quiet things instantly become.

That is the kind of[2] difference Interboro Ceilings will make in your home. The tiny openings in Interboro Ceilings actually[3] absorb up to 75 per cent of the room noise that strikes them.

Interboro Ceilings have an[4] attractive pattern that introduces new beauty into the interior of your home. You will be interested[5] to know, though, that they are economical to install.

You can, of course, easily install these ceilings without[6] help; but if you want the work done for you, just call one of the dealers listed on the enclosed folder. Many[7] of these dealers can be reached evenings until nine. Yours very truly, (153)

328. Dear Mr. Billings: For a long time I have had it in mind to write you this letter telling you some of the things[1] your bulletin, The Financial Weekly, has been able to do for me. Since I entered my order for The[2] Financial Weekly three or four years ago, my earnings have increased from $9,000 to $14,000.[3] My increased earnings, though, do not quite tell the whole story.

The Financial Weekly also tells me how to get[4] more value from the purchases I make.

In one of the spring issues, for example, you had an interesting[5] report on cars. That report helped me trade in my car at the right time. Another issue had an interesting,[6] entertaining, and practical article on home furnishings that helped me make considerable savings when[7] I built an addition to my house.

Please continue sending me The Financial Weekly without interruption![8] Yours very truly, (164)

329. Dear Mr. Turner: We want to welcome you to our family of stockholders of the Western Medical Supply[1] Company.

The enclosed booklet will tell you in non-technical terms all about our line of chemical,[2] medical, and surgical products.

We have begun the preparation of our annual report, which you will receive[3] in March. It will explain our plans for the future. Yours very truly, (73)

Assignment 36

330. *Recall Chart*

1. Merchant, merchandise, recognize, never, experience, between.

2. Short, quantity, situation, railroad, world, throughout.

3. Object, objective, character, characters, govern, government.

4. Introduces, introduced, introduction; interpret, interpreted, interpretation.

5. Entertain, entertains, entertainment; proceed, procedure, proceedings.

6. Term, termed, termination; alter, altered, alteration.

7. Furnish, unfurnished, furnishings; inform, informed, information.

8. Misplace, displace, replace; become, outcome, income.

9. Announce, pronounce, renounce; schedule, schedules, scheduled.

10. Yell, yelled; enjoy enjoyable; tax, taxes.

11. Chemical, article, radically; steady, steadier, steadily.

12. Weeks ago, days ago, hours ago, I want, you want, he wanted.

13. Some of the, many of the, one of the, of course, I hope, as soon as.

332. *How Do You Look?*

A short time ago, the staff of one of the Chicago newspapers undertook a comprehensive study in[1] which they asked businessmen to state the particular pet peeves they had about the appearance of their secretaries.[2] Here are some of the frank answers these businessmen reported:

1. "My secretary wears altogether too[3] much make-up."

2. "My secretary chews gum. Her jaws are never still. They seem to be moving morning, noon, and night."[4]

3. "My secretary, a young man, doesn't know how to match colors. He is likely to wear a yellow tie with[5] a blue suit — and red socks!"

4. "I can always tell when my secretary has a date for the evening. She comes to[6] work with her hair in pin curls."

Don't get the mistaken idea from these statements, though, that the businessman insists[7] on glamour. Far from it. He values his secretary for her excellent grooming, her tasteful choice of clothing,[8] and her cheerful manner.

To achieve a smart appearance, you will find that attention to every detail of[9] your personal appearance must become a natural, daily routine. Any successful secretary will[10] tell you that personal details are indispensable factors in job getting, in job holding, and in job[11] promotion. (222)

333. *Courtesy*

Whenever people work togeth-er, there is certain to be occasional friction. All it takes, though, to keep this[1] friction to a minimum is common courtesy.

Courtesy is a queer thing. We give it freely to strangers;[2] yet the better we know people, the less we think about using it. This is too bad, because courtesy — the same[3] kind we gladly accord to strangers —is a fine way to win co-operation and good will from the people with[4] whom we work.

Courtesy shows up every day in many ways. It shows up in the way we greet people in the[5] morning, in the pleasant tone we use over the telephone, and in the considerate way we answer questions.[6]

People are conscious of courtesy. They are quick to notice its presence or absence. Courtesy costs us nothing;[7] yet it can be an important factor in helping us succeed or fail in business. (155)

334. *Business Dress*

The subject of dress is of interest to every person. There are clothes for every occasion—and there[1] are many occasions.

It is of the utmost importance that you select appropriate dress for one of those[2] occasions — your daily business appointment with your fellow workers and your boss.

Appropriate clothes are one of[3] the businesswoman's most valuable assets. She can work better, she is more cheerful, and her boss is pleased if⁴ she is dressed neatly and attractively.

But the wise business girl guards against being overdressed. It is far better⁵ to be conservative in dress than to be carried away by the extremes of fashion. A business girl who⁶ comes to work as though she were ready to give a performance on the stage not only is violating the rules⁷ of business dress but is endangering her position with the firm as well. (154)

335. *Chuckle*

A five-year old boy came to visit his grandmother. Toward the end of the afternoon, she telephoned his mother¹ to ask her when she should bring him home. Without a moment's hesitation, the mother answered, "When he is sixteen!"² (41)

CHAPTER 7

Assignment 37

341. Dear Mr. Star: In previous years owners of various types of stores in Los Angeles had a genuine¹ problem in the warm weather. They found that their sales dropped seriously in the summer. It was becoming increasingly² evident that people would not willingly shop in the discomfort of warm, humid weather.

A few years³ ago, though, the progressive stores in Los Angeles found an exceedingly practical and simple solution⁴ to this seemingly impossible situation. They installed an Empire Air Conditioner. Sales immediately⁵ improved.

If your store does not have an Empire Air Conditioner, you are losing an extremely fine⁶ opportunity to improve your sales picture in the summer months. If you are interested in learning how⁷ surprisingly inexpensive an Empire Air Conditioner is to install, just return the enclosed card. Yours very⁸ truly, (162)

342. Dear Mr. Green: I was exceedingly happy to read your letter of Friday, August 15, telling me how¹ impressed you were with the courteous service you received from some of the employees in our Import and Export² Department.

It is not often that customers willingly write us about our service. That is why a letter³ like yours is genuinely appreciated.

I want to share your letter, Mr. Green, with the employees of⁴ the Import and Export Department. Accordingly, I am referring your letter to the head of that department⁵ with the suggestion that he put it on the bulletin board.

If you ever have any suggestions that will⁶ help us improve our services further, please be sure to let us know. Yours very truly, (136)

343. Dear Mr. Day: The

amount of money you make in a year, Mr. Day, does not indicate how much you improved[1] your net worth in that year; it is what you save in that period that will decide what your financial future will[2] be.

It is surprisingly easy to save at the Empire Savings Bank. You will be exceedingly impressed and[3] delighted as you watch your account grow with the help of our generous quarterly dividends.

If you would like[4] to take steps to improve your financial future, come to the Empire Savings Bank, this city's leading bank.

A friendly,[5] courteous, and cordial welcome by the employees of the Empire Savings Bank awaits you. Cordially yours,[6] (120)

344. Dear Mr. Green: I was exceedingly embarrassed to discover this morning that I had not answered your[1] courteous note of Monday, April 16, inviting me to dinner on May 10. I would not, of course, knowingly[2] be so discourteous; but your note was misplaced among some papers on my desk and just came to light today.

I[3] am genuinely sorry that it will be impossible for me to accept because of a previous[4] engagement I made for May 10 in Dallas. For many reasons it is imperative for me to keep that engagement.[5]

I hope that you will give me another invitation for some day after my return to New York on May[6] 20. Yours very truly, (125)

Assignment 38

350. Dear Mr. Owen: Thank you for submitting your application for membership in the National Radio[1] Association and for sending us your check for $10. Your membership card is attached.

As you may know,[2] your membership automatically entitles you to a subscription to our bulletin.

As you will see[3] by the enclosed report, our plans for our annual convention on June 16, 17, and 18 are[4] substantially complete. If all goes well, you should receive final details in a few days.

We hope, Mr. Owen, that[5] your membership in our association will be the source of many lasting friendships and profitable business[6] relationships. Very truly yours, (127)

351. Dear Mr. Billings: As we wrote you on April 16, we are granting 100 scholarships to high school seniors[1] who show unusual promise of leadership. At that time we suggested that, if you wanted any of[2] your seniors to compete for these scholarships, you were to fill out and submit to us the report form that we enclosed.[3] We have not yet heard from you.

If you plan to have your students enter the competition, may I impress on[4] you that all applications must be submitted by Friday, July 10.

As we also wrote you, we feel that the[5] seniors of Baker Township High School would profit substantially by competing for these scholarships. We hope, therefore,[6] that you will submit your applications promptly. Cordially yours, (133)

352. Dear Mr. Owens: As you can well imagine, this letter is a difficult one for me to write because I[1] must collect the overdue balance that you owe us without jeopardizing your friendship. I know, of course, that by[2] writing this letter I run the risk of disturbing our pleasant relationship on which the success of our[3] partnership depends.

I hope that this letter will not only persuade you to pay your account but will also preserve[4] that pleasant relationship.

Your check for $550 or a substantial part of it will bring your[5] account up to date. May we hear from you soon. Very truly yours, (112)

353. Dear Leo: As you know, I have just purchased a house in the suburbs on the former Baker estate, which was[1] subdivided two years ago into 15 one-acre plots.

This means, of course, that I shall have to sublease my[2] five-room apartment at 415 East 18 Street, in New York. Do you have anyone on your lists who would be[3] interested in subleasing the apartment for six months, the term that my lease has still to run? I am paying[4] $120 a month rent but would willingly sublease it for substantially less in order to[5] get it off my hands immediately. Yours very truly, (111)

354. Dear Subscriber: As you know, your subscription has expired; but there is still time to keep the News Magazine coming[1] to your home without interruption! All you have to do is mail the enclosed card today.

Normally, we could send[2] the next issue even though your subscription had expired, knowing that your renewal would be coming along sooner[3] or later. But now, with our presses already operating at their fullest capacity, we regret[4] that we cannot continue your subscription unless we hear from you right away.

Send no money now. Just fill out[5] and mail the enclosed card. Very truly yours, (108)

355. Mr. Ferris: I have decided to schedule our annual sales meeting for sometime between Monday, May 10,[1] and Friday, May 14, in Miami.

Actually, we have never held our annual sales meeting so early[2] in the year; but the week of May 10 is the only week in which I shall be free before the end of September.[3]

I am gradually getting our plans for the annual sales meeting in shape. I shall mail you a copy[4] of the final plans shortly.

When you receive them, please see that all our men receive an announcement. A. H. Allen[5] (100)

356. *Chuckle*

After being married and moving into a new apartment, a young lady phoned the Subscription Department[1] of a magazine to which she subscribed.

"I should like to change my name and address," she explained.

There was a sigh; then[2] a sweet, young voice replied emphatically, "Who wouldn't!" (50)

Assignment 39

363. Dear Mr. Knox: What is it that brings one man success, happiness, and prosperity in life and mediocrity[1] or failure to his brother?

The answer is that some men willingly and cheerfully pay the price of success,[2] while others make the mistake of doing nothing to improve themselves. Every man should ask himself this question:[3] "Am I willing to force myself to work for success and security?" When you can with sincerity say "yes"[4] to yourself, then our course in modern business methods can help you.

Our booklet, "Preparing Yourself for Business," describes[5] our courses, our facilities, and our faculty.

If you want to prepare yourself for a position of[6] responsibility, be sure to send for a copy. Yours very truly, (134)

364. Dear Mr. Smith: Do you know that you are doing an injustice to yourself? When you delay paying your account[1] after it is due, you endanger your reputation as a man of integrity and responsibility.[2] You are also endangering our friendly relationship.

I know, of course, that you intend to pay your bills[3] eventually; but the sensible thing to do is to pay now.

In justice to yourself and the future[4] prosperity of your business, send us a check now. Yours very truly, (93)

365. Dear Mr. Baker: Here is an opportunity that will be of interest to music lovers like yourself.[1] We will send you your choice of any one of the high-fidelity records listed on the enclosed folder for[2] only $1.

We make this special offer to demonstrate the fine quality of these high-fidelity[3] recordings. Simply indicate on the enclosed card the high-fidelity record you want, and return the card[4] to us.

When your record arrives, you may keep it for five days. If in that time the record does not prove itself to[5] be the finest in tonal quality and clarity, you may return it to us and your money will be[6] refunded readily. Very truly yours, (127)

366. Dear Mrs. Jones: When you are looking for some reasonably priced article to give your husband or other male[1] member of your family, you are sure to find it in our store.

Our store is crammed with all kinds of quality gifts.[2] The wide selection enables you to choose gifts that reflect your personality, originality, and[3] individuality.

On our third floor you will find a large selection of Meade Watches that you can purchase[4] at substantial savings. The Meade Watch has won wide popularity with men because it winds itself as it is[5] worn.

You will enjoy the quiet surroundings of our store. Why not come and see for yourself. Yours very truly, (119)

367. Dear Mr. Gray: Our advertising manager resigned a week ago because of ill health. This means that we have[1] an opening that we believe, with all sincerity, to be a wonderful opportunity for the man[2] who has the following traits:

1. Familiarity with all phases of advertising.

2. A pleasing[3] personality.

3. Ability to inspire loyalty in the large staff of assistants over whom he will[4] have authority.

With your years of experience in advertising, we thought there was a possibility[5] that you might know of some person of outstanding ability who would be interested in making a fine[6] future for himself with us.

If you do, please have him get in touch with us. Very truly yours, (137)

368. *Chuckle*

A seventh grade class was holding a magazine-subscription sale. The morning after the sale started one boy came[1] to class and said that he had sold twenty dollars worth of subscriptions.

"How did you manage to sell so many so[2] quickly?" the teacher asked.

"I sold them all to one family," the boy replied. "Their dog bit me!" (57)

Assignment 40

372. Dear Friend: For almost fifty years the Smith Company has been taking care of the fuel requirements of the people[1] in this county. We have always maintained a policy of selling top-quality products. Consequently,[2] we have won for ourselves a host of friends in the years that we have been fuel distributors.

It is with a great[3] deal of pleasure at this season of the year that we extend our gratitude to you and to all our other[4] customers whose good will has contributed so much to our success.

If there is any way in which we can meet[5] your requirements more completely, we hope you will be sure to let us know. Yours very truly, (117)

373. Dear Mr. Davis: About eight months ago I was introduced to a young man by the name of Henry Gray. He[1] was interested in joining our organization as a salesman. He had all the attributes of a good[2] salesman, and I was exceedingly impressed by his attitude and sincerity. Consequently, I was ready[3] to place him in an opening that was available at that time. Unfortunately, he was taken[4] seriously ill before he could report; and it was subsequently necessary for me to find another[5] person for the vacancy.

When Mr. Gray recovered, we had no openings available.

If you require[6] a competent salesman for your staff, I can recommend Mr. Gray without hesitation. Very truly yours,[7] (140)

374. Dear Mr. Blair: If part of your sales are made on credit, you, like the rest of us, have no doubt had your share of[1] delinquent customers. When accounts are delinquent, they require a great deal of extra attention. Consequently,[2] you can appreciate the satisfaction that a distributor like yourself, who pays his bills promptly, gives[3] to the credit department.

Unfortunately, we frequently take friends like you for granted and fail to express[4] our gratitude. The only purpose of this letter, therefore, is to express our gratitude for the way in which[5] you co-operate with us. Cordially yours, (108)

375. Mr. Farmer: I frequently receive inquiries about sales aptitude tests; in fact, in the last week I received[1] ten such inquiries. In view of the increasing interest in sales aptitude tests, I wonder whether we[2] shouldn't consider once again the practical possibility of adding them to our list of materials.[3]

It would not require very much time and effort to obtain a set. As you know, last spring we had a fine set[4] of aptitude tests submitted to us. I am sure we could easily acquire the distribution rights to them.[5]

Consequently, I suggest that we reconsider the whole matter of sales aptitude tests at our next meeting.[6] H. G. Baker (123)

376. Dear Mr. Parks: May I express our sincere gratitude for the way you have taken care of your account with us.[1] Too frequently, a credit department is concerned only with writing letters to customers, reminding them[2] that their accounts are delinquent.

In your case, though, we find that you always pay your invoices promptly. This is a[3] record of which you may be justly proud.

It is a genuine pleasure for us to take care of your requirements.[4] If there is any further way in which we can serve you, please do not hestitate to call on us. Yours very truly, [5] (101)

Assignment 41

382. Mr. Brown: The plans and specifications for our new transportation building were transmitted to me several[1] days ago by your secretary, Miss Green. After studying them carefully, I find that several[2] significant modifications were made without my knowledge or permission.

While there may actually be some[3] justification for making these modifications, there is no justification for your making them without[4] letting me know.

I am exceedingly reluctant to approve these plans and specifications in their present[5] form. If it is convenient, I should like to discuss them with you on Friday, June 15. Frank J. Smith (118)

383. Dear Miss Cummings: We are seeking a competent girl to fill the opening as secretary to the head of[1] our Translation Division. As your school has supplied us with fine girls in the past, we are hoping that you will be[2] able to help us again.

The girl we want should have the following qualifications:

1. She should be between[3] the ages of 18 and 25.

2. She should be able to get along well with people.

3. She should be[4] able to take dictation easily at 100 words a minute and also be able to transcribe with[5] facility.

If you have a girl who meets these qualifications, please have her submit her application to[6] us at her convenience. Very truly yours, (128)

384. Dear Mr. Smith: I have just learned with gratification that you have opened a charge account with us. I know[1] you will find it a convenient, quick, and practical way to buy. I know, too, that you will enjoy shopping in the[2] atmosphere of friendship in our store.

In a few days you will receive your charge identification card; you will[3] find it convenient in transacting business at Stern's. When you receive the card, please sign it. This identification[4] card is for your use only. Consequently, it is not transferable.

Thank you for your confidence in Stern's.[5] Our employees will consider it a privilege to serve you. Cordially yours, (114)

385. Dear Mr. Green: I am returning for clarification your bill covering the cost of the transcript you prepared[1] for us in the case of the New York Transportation Company versus Transcontinental Airlines.

On the[2] bill you indicate that you transcribed 120 pages at the rate of $1 a page, making a[3] total of $120. Yet the transcript itself contains only 110 pages. Shouldn't[4] you, therefore, have billed us for $110?

Please let me know whether your bill is incorrect or whether[5] the difference of $10 represents a charge for some other service in connection with the transcript. Very[6] truly yours, (123)

386. Dear Mr. Baker: You will be interested to know that today the Air Transport Company celebrates an[1] anniversary, its tenth. We look with gratification upon the significant progress we have made in[2] those ten years; we feel we have every justification to be proud of it.

On this tenth anniversary[3] we want to thank you with all sincerity for the part your organization has played in the growth of the Air[4] Transport Company and for the confidence you have shown in us. Yours very truly, (95)

387. Dear Mrs. Casey: Would you like to take care of your bills at one time? Naturally you would! You can enjoy this[1] pleasant experience by taking out a low-cost loan from the Mutual Bank and Trust Company.

This is all[2] you have to do:

Figure out the actual sum you will need to pay all your bills; then visit your local branch of[3] the Mutual Bank and Trust Company. There you will simply fill out a short blank, and you will immediately[4] be given a check for the amount you need. You repay the loan gradually, as your income permits. Very[5] truly yours, (102)

388. *Chuckle*

The doctor was trying to encourage a gloomy patient. "You're in no real danger," he said. "Why, I have had[1] the same complaint myself."

"Yes," the patient moaned, "but you didn't have the same doctor!" (34)

Assignment 42

389. *Recall Chart*

1. Myself, yourself; security, authority; facility, nationality.

2. Improve, improvement; employ, employment; willingly, seemingly.

3. Submit, submission; relationship, friendship; introduce, introduction.

4. Entertain, entertainment; interest, interested; bearings, clippings.

5. Technical, technically; inform; informed; displace, misplace.

6. Alters, altered; steadily, speedily; actual, actually.

7. Procedure, procedures; careful, carefulness; express, expresses.

8. Enforce, enforcement; transport, transportation; gratification, notification.

9. Unpaid, unfair; contain, detain; comfort, comfortable.

10. Mother, further; perform, performance; personal, personally.

11. Debate, depress; purchase, purchased; become, before.

12. Rebate, replacement; reliable, terrible; mention, termination.

13. Special, especially; neatly, clearly; faculty, penalty.

14. Proficient, deficient; efficiency, deficiency; ourselves, themselves.

391. *How Is Your Vocabulary?*

If you want to get ahead in the business world, you must pay attention to your vocabulary. As many[1] tests have shown, good students almost always have a better working vocabulary and read faster than the weaker[2] students. Good students can recognize, define, and use more words than their weaker brothers.

This helps them read[3] faster because they understand the meaning of words at a glance. To become a fast reader, therefore, you must become a[4] master of the words you read. There are a number of ways you can do this.

Get the Dictionary Habit. Be[5] constantly on the lookout for new words. When you see a new word or encounter one that is only vaguely familiar[6] to you, don't pass it by, thinking you can get along without it. Often the meaning of a whole sentence may[7] hang on the new word. If you are going to read efficiently, you need to know well all the words you read.

When you[8] come across a new word, the first thing to do is look it up in the dictionary. Have a good dictionary[9] handy at all times.

Successful writers, who probably have a better command of the language than most people,[10] usually have two or three dictionaries for different purposes where they can reach them readily.

Use[11] New Words. Besides looking up new words, take steps to add them to your working vocabulary. It is a good idea[12] to write down these new words on a card or on a piece of paper. During the course of a day in which you read[13] for perhaps an hour or two, you can probably compile a list of eight or ten new words. When a dictionary[14] is available later, look them up. Finally, try to use these words in your everyday conversation and[15] writing.

If it is your ambition to become a successful secretary, you must remember that you will[16] constantly be working with words. The more words you know and can use, the easier will your secretarial work[17] be and the more rapidly will you progress. (350)

392. *Economy*

The most economical person I ever knew was a big spender — "investor" would perhaps be a better word.[1] He never let his money lie idle but was always finding ways and means to make it earn a good income.

This[2] man realized that economy is the careful use of anything. Many people think of economy[3] as refraining from spending. That is merely stinginess.

To be really economical, you must learn to spend[4] wisely. Once you learn to do this, you are on the high road to becoming truly economical.

There are more[5] kinds of economy than economy of money. There is economy of time and economy of[6] energy. These are most important; for unless you use time and energy properly, you will have no money[7] on which to practice economy!

To economize on time means to use your time to best advantage. To do[8] this, you must economize on energy. In turn, this means that you must work on a plan and a schedule. (178)

CHAPTER 8

Assignment 43

399. Mr. Kelly: As I suggested to you yesterday, I believe that we should not postpone any longer the[1] appointment of Mr. Harry Nelson, my assistant, as supervisor of our magazine's Circulation[2] Department. He has done a superb job as acting supervisor. When he took over the job two years ago,[3] our circulation was 80,000. Our circulation today is more than 100,000.

I realize[4] that you may feel that Mr. Nelson is too young for the job of supervisor of our Circulation[5] Department, but I am confident he will do a superior job for us.

May I have your permission to make[6] Mr. Nelson's appointment official? Robert S. Griffin (131)

400. Dear Mr. Green: Here is what a Superior Postage Meter will do for you:

1. It will print postage on your[1] letters, circulars, and other mail.

2. It will give you close supervision over postage expenditures.

If[2] you have been postponing the purchase of a postage meter because of the expense, postpone no longer. You can[3] now purchase a Superior Postage Meter that exactly fits the needs of your office, and you can do so[4] at a surprisingly low cost.

After your staff has used the

Superior Postage Meter for a few days, you[5] will congratulate yourself on the savings you will make. Sincerely yours, (113)

401. Dear Mr. Casey: The postman just delivered your manuscript for the second edition of your book, "Tabulation[1] Made Easy." May I congratulate you on a superlative job. You have justification to be[2] proud of its quality.

I want to congratulate you also on keeping to the schedule that we set up last[3] spring. I realize that it took superhuman effort on your part, and I appreciate it.

If my calculations[4] are accurate, next year we should sell at least fifteen thousand copies of "Tabulation Made Easy." Very[5] cordially yours, (104)

402. Dear Mr. Dean: Your subscription to the Transportation Supervisor's Monthly has expired, and the January[1] issue is the last one we can send you without a renewal.

I am reluctant to remove your name from[2] our file because I know that, as a railroad superintendant, you will benefit from the stimulating and[3] interesting issues we are planning for the future.

It is so easy to keep the Transportation Supervisor's[4] Monthly coming. Send no money now, but return to us the enclosed post card. Please do it today, Mr.[5] Dean, so that you will not miss the February issue. Yours sincerely, (113)

403. Dear Mr. Jones: The Journal of Commerce is the only publication that can supply businessmen everywhere[1] with the facts they must have today in order to supervise their businesses properly. How can the Journal[2] do this?

We have on our staff more than 250 superior reporters and editors who accumulate[3] and tabulate up-to-the-minute information about population trends and other factors of[4] interest to businessmen.

Our publication has grown more than any other similar publication in[5] the field. Our circulation is more than 200,000.

If you are interested in receiving current[6] information that affects your business, you need the Journal of Commerce. The subscription price is only $6[7] for one year.

All you have to do to start your subscription is to fill out and return the enclosed post card. Don't[8] postpone taking action; mail the post card today. Yours very truly, (173)

404. Dear Mr. Drake: I was sorry to receive your letter telling me that you will be unable to have dinner[1] with us on June 15. I realize, though, that you have a busy schedule.

I hope that the next time you are in[2] New York you will reserve a few hours for us. Sincerely yours, (51)

Assignment 44

411. Mr. Macy: When I was in New York a few days ago, I learned of a manuscript for a modern, up-to-date[1] book entitled "Self-Teaching Course in Typing." It occurred to me that "Self-Teaching Course in Typing" would be a[2] fine addition to our self-improvement series. Under the circumstances, I asked the author to submit the[3] manuscript to us, which he has done.

I assume that you will want to examine this manuscript yourself to see[4] whether it meets our specifications. I am, therefore, sending it to you along with the author's letter, which is[5] self-explanatory.

Please let me know as soon as possible whether you agree that "Self-Teaching Course in Typing"[6] should be made a part of our practical self-improvement series so that I can offer the author our[7] regular authorship contract. A. H. Taylor (148)

412. Dear Mr. Smith: Am I correct in assuming that our conference on consumer education will run from[1] 9 to 5 on Friday, April 16, and will resume at 9 on Saturday, April 17?

If this[2] assumption is correct, I shall reserve Parlors A, B, and C of the Baker Hotel for those two days.

Because of[3] the interest in consumer education, we should have a profitable, well-attended conference.[4] Sincerely yours,

P.S. A stamped, self-addressed envelope is enclosed for your convenience in writing me. (98)

413. Dear Mr. Davis: If you are like most persons, we may assume that you wish you had more self-confidence and[1] self-assurance when you get up to address a gathering. You wish you could overcome the feeling of stage fright.

There[2] are two ways to defeat stage fright. One way is by striving for self-improvement by yourself. As I am sure you will[3] agree, this is a tedious, difficult way. A better way is to take the Johnson Public-Speaking Course. In[4] this course you will develop self-expression and self-confidence under the supervision of a skilled instructor.[5]

If you would like to have more information about our course, fill in and return the enclosed stamped, postage-paid[6] card. Yours very truly, (124)

414. Dear Friend: Our airline has resumed operations, and we are once again serving cities from coast to coast.

We[1] sincerely regret the inconvenience you may have been caused by this interruption in service, but circumstances[2] beyond our control required us to stop operations for almost two weeks. We are grateful for your patience under[3] the circumstances.

With the resumption of full schedules, we offer you the finest transportation at the[4] lowest cost in history. We hope you will have frequent occasion to use our airline. Cordially yours, (98)

415. Mr. Smith: As the January and February issues of the National Consumer Reports have not[1] reached my desk, I assume that we have let our subscription expire.

My assistant and I have always read these Consumer Reports[2] as a matter of self-interest, and we should like to see our subscription resumed. Under the circumstances,[3] will you please place an order for a two-year subscription to the Consumer Reports beginning with the current[4] issue. Harry J. Wilson (86)

416. Dear Reader: According to our records, your remittance for the book you ordered on May 15 is still outstanding.[1]

It may be that you have already sent us your check and that our letters have crossed in the mails. If that is the[2] case, please disregard this note.

If you have not yet sent us your remittance, I should appreciate your taking care[3] of this little detail.

A stamped, self-addressed envelope and a duplicate invoice are enclosed for your convenience.[4] Sincerely yours, (84)

423. Dear Mr. Baker: Frankly, I find myself in an awkward, uncomfortable situation. I have to tell[1] you that unless I receive your check for $500 by June 6 it will be my responsibility[2] to turn your account over to our attorneys. I assume you do not want this to happen.

As you know, this[3] $500 covers your purchases on January 2 of 300 pounds of grass seed, 800 feet[4] of lumber, and 500 feet of wire.

Under the circumstances, Mr. Baker, won't you please help me out of[5] this awkward situation by sending me your check for $500.

I shall look forward to receiving[6] your check without delay. A self-addressed, postage-paid envelope is enclosed for your convenience. Yours very truly,[7] (140)

424. Gentlemen: For the past twelve weeks I have been teaching typing in the adult-education school in my neighborhood.[1] It has been a rewarding experience indeed, and I look forward to each session.

Already most of[2] these adults are typing 40 words a minute. I attribute these fine results in large part to your textbook, "Typing[3] for Adults." I selected this book after examining, backwards and forwards, more than ten books on the market.[4]

I thought the authors would be

interested in knowing about the superior results I have been getting[5] with their fine book. Please offer them my congratulations for producing such a fine book. Yours very truly,[6] (120)

425. Dear Sir: Over a million depositors of the Mutual Savings Bank increased their savings last year by more[1] than a billion dollars. As a result, they have on deposit at our bank almost two billion dollars.

These depositors[2] received in the neighborhood of forty million dollars in dividends last year.

If you do not have a[3] savings account, this is the time to open one. You will find it a rewarding experience to watch your savings[4] multiply from month to month.

Why not call at our branch in your neighborhood and let one of our officers show[5] you how simple it is to open an account. When you call, also consult him about any banking problems[6] you may have.

May we look forward to seeing you soon. Very truly yours, (133)

426. Dear Mr. Weber: As you requested, we have reserved two large rooms for you for the week of April 28.[1] We are confident that you will find these rooms suitable for your purpose. The cost of these two rooms for one week is[2] $75.

If we can be of assistance to you in any other way, please do not hesitate[3] to let us know. Yours very truly, (67)

427. *Housing for the Future*

When a couple marry, they need a place to live. (One million five hundred thousand couples will marry this year.) When[1] they achieve parenthood, they need a bigger house. (Four million babies will be born this year.) When a house is demolished,[2] the family needs a new home in a new neighborhood. (Seven hundred thousand houses will ultimately be[3] demolished this year.)

As a result, our housing needs will multiply many times; we shall need at least twenty million[4] new homes during the next ten years. We shall need:

1. Seven million five hundred thousand new homes to meet the demands[5] of a growing population.

2. Seven million more new homes to replace demolished homes.

3. Five hundred[6] thousand new homes to replace those destroyed by fire, flood, and other causes.

4. One million additional homes for[7] our rapidly increasing old-age population.

These are minimum needs. In all likelihood, our actual[8] needs will be greater. (164)

Assignment 46

435. Dear Friend: No doubt

your lights went out on Saturday during the electrical storm that started at 10 a.m. and[1] lasted until about 5 p.m.

When this electrical storm hit us, we immediately alerted all[2] our repairmen, electricians, and supervisors. Notwithstanding the high winds, they worked at great sacrifice right[3] through the storm.

As you may have read in the newspapers, in your neighborhood alone there were over a thousand breaks[4] in transmission wires caused by the trees that crashed down on our lines. Within twenty-four hours, however, electricity[5] had been brought back to more than three hundred thousand of our customers.

To the thousands of customers like you[6] who were without electricity, we extend our sincere, grateful thanks for their patience. Very truly yours,[7] (140)

436. Dear Mr. Abbey: Perhaps it has escaped your attention that your subscription to the Radio Program Guide[1] expired with the July issue. We are, however, sending you the August issue because we assume that you[2] will want to receive this program guide without interruption.

Within the last year we added more than 60,000[3] people to our list. Many of them have written us that they find this program guide very much worthwhile because[4] it helps them enjoy the pro-

grams of our station more completely.

If you haven't yet sent us your renewal, why[5] not do so today. Cordially yours, (107)

437. Dear Tenant: It will be necessary for us to cut off your electric service from 11 a.m. until[1] 1 p.m. on Thursday, June 16, while our electricians repair the electrical wiring on your floor[2] of the Chamber of Commerce Building. This is part of our general program of building improvement.

We are sorry[3] to have to deprive you of electric service for this period, but we are confident that you will be[4] pleased with the more efficient electric service you will receive as a result of this work.

Under the[5] circumstances, we know that you will bear with us while these repairs are being made. Yours very truly, (117)

438. Mr. Harris: Within the next day or so I shall forward to you the diagram I prepared for the location[1] of furniture and equipment in our new quarters in the Chamber of Commerce Building.

After you and your[2] staff have had an opportunity to study the diagram, I should like to discuss with someone on your staff[3] the installation of electrical outlets for our electric typewriters.

Any time after 4 p.m.[4] on Wednesday, May 8, will be satisfactory for me. A. J. Barnes (83)

439. Dear Friend: Thanks to the miracle of electronics, you can now have a fine organ in your home for less than the[1] price of a piano. The science of electronics, which has already brought radio and television[2] within the reach of everyone, now brings you another delightful instrument—the Nelson Electronic[3] Organ.

This exciting electronic instrument develops far richer tones than are possible with other[4] types of organs. However, its cost is well within the reach of the average family budget.

See and play[5] the Nelson Electronic Organ today. Your neighborhood Nelson dealer will welcome your call. Very truly[6] yours, (121)

440. *Chuckle*

As the young wife came home with a hatbox in her hand, she received a menacing look from her husband.

"Darling," she[1] hastily explained, "I was down in the dumps today, so I bought myself a new hat."

"Oh," he growled, "so that's where you[2] get them!" (41)

Assignment 47

444. Dear Mr. Wellington: You will find something new and convenient waiting for you the next time you drive to the Pittsburgh[1] National Bank. Our parking lot on Danville Place has been completely repaved, enlarged, and generally improved.[2]

No bank or business can solve the complicated parking problem for all of Pittsburgh, but we are doing our[3] utmost to make sure that the customers of the Pittsburgh National Bank will have plenty of free parking space while[4] they take care of their banking business.

Parking, Mr. Wellington, is part of the service of the Pittsburgh National[5] Bank, Pittsburgh's leading bank. Yours very truly, (109)

445. Dear Mr. Green: If you have not already made final arrangements for moving from Pittsburgh to your new home on[1] 18 Farmington Road, may we have an opportunity to send one of our representatives to give you[2] an estimate.

We are an established, well-known moving and storage firm and have an enviable reputation[3] for doing an efficient job.

Our representative, as well as our managers, is looking forward to[4] the pleasure of serving you. Cordially yours, (88)

446. Dear Mr. Buckingham: Don't run the risk of theft or loss by carrying around large sums of cash. Use a Nashville[1] Trust Company special checking account. You can open an account with any amount; no minimum balance[2] is required.

No matter how many checks you draw, the maintenance fee is only 25 cents a month. Your statement,[3] along with your canceled checks, is mailed to you every three months without charge.

When you are in our neighborhood[4] again, open a special checking account at the Nashville Trust Company. If it is more convenient, you can[5] open an account by mail. Cordially yours, (108)

447. Dear Mr. Lexington: We have just learned that you have moved to Greensburg, and we should like to be among the first to[1] wecome you to our city.

We extend to you a cordial invitation to use the facilities of the[2] Greensburg National Bank whenever you need them. As you may already know, the main office of the Greensburg[3] National Bank is on Danville Road and Washington Street. We also have a branch at the other end of town, across[4] from the Greensburg railroad station.

We should welcome the opportunity to meet you personally, Mr.[5] Lexington. We want to do all we can to help you get settled in Greensburg. Yours very truly, (115)

448. Dear Mr. Cummings: It is my pleasure to notify you that at a recent meeting of the board of directors[1] I was authorized to invite you to continue as a season member of the Huntington Country Club[2] during the coming year.

The dues for the season have been set at $200, to which a Federal tax[3] of 20 per cent should be added.

Please indicate on the enclosed card whether you wish to accept this invitation,[4] and return the card on or before April 5. If we do not hear from you by that time, it will be our[5] understanding that you do not wish to continue your membership in the Huntington Country Club during the[6] coming year.

It is our sincere hope, Mr. Cummings, that you will be with us again. Very truly yours, (138)

449. Dear Mr. Gray: Sales letters, news releases, or any other material that you duplicate will get better[1] attention if they are bright, clear, and easy to read.

You can make your messages more inviting by putting[2] them on Nashville Duplicating Papers. They are made especially for stencil work.

We should like to send you our[3] folder of duplicating papers. We are confident that once you have examined them you will want to use one[4] or more of them on your next job. Cordially yours, (89)

450. *Recall Chart*

1. Harm, becoming, justification, impending, exceedingly, checks.

2. Appears, called, qualify, misinform, encourages, young.

3. Program, furniture, consumed, names, skates, authorities.

4. Altogether, circulation, shown, amounts, utilities, subdividing.

5. Hopeless, savings, ounces, kingdom, ultimate, zealously.

6. Thin, pursued, terminations, childhood, family, earth.

7. Perplexing, respectful, forwarded, yelled, skillful, musical.

8. Confused, function, joining, threads, township, costly.

9. Distribution, surest, distract, afternoon, psychology, desired.

10. Themselves, notify, conveniently, patiently, creative, encounter.

11. Exportation, quiet, including, dependable, whenever, electric wiring.

12. Scheduled, postponed, circumstantial, awakened, introduces, supervisor.

13. Self-made, compliance, entertain, investment, transportation, maintaining.

14. Louisville, emphatic, uncompromising, Washington, Birmingham, Nashville.

15. $3; $500,000; 3,000,000; 4 pounds; three o'clock; $8 billion.

16. To be, have been, has not been able, to know, to me, years ago.

17. Let us, to do, of course, at a loss, one of the, if you want.

452. *Pride*

Every one of us would like to be proud of himself. We all like to know that we really matter, that we[1] are needed, and that we are important to someone.

When and if you rise to an executive position, this[2] is an important fact to remember every day of your life. If you can make people feel that they are[3] really needed, wanted, and important, they will always do their best for you.

The trouble with most of us is that we[4] take too much for granted. As long as others perform their jobs satisfactorily, we tend to forget how[5] important they are to us.

Who, for example, gives much thought to the people who do the cleaning in an office, in[6] a factory, or in a school? Yet, the work that these people do is vital. If offices, factories, and schools[7] were not cleaned, work would come to a standstill.

When you stop to think about it, every employee, no matter how[8] humble his position, is important to the company. Do not forget it, and don't let him forget it. People[9] never get tired of hearing that they are important.

The person who takes pride in himself and in his work is[10] a happy worker and a productive worker. (209)

453. *Self-Control*

One of the most important qualities a person must possess if he is to assume a position of[1] leadership in business is self-control. He must be able to control his temper even when others are losing[2] theirs. Before a person can control others, he must first learn to control himself.

If you will examine the traits[3] of men who have made good in business, you will find that they have also schooled themselves against making snap decisions.[4] They have made it a habit to consider things calmly and carefully. In addition, they keep their personal[5] feelings out of the picture.

A person is not born with this type of self-control. In fact, it is contrary to[6] the nature of most people. It takes practice to acquire it. Those who acquire it move ahead fast. There is always[7] a place at the top in business for them. (147)

454. *Faithful Servant*

The postman who puts the mail in your mailbox day after day is sort of a permanent soldier. He outwalks many[1] of the soldiers and marines in the armed services and keeps right on hiking along, rain or shine, day in and[2] day out. We know a postman who has been making his daily rounds for twenty-eight years, and in making those rounds he[3] has walked the equivalent distance of five times around the earth at the equator!

There are many people who[4] say that there is no indispensable man. But if there is one, it's the postman! He is our connecting link with[5] the rest of the world. Through the magic of his daily delivery of the mail, he brings minds and hearts closer[6] together. He speeds business, because more business is handled through letters than by any other way.

Postmen take millions[7] of footsteps each day to serve us. The mail, through the miracle of the postman's loyalty and spirit, always[8] comes through. (161)

CHAPTER 9

Assignment 49

457. Dear Mr. Farmer: On Friday, March 15, we appointed a new man to represent in your territory.[1] May I tell you a little about him?

His name is Harry H. Barnes, and he is a recent graduate[2] of Baker College. Before he joined our staff, he was a teller in a Dallas bank.

If you like an ambitious,[3]

friendly young man, you will like Harry. You will find that he is easy to get along with and that he has a thorough[4] knowledge of our line of goods.

When a tall, good-looking fellow appears at your door in the near future, I should[5] consider it a personal favor if you would give him a friendly welcome. Better still, why not give him an[6] initial order to start him off on his new vocation. Sincerely yours, (134)

458. Dear Miss Parks: Each time you receive a pay check, you must make an important decision; you must decide whether you[1] will set aside a certain amount for rainy days or whether you will simply spend everything you earn.[2]

Everyone believes in saving; but many people put off opening an account until next week, next month, or[3] next year — and often they never get to it.

When you receive your next pay check, take a step in the direction of[4] financial independence. Open a savings account at our bank, and make regular deposits an important[5] part of your savings plans. Yours very truly, (109)

459. Dear Mr. Jones: At this time of the year we must dispose of all our winter merchandise in order to make room[1] for our spring and summer line.

During the week of February 15, therefore, we are holding a private sale[2] for our customers at which all our winter clothes will be offered for sale at low prices.

Set aside an hour or[3] two during the week of February 15 to come in to see us. Yours very truly, (77)

460. Gentlemen: On Thursday, March 15, I wrote you that I had not received the pen I ordered on February[1] 15. The pen arrived this morning, and I am very well pleased with it. I am so pleased, in fact, that I should like[2] to order another like it. This will be a Christmas present for my sister.

I am enclosing my check for[3] $12 in payment for the two pens. Very truly yours, (71)

461. Dear Mr. Gates: I am happy to announce that Mr. George Smith has just been appointed as our salesman in Dallas.[1]

George has been with us for many years, but this will be his first experience in selling. One of his first[2] positions with us was in our Purchasing Department. Later, he was in charge of office personnel in New York.[3] This experience has given him a thorough grasp of our problems.

As a favor to me, won't you be good enough[4] to give George a pleasant reception when he visits your territory in May. Cordially yours, (97)

462. Dear Mr. Casey: This is the fourth letter we have written you reminding you that your account is past due. I[1] am sorry to say that we have received neither a check nor an answer to any of our letters.

As you may[2] know, our accounts are insured by the National Credit Bureau. When an account is as long overdue as yours,[3] we must report this fact to the Bureau. We do not like to do this because of the bad effect our action would[4] have on your credit rating. Unless we hear from you soon, however, there is nothing else we can do.

Won't you send[5] us a check for $200 now. It is vitally important to both of us that you do so. Yours very[6] truly, (122)

463. Gentlemen: Thank you for your letter reminding me that I have not made a payment on my account for some time.[1]

I have been ill for the past three weeks and have not been able to look after my business affairs.

I hope to be[2] able to send you a check for $100 on May 15 and another for $150[3] on June 15. Yours very truly, (67)

Assignment 50

466. Dear Mr. Mild: This morning my secretary asked me, "Why don't the Smith people pay their bills or at least answer[1] our letters?"

I had to confess that I didn't have the answer. I must have the answer soon, however, for I[2] am getting ready to place your account in the hands of a collection agency. This is a step I should be[3] loath to take, but it is the only course open to me if I do not hear from you by August 15.

That gives[4] you 15 days in which to send me your check for $150 or at least to write me.

I am sure[5] that both of us will be relieved when this matter has been settled. Sincerely yours, (114)

467. Dear Mr. Small: As I am sure I need not remind you, your check should have been in our hands by April 16. Here[1] it is May 20, but we have no record of having received a check or letter from you.

Don't you agree that[2] we have been most patient and have sincerely tried to be co-operative and friendly?

If you cannot send the[3] entire $350, at least make a partial payment and let us know when you will be able to[4] pay the rest.

Please don't put this matter off; take action now to preserve your good credit rating with our store. Sincerely[5] yours, (101)

468. Dear Sir: More and more people are learning that it pays to take their vacations in Miami in June. Taking their[1] vacations in June enables them to take advantage of the special rates that prevail at that time.

Why not plan[2] to take your next vacation in Miami in June?

The attached folder will prove to you that you can save at least[3] 20 per cent on your vacation costs by staying at the Miami Hotel.

I shall be glad to make a[4] reservation for you. Sincerely yours, (87)

469. Dear Mrs. Willis: With the fall clothing season starting and with stocks at the Baker Clothing Mart at their peak, you[1] couldn't select a better time to choose your fall wardrobe.

The chances are good that you will be able to find just[2] the coat or suit that really appeals to you in the large selection that our store offers. Our prices range from[3] $50 to $100.

If you would prefer to do so, you can pay for the garments you choose on[4] our special charge plan. Sincerely yours, (87)

470. Gentlemen: It is a pleasure to give you the information you wish about Mrs. Mary Strong, who has been[1] with us since 1960. Mrs. Strong was hired as a clerk and rapidly rose to the position of buyer.[2] She made many friends for our store, and we are very sorry to lose her services.

We realize, however,[3] that your offer is a fine promotion for her; therefore, she leaves our employ with our good will.

I know that Mrs.[4] Strong will do a fine job for you and that she will be an asset to your organization. Sincerely yours, (99)

471. Dear Mr. Lee: You will recall that on November 16 you left a $10 deposit with us on a[1] ring you planned to give your niece as a Christmas present. Will you please let us know whether you still want the ring or whether[2] you have changed your mind.

If we do not hear from you by December 16, we shall assume that you do not want[3] it and will place it back in stock. Sincerely yours, (69)

472. Dear Mr. Barry: No doubt by this time you have received the catalogue that we sent you on August 15. We[1] hope that you have had an opportunity to look through it. If you have, we are sure that you must have been impressed[2] by the large selection of goods and by our low prices.

In the back of the catalogue there is a convenient[3] order blank. The next time you are in the market for office supplies, we hope that you will use this blank. Yours very[4] truly, (81)

473. Dear Mr. Smith: Wouldn't you like to live in a house in the country? I am sure you would.

Why not let me show you[1] some of the homes that are on the market in this section of the state. I know of several homes that are for sale[2] at a reasonable price. Very truly yours, (49)

Assignment 51

476. Dear Friend: It has been more than six months since we have seen you in our store or had the pleasure of serving you in any[1] way.

We have always tried to keep our store a friendly place in which to shop, and we are wondering whether[2] we have failed in our aim or have not given you the service that you have a right to receive. If we have offended you[3] in any way, won't you please tell us.

As you know, your credit rating with us is A1.

It is our sincere[4] hope that you will visit us soon so that we may show you the many fine bargains we have on our racks. Yours very[5] truly, (101)

477. Dear Friend: This year's Handbook of Business will be available on or before March 15. This handbook will provide[1] a wealth of valuable financial and business statistics that are of great importance to you in the[2] operation of your manufacturing business.

As we know that the limited number of copies we are printing[3] will go quickly, we urge you not to delay placing your order.

If you will mail the enclosed card, we shall be[4] glad to send you a copy for only $3. Very truly yours, (93)

478. Dear Sir: Perhaps you may think it strange that we should be talking about Christmas so early in the year; but just before[1] the holidays, we are always faced with more orders for our products that we can fill. We are, therefore, writing[2] you today to be sure that we can take care of your needs.

As you know, we have many Christmas packages of candies,[3] attractively wrapped for the Christmas season, at prices ranging from $1 to $10.

If you will[4] mail us your gift list soon, we will enclose a name card with each gift. Cordially yours, (94)

479. Dear Friend: There is nothing like getting your paper the first thing in the morning. That is why so many people have[1] us deliver the Troy Post to their door bright and early each morning. They find that this service helps them start their day[2] off right—and it costs only a few pennies a week.

There are two ways that you can order delivery service:[3]

1. Call Main 3-4414 and tell the operator that you would like the Troy Post delivered each morning.[4]

2. Mail the enclosed coupon, and we will take care of all the necessary details.

Why not call or write us to[5] begin this service for you at once. Very truly yours, (110)

480. Dear Friend: Enclosed is a sticker that entitles you to park free of charge in our parking lot on Baker Road and[1] Woodland Square. Just place this sticker on your car when you do your shopping.

Please feel free to park in our lot any evening[2] that you go to a movie or visit friends.

When you plan to park in the lot, drive in on the Baker Road side.[3] The section on the Woodland Square side is reserved for those who work in our store.

This is just one more illustration[4] of the way in which we try to be of service to those who do business with us. Sincerely yours, (97)

481. Dear Mr. Best: There is a serious problem on my mind right now — the loss of your business. I should very much[1] like to know why we have not received any orders from you recently.

As I am sure you realize, we must[2] depend on firms like yours to distribute our products. We want your business. We cannot afford to lose it. If our[3] service or the quality of our products is responsible for the loss of your business, we should like to know[4] about it so that we can make a real effort to improve.

Won't you write me a personal note, Mr. Best,[5] and tell me why we have lost your business. Also, I should welcome any suggestions you may have on how we can[6] improve our service or our products so that you will once again buy from us. Very truly yours, (137)

Assignment 52

485. Dear Mr. Hughes: At the present time we have no opening in our Accounting Division, and there seems little[1] chance that such an opening will occur before September or October.

If you would care to consider a[2] position with our company as a correspondent, I should be glad to have you fill out and mail to me the[3] enclosed application.

After I have had an opportunity to study your application, I will write[4] you about a possible conference with the head of the Correspondence Department. Cordially yours, (98)

486. Gentlemen: This is just a note to tell you how happy we are with our advertising in the Times.

Recently[1] we had an illustration of the value of advertising in the Times. In our last series of advertisements,[2] we stressed our new paint-job service for automobiles, which we are offering for $49.50.[3] The number of replies has been very gratifying. Definite proof of the pulling power of the[4] Times is provided by the number of customers who came in with a copy of our advertisement in their[5] hands.

You may be sure that we shall continue to make provision for advertising in the Times. Cordially yours,[6] (120)

487. Dear Mr. Temple: Do you know why people who really want their money's worth buy a Trenton Television[1] Set? The answer to that question is this: they know that by paying a little more for a Trenton than they would for[2] another make they definitely save money in the end.

A Trenton costs a little more, but it seldom needs[3] servicing. A set must meet our rigid tests before it leaves our factory.

If you have not yet seen and heard a[4] Trenton, may we suggest that you stop in to see your local Trenton dealer and look over his complete line.[5] Yours very truly, (104)

488. Dear Mr. Powers: In July, 1925, the Davis brothers were building their new hotel in Clinton.[1] They came to us and said, "Give us a heating system that will stand the test of time."

Now, nearly forty years later,[2] the heating system that we put in is still serving that hotel, giving fine service at a minimum of cost.[3] What is more, that system is now serving the five floors that were added in 1960.

When you reach a decision[4] to purchase a new heating system, write or call us. We can help you get the most for your heating dollars.[5] Cordially yours, (102)

489. To the Staff: During the past few weeks I have had several inquiries about the discounts that are available[1] to members of the staff on the books that we publish. With the thought that some of you may not be familiar with[2] our policies on discounts, I am summarizing these policies here:

1. Members of the staff are entitled[3] to a discount of 40 per cent on all trade books that we publish.

2. On textbooks, technical books, and special[4] editions, members of the staff are entitled to a discount of 20 per cent.

Now that the Christmas season[5] is approaching, you may wish to give our books as Christmas presents — and enjoy a considerable saving over[6] the regular retail prices. Harry H. Bates (130)

490. Dear Mr. Wilson: Thank you for the information you sent me about your products. It is just what I wanted.[1]

We are planning to buy some new equipment soon, and this information will help us decide what we should get.[2] Cordially yours, (42)

Assignment 53

493. Gentlemen: Our idea of a collection letter may be summarized as follows:

1. It should be brief.
2.[1] It should be friendly.
3. It should be successful.

This letter is brief; it is friendly. Whether it is successful[2] depends on whether you send us your check to take care of your unpaid invoices. Very truly yours, (58)

494. Dear Mr. Dexter: In 1910 the National Bank of New York was a successful pioneer in the field[1] of foreign banking.

Recently we added another country to the long list that we serve. On April 10 we[2] opened an office in Paris.

If you would like to have all the facts about the helpful services that this new[3] bank can render your organization, you can obtain them by writing to us. We will send them to you promptly.[4] If you prefer, you can pay a visit to our main office at 300 State Street, in New York.

We shall be happy[5] to see you. Yours very truly, (107)

495. Dear Mr. Banker: As a regular reader of the Miami Times, you will be particularly happy[1] to learn of a novel service that we are starting next Monday. Beginning with that issue, the Miami Times[2] will publish daily a civil service section that will provide a complete list of positions that are open,[3] public examinations that will be held, and appointments that have been made in the civil service.

If you have[4] any suggestions on other ways in which we can increase the usefulness of our newspaper in the days ahead,[5] please be sure to let us know. Very truly yours, (110)

496. Dear Mr. Yale: No matter where you go on your vacation in this country, you can get your regular copy[1] of the Miami Times. If Uncle Sam can find you, we can see to it that you enjoy your regular newspaper[2] each day. We are ready to enhance your vacation enjoyment without any additional expense to[3] you.

Before you get into the packing rush, mail the enclosed blank to us and let us be responsible for all[4] the details.

Do it now so that you won't miss a single issue. Cordially yours, (94)

497. Dear Mr. Rush: We are sorry that you have been experiencing difficulty receiving copies of our[1] magazine. Upon checking with our Mailing Department, we find that magazines have been mailed regularly to[2] your Chicago address. As no magazines came back to us, we had no way of knowing that you had changed your address.[3]

As you request, we are sending you duplicate copies of the March and April issues, which you did not receive.[4]

Your stencil is now correct, and you should receive your magazines promptly as they are published each month.

We hope[5] that our magazine is bringing you both pleasure and enjoyment. Yours very truly, (115)

498. Dear Mr. Barnes: Five of the six pieces of the dining room set I ordered from you arrived today in good[1] condition. The sixth piece, the serving table, was damaged. The top has been badly scratched by a nail in the packing case.[2]

Unfortunately, your delivery truck left before we could unpack the furniture. We could not, therefore, have[3] your driver take the serving table back. I should appreciate it if you would replace this serving table with[4] a new one. When your truckman delivers it, he can pick up the damaged table. Cordially yours, (97)

499. Dear Friend: Thank you very much for your order for the Science Monthly. Your subscription was entered promptly.

Your bill[1] is enclosed. Would you be good enough to return the bill with your payment so that I can see to it that your account[2] is promptly and properly credited.

I know that you are going to enjoy Science Monthly. Yours very[3] truly, (61)

Assignment 54

503. Dear Miss Gates: Would

you like to know an easy way to achieve peace of mind? All you need do, Miss Gates, is put aside[1] a small amount each week from your earnings to make it possible to get what you want out of life.

Put part of your[2] earnings each week in a savings account at the Chemical Bank and Trust Company, Springfield's foremost bank.

You will[3] experience a feeling of confidence, freedom, and well-being as you watch your savings account grow. Very[4] truly yours, (82)

504. Dear Mr. Thomas: As you know, on the southeast corner of your lot there is a large elm tree. It is a beautiful[1] tree. Unfortunately, though, it is a traffic hazard. The tree is so located that cars coming from the south[2] on Fourth Street cannot easily be seen by drivers of cars coming from the west.

The Town Board suggested at its[3] meeting several days ago that, with your permission, this tree be cut down. We hope that you will have no objection[4] to this suggestion in the interests of greater safety. The Town will, of course, pay the bill.

May I discuss[5] this matter with you some evening next week? Yours very truly, (111)

505. Dear Mr. Samuels: Thank you for the nice order we received from you a few days ago for a quantity[1] of our sporting goods.

I am sorry to report that our credit file on your organization is not complete;[2] we cannot, therefore, ship this merchandise to you on open account.

As time is short, Mr. Samuels, may we[3] suggest that on this order you send us your advance check for $480. Then, after this merchandise[4] has been manufactured and we have the actual cost figures, we will immediately reimburse you[5] for the amount of any overpayment.

We shall, of course, continue our credit investigation in the[6] hope that we can offer you our regular terms on future orders. Cordially yours, (135)

506. Dear Miss Brown: Have you seen the new Chester Camera, which makes taking pictures even more fun? With this practical[1] camera, you snap your picture, press a button, and a few seconds later lift out a beautiful print—regardless[2] of the weather.

You will experience a real thrill when you see the picture you have taken shortly after[3] you have taken it. You will never again have to wonder how your pictures will turn out; you will know at once.[4]

The Chester Camera takes pictures indoors as well as outdoors. It makes no difference whether the sun is shining,[5] whether it is cloudy, or whether it is raining.

If you would be interested in receiving our free descriptive booklet,[6] "Cameras Can Be Fun," just return the enclosed card. The booklet contains full information about the new[7] Chester Camera. You will be amazed and pleased at how simple and economical the camera is to[8] operate. Yours very truly, (166)

507. *Chuckle*

A college teacher had just moved across the country with all her possessions, including box upon box of books.[1] As the burly van driver deposited the last heavy box on the third-floor landing of her apartment building,[2] he grumbled, "For goodness' sake, lady! Why didn't you read them before you moved?" (54)

Assignment 55

511. *Your Telephone Voice*

Have you ever "met" a person for the first time over the telephone? Usually, you could tell by his voice[1] the kind of person he was. If his voice was pleasant and his tone friendly, he impressed you as a nice person to[2] know and to do business with. If his voice was gruff and unfriendly, you completed the call with the feeling that he[3] is probably a difficult person to get along with.

What impression do *you* give people over the[4] telephone? You cannot, of course, be seen. You can only be heard, and your voice must convey your personality.

Do[5] you speak with clarity? Are you logical in expressing your thoughts? Are you tactful? Do you have "the voice with a[6] smile"?

Over the telephone, you will represent your company. By speaking softly, by choosing words that convey[7] your thoughts clearly, and by giving the caller the feeling that you are sincerely interested in helping him,[8] you will make friends for your organization. (168)

512. Dear Mr. Abbey: A man is judged by his letters, and so is his company. After all, a business letter[1] is a representative you send to speak for you and your company.

When your letter looks sloppy, it makes a[2] very poor impression. That is one good reason why you should trade in your old typewriters on new Nelsons.

Surprisingly[3] enough, new Nelsons will save you a great deal of money because they require very little servicing.[4]

Our representative in your locality, Mr. E. H. Green, will be glad to submit to you a plan that[5] will tell you just when it will pay you to trade in your old machines for more efficient Nelsons. Very truly yours,[6] (120)

513. Dear Mr. Evans: How would you like to have a brand-new $20 coffee table for less than $5[1] or a new $150 cabinet for only $15?

You can have these things and many[2] others once you start the fascinating hobby of making things for yourself. It is fun to make things for yourself[3] once you have learned how. Learning how is amazingly simple if you have a copy of our book, "Using Your Hands."[4] You need no previous experience, training, or special aptitude. The book outlines each operation with[5] such clarity that you will have no difficulty with it.

Read the full description of "Using Your Hands" in the[6] enclosed folder. Then send for a copy. Cordially yours, (130)

514. *Chuckle*

One day a young wife was playing hostess to her bridge club. One of the unwritten rules was that on the evenings that[1] the wives entertained, the husbands were to stay away. This particular evening, though, the game was long, so that the[2] husband returned before the girls left. His wife introduced him to everyone, after which he went into the[3] bedroom and read, apparently taking no interest in the rapid-fire conversation downstairs. But after[4] the last guest had left, he said, "I have just one question. Who listens?" (92)

518. Dear Mr. Rich: No two successful businessmen look alike, dress alike, or work alike. When you see a man who[1] fits a certain pattern, however, the chances are that you are looking at a superior executive.[2] Here are some of the ways to spot him:

1. He has self-confidence and does not shirk responsibility.

2. He[3] is able to supervise several jobs simultaneously without becoming flustered.

3. He has an[4] office that helps him to work efficiently.

It is in this last point, Mr. Rich, that our furniture helps. Our[5] equipment gives the executive or supervisor an office that looks attractive. An attractive, efficient[6] office helps him sell himself and his ideas.

When you are in the market for new office furniture, let us[7] show you our line and tell you how it will be a real asset to your business. Cordially yours, (157)

519. Dear Mrs. Harrington: Recently we forwarded to you a Maintenance Service Agreement for your electric[1] machines. As we have not received a signed copy from you, we again bring to your attention the benefits that[2] will accrue to you from our maintenance program.

The great majority of our customers now avail themselves[3] of the Maintenance Service Agreement, for they find that it reduces to a minimum the expense and[4] inconvenience caused by service calls.

We should appreciate your returning to us one signed copy, retaining the[5] duplicate for your files. Cordially yours, (107)

520. Dear Mr. Jones: Without a doubt the most welcome and most appreciated check that reached my desk this morning was[1] yours for $200 covering your April, May, and June balances. Our sincere congratulations, Mr.[2] Jones.

Thanks for working with us so thoughtfully in setting up a payment program that met our requirements and[3] yet did not ultimately place too great a burden on your finances. May I congratulate you, too, on having[4] overcome the trying circumstances that made things so difficult for you during the past few months.

It was a pleasure co-operating with you. Very[5] truly yours, (102)

521. Dear Mr. Green: Now every office can have a postage meter. Even if you average $1 a[1] day or less for postage, you can have a Harper desk-model postage meter.

The postage meter is set by the[2] post office for any amount of postage you need. Your postage in a meter is protected from damage, loss,[3] and misuse.

There is a postage meter model for every office, large or small. Under the circumstances,[4] it is a matter of self-interest for you to see our dealer in your neighborhood and have him show you the[5] models that are available. Do it today. Very cordially yours, (113)

522. Dear Mr. Dayton: Ellis Self-Service Elevators have been in successful operation for many years[1] in busy office buildings throughout the country. These self-service elevators can be operated either[2] by tenants or by regular attendants in the cars.

Building owners make real savings, too, as these self-service[3] elevators enable them to cut from $5,000 to $10,000 a year from their[4] operating costs.

Why not look at an actual installation in one of the newer buildings in your city.[5] If you would like to have the name of a building in your city where Ellis Self-Service Elevators have been[6] installed, return the enclosed card. Very truly yours, (130)

523. Dear Mr. Hunt: I have just learned that you have not used your charge account with us for several months. I am naturally[1] very much interested to find out why. Have you found our goods unsatisfactory?

Won't you take a[2] moment to write me. A stamped envelope is. enclosed for your convenience. Yours very truly, (57)

524. *Chuckle*

The self-made millionaire was addressing a graduating class. "All my success in life," he said, "I owe to one[1] thing — pluck, pluck, pluck."

"That's great, sir," spoke up a voice from the rear, "but will you please tell us something about how and whom to[2] pluck?" (41)

Index of Gregg Shorthand

In order to facilitate finding, this Index has been divided into six main sections — Alphabetic Characters, Brief Forms, General, Phrasing, Word Beginnings, Word Endings.

The first figure refers to the assignment; the second refers to the paragraph.

INDEX OF BRIEF FORMS

The first figure refers to the assignment; the second to the paragraph.

INDEX OF BUILDING YOUR TRANSCRIPTION SKILLS

The first figure refers to the assignment; the second figure to the paragraph.